POLITICAL REPRESENTATION AND ELECTIONS

D1799342

STUDIES IN POLITICAL SCIENCE

already published

POLITICAL REPRESENTATION AND ELECTIONS IN BRITAIN

Peter G. J. Pulzer

Student of Christ Church, Oxford
University Lecturer in Politics

Author of 'The Rise of Political Anti-Semitism
in Germany and Austria'

THIRD EDITION

London

GEORGE ALLEN & UNWIN LTD
RUSKIN HOUSE · MUSEUM STREET

FOR GILLIAN

FIRST PUBLISHED IN 1967
SECOND IMPRESSION 1968
SECOND EDITION 1972
THIRD EDITION 1975

*This book is copyright under the Berne Convention. All rights
are reserved. Apart from any fair dealing for the purpose of
private study, research, criticism or review, as permitted under
the Copyright Act, 1956, no part of this publication may be
reproduced, stored in a retrieval system, or transmitted, in any
form or by any means, electronic, electrical, chemical, mechanical,
optical, photocopying, recording or otherwise, without the prior
permission of the copyright owner. Enquiries should be addressed
to the publishers.*

© *George Allen and Unwin Ltd., 1967, 1972, 1975*

This book is published in the United States of America
by Frederick A. Praeger, Inc.
under the title POLITICAL REPRESENTATION
AND ELECTIONS: PARTIES AND VOTING IN
GREAT BRITAIN

ISBN 0 04 329023 X

PRINTED IN GREAT BRITAIN
in 10 point Plantin type
BY LOWE AND BRYDONE (PRINTERS) LTD
THETFORD, NORFOLK

INTRODUCTION TO 1974 EDITION

Having extensively revised this book in 1971, I have decided to let the body of the text stand, and to precede it with some hints on how the election of February 1974 has affected its main arguments.

The election of February 1974 extended to Parliament the deadlock that many observers had long detected in British society and, in particular, in British industrial relations.[1] In doing so, it brought into line, however temporarily and unsatisfactorily, the political and the socio-economic institutions that had, in the preceding two decades, been subjected to increasingly divergent expectations. Elections had been fought on the assumption that their outcome was to produce responsible party government, resting on coherent, disciplined majorities. Coalitions were bad because they diffused responsibility, involved excessive compromise, and could not be accurately related to the will of the electorate. Minority governments were a lesser evil, inviting, as they did, instability, but having at any rate the merit of clarifying who ran the country and who did not.[2] Responsible party government was designed, and expected, to provide strong leadership, coherent policies and, above all, to arbitrate between the competing organized interests that are the hallmark of an advanced industrial society. This view was accepted by the exponents of the 'smack of firm government', the Wilson administration of 1964–70. *In Place of Strife*, the White Paper introducing the 1968 Industrial Relations Bill, demanded 'the active support and intervention of the government' to regulate 'the necessary conflicts of interest in industry'.[3] *In Place of Strife* was based on a preference for formal institutions over conventions, for tidiness over untidiness, preferences that Mr Heath showed even more strongly when he became Prime Minister in 1970 and deduced, from the unexpected result of the 1970 election, that he had a mandate to carry into effect.

Yet decisive government, especially in socio-economic matters, also means divisive government; it means a challenge to the stalemate in British class relations, to the widespread fear of the consequences of an ultimate show-down, to the faith that many participants in industrial conflict had in 'beer and sandwiches' solutions, perfected by Mr Macmillan.[4] The Donovan Report, commissioned by the Labour Govern-

---

[1] e.g. Professor S. H. Beer, quoted on p. 154; and Peter Jenkins, summarizing the psychology of the Donovan Report, *The Battle of Downing Street* (London, 1970), pp. 22–25.

[2] See pp. 40, 42–3.

[3] *In Place of Strife: A Policy for Industrial Relations,* Cmnd. 3888 (London, 1969), p. 5.

[4] 'The Unions asked a lot of questions . . . but in a very amicable and reasonable tone. A good deal of whisky was consumed.' Macmillan, H. *Riding the Storm, 1956–1959: Memoirs,* Vol. IV (London, 1971), pp. 710–12.

ment, but repudiated in its own Industrial Relations Bill, had given the most eloquent justification of this private world of complex bargaining. Rather in the manner of Bagehot, it distinguished between the dignified parts of our industrial constitution – the 'formal system' – and its efficient secret – the 'informal system'.

'The formal system assumes that collective bargaining is a matter of reaching written agreements. The informal system consists largely in tacit arrangements and understandings, and in custom and practice . . .

[The] lack of intention to make legally binding collective agreements, or, better perhaps, this intention and policy that collective bargaining and collective agreements should remain outside the law, is one of the characteristic features of our system of industrial relations which distinguishes it from other comparable systems. It is deeply rooted in its structure . . .

The British system of industrial relations is based on voluntarily agreed rules which, as a matter of principle, are not enforced by law . . .

Any suggestion that conflict between the two systems can be resolved by forcing the informal system to comply with the formal should be set aside. Reality cannot be forced to comply with pretences.' [1]

There was every reason to believe that these principles were accepted, if only *faute de mieux* and with a shrug of the shoulder, by the majority of the population. Reflecting on the reasons for expected defeat of Mr Heath in 1970, *The Economist* wrote,

'For many years now, certainly since 1945 if not 1914, the British public has placed greater importance on the stability of its society, on the gradualness of economic and social change, on resistance to political zeal and violence . . . than most other similar political communities have done. For this it has been prepared, apparently deliberately, to forfeit the rate of economic growth, and thereby in part the opportunity for personal acquisition that a country with so developed an economy . . . could have achieved had it wished.' [2]

If this assertion is true – and it is an important part of my argument that it is – then there was no occasion for surprise at the outcome of the February 1974 election. For a politically decisive answer to the question 'Who governs Britain?' would have damaged, if not broken, the *de facto* permanent coalition of the major producer groups that has been Britain's other government since World War II. It would have exposed, irremediably, the contradictory expectations we have hitherto harboured of strong, single-party government and pluralistic conciliation. Thus, the negative explanation for the election result – that most people in Britain did *not* want a show-down between the Government and the unions, or at any rate that they were not prepared to pay the price for one – is the one we can offer most confidently. More positive explanations must be more speculative. How many of the factors in February 1974 were special and temporary, how many of them have become major and long-term features

[1] Royal Commission on Trade Unions and Employers' Associations, Cmnd. 3623 (London, 1968), pp. 36, 126.
[2] *The Economist,* 13 June, 1970, p. 10.

of British electoral behaviour will be clearer by the time of the next election (which may well be over by the time these words appear in print).

First, the short term factors. Here again it is easier to demonstrate negative than positive propositions. The most obvious conclusion is that it is almost impossible to turn a British general election into a referendum on a particular issue. The occasion for the election was the miners' strike, leading to the three-day week in industry. But in the course of a campaign such specific preoccupations are swamped by the more general questions of the parties' record. At the beginning of February voters ranked strikes equally with prices and the economy as the most important issue; by the end of February there was a two-to-one majority for the economy.[1] The second most obvious conclusion is that 'the electorate', not being a cohesive body with a collective mind and will, cannot possibly have wanted a deadlocked result. Common sense as well as limited survey evidence suggests that those who voted Labour or Conservative – which was still three out of every four voters – did so because they wanted their party to form the Government.[2]

A much more important question, then, is why only three out of four voters – fewer than at any time since 1931 – favoured the major parties. Here, too, there are short- as well as long-term factors, for the tidy alternation in office of Government and Opposition requires firstly, discontent with the incumbent administration, secondly, confidence in the alternative, and thirdly, overriding faith in this particular method of providing good government. There was little doubt of the unpopularity of the Government during most of its period of office; there was equally little doubt of the unpopularity of the Opposition. In so far as not merely Mr Heath but many non-Conservative observers expected Labour to be defeated again in 1974, the main reason lay not in Mr Heath's merits, but in Mr Wilson's defects.[3] Throughout the 1970–4 Parliament, Labour had succeeded in gaining only one by-election seat from the Conservatives. The remaining four Conservative losses had been to the Liberals, and Labour in turn had lost three seats, one to the Liberals, one to the SNP and one to the former Labour MP, Dick Taverne. In the last six months of 1973 favourable answers to the question 'Do you think the Labour Party would run the country well or badly if it were re-elected?' ranged from 34 per cent to 27 per cent; favourable answers to the question, 'Do you think Mr Wilson would do a good job or a bad job as Prime Minister?' ranged from 42 per cent to 33 per cent.[4] Though Labour did, in the end, emerge with the greatest number of seats, it did so with only 37.2 per cent of the total vote, its lowest share for forty years.

The reason for that must, in turn, be sought in some of the longer-term electoral developments in Britain, for though these did not preclude a decisive outcome, they made the present fragmentation of the electorate –

[1] ORC survey, *The Times,* 27 Feb., 1974; Gallup Poll, *Sunday Telegraph,* 24 Feb., 1974.
[2] 'Wilson is Favourite for Number Ten', *The Sunday Times,* 3 March 1974.
[3] For the importance of this criterion, see p. 148.
[4] ORC poll, *The Times,* 7 Dec. 1973.

unthinkable twenty years ago – possible. In the mid-fifties it had looked as though the British electorate was being increasingly absorbed in two stable, disciplined class-based voting armies. The principal change since then has been ever-increasing electoral volatility. The main side-effects of this are increasingly violent fluctuations between the major parties, increasing support (in short or long bursts) for third and minor parties, and a general decline in turn-out, halted only in 1974.

The first and most obvious symptom of this is the rate at which swings between the parties at general elections increased from 1950 to 1970.[1] The cumulative swing to the Conservatives at the three elections between 1950 and 1959 was 4.0 per cent, less than the swing in 1970 alone. In February 1974 it was lower – 0.7 per cent from Conservatives to Labour – but that was because both parties lost in more or less equal amounts to smaller parties. Indeed the 1974 figures show that 'swing', which implies regular and uniform movement from one major party to another, is an unsatisfactory measurement for these purposes, for it tends to disguise the extent of the cross-currents. A better indicator is the steadily declining share of the total *electorate* polled by both major parties since 1950, for this takes into account both changes in turn-out and the shares of minor parties.

Percentage of Total Electorate Supporting Major Parties, 1950–1974

	Con.	Lab.	Con.+Lab.	Turn-out
1950	37.6	39.9	77.5	84.0
1951	39.6	40.3	79.9	82.5
1955	38.1	35.6	73.8	76.8
1959	38.8	34.5	73.4	78.8
1964	33.4	34.0	67.5	77.0
1966	31.7	36.3	68.0	75.8
1970	33.2	31.5	64.7	72.0
1974 (Feb)	30.0	29.3	59.3	78.9

This is, cumulatively, a major change.

The decline in turn-out has been fairly steady[2] and was halted only in 1974. It is one symptom of the loosening of bonds between the voter and those who claim to carry out his wishes. Another symptom has been the increasing rate of dissatisfaction with the Government as revealed at by-elections. The normal pattern of a government's mid-term unpopularity began to emerge much more sharply after 1955.

[1] p. 120.

[2] For a discussion of this and related phenomena, see pp. 148–9.

Median Drop in Pro-Government Vote
at By-Elections, 1955–1973 [1]

1955–6	6%
1957	9%
1958	10%
1959	3%
1960	6%
1961	16%
1962	19%
1963	11%
1964	9%
1966–7	17%
1968	20%
1969–70	15%
1970–71	9%
1972	10%
1973	17%

Until 1970 this protest vote was divided between the main Opposition party and the Liberals; only from 1966 onwards did some of it also go to the Scottish and Welsh Nationalists. Except at Orpington, seats gained by minor parties at by-elections always reverted to the major party at the subsequent general election, in line with a general reassertion of traditional loyalties. Even so, there were signs of further fissures in the party structure by 1970. In the doldrums of the Macmillan Government the Liberals alone had been able to rival the official Opposition as the beneficiaries of discontent. Under the Wilson Government it was the Nationalists who managed to exploit the traditional weakness and unpopularity of the other established parties in industrial Scotland and Wales. For that reason, it was tempting to interpret this upsurge as a purely temporary phenomenon, explicable by the existence of an exceptionally unpopular Labour Government,[2] different in kind from the predictable epidemics of Liberal revival. The reversion to Labour of the two Nationalist by-election successes (Hamilton and Carmarthen) seemed to confirm this hypothesis. But the 1970 election also saw the election, for the first time since 1945, of two MPs not belonging to the three established parties, one Scottish Nationalist and one Labour Independent, S. O. Davies of Merthyr Tydfil, a popular incumbent MP who had been denied renomination by his party on the grounds of old age. And even though his seat, too, reverted to Labour on his death, these were straws in the wind.

Since 1970 all these deviations from loyalty to the major parties have reappeared in greatly magnified form. Firstly, the Liberals revived more strongly than ever before. In 1973 their median votes in by-elections

[1] See Cook, C. and Ramsden, J. (eds), *By-Elections in British Politics* (London, 1973), esp. Appendix A.

[2] See p. 119.

were 37 per cent, compared with medians of 25–7 per cent in 1957–8 and 1961–3. They gained five seats, including one from the Opposition, and held three of these (Rochdale, Isle of Ely and Berwick) at the general election. Secondly, there was a renewed Nationalist revival, stronger in Scotland than in Wales, falsifying earlier hypotheses. And though the SNP lost its by-election gain of Glasgow Govan, it gained six new seats, four from the Conservatives and two from Labour. Throughout Scotland the SNP polled 21.8 per cent of the vote (compared with 11.5 per cent in 1970 and 5.1 per cent in 1966) and is now implanted as a major force in all parts of the country. Plaid Cymru in Wales, polling less well than in 1970 (10.0 per cent instead of 11.5 per cent), its bridgehead restricted to the rural, Welsh-speaking parts, also gained two seats and missed a third by three votes. Thirdly, Dick Taverne, a Labour MP, whom his constituency party had declined to readopt for the coming election on doctrinal grounds, resigned his seat, won resoundingly at a by-election and narrowly held it at the general election.[1] He was joined by another disavowed Labour MP, Edward Milne of Blyth, whose disagreement was, however, organizational, not doctrinal. If we add to this the collapse of 'official', i.e. Conservative-supported, Unionism in Northern Ireland, leading to eleven independent 'loyalist' MPs where there had previously been one, we come to a total of thirty-seven minor party MPs, belonging to six groupings and representing $7\frac{1}{2}$ million voters:

Liberals	14
United Ulster Unionists	11
SNP	7
Plaid Cymru	2
Democratic Labour (Taverne)	1
Independent Labour (Milne)	1
SDLP (Fitt)	1

Why? The hypothesis that we are here dealing with a long-term, structural phenomenon is confirmed by experience from other advanced countries. In most Western industrial countries the sixties have seen some major realignment of party loyalties, either in the disappearance of old parties and the rise of new ones, or in a radical abandonment of traditional ideologies as the price of survival, or in a major shift in the sources of support. All this has happened in societies where the sources of political cleavage generally reach back to the beginnings of indus-trialisation and democracy and which have, in the main, been characterized by a stability of political loyalties sometimes bordering on paralysis.

The most outstanding example is that of France, where the unstable multi-partism of the Third and Fourth Republics gave way to a bi-polar equilibrium, based on Gaullism and an alliance of the old Communist and a reconstructed Socialist party, only to see the Gaullist electoral front disintegrate for the benefit of a new majority of the Centre-Right.

---

[1] See his own account of the episode, Taverne, D. *The Future of the Left* (London, 1973).

Other examples could be multiplied – the abandonment of Marxism by the German and Austrian Social Democratic parties, both rewarded, within a decade, with electoral office; the secularisation of Dutch politics; the sudden fragmentation in Scandinavian party life after decades of Social Democratic hegemony; the realignment of American party loyalties – the survival of party labels notwithstanding – following the defection of the South from the Democratic Party, at least in presidential elections.

No doubt each of these realignments has its own, local explanation, as issues have arisen that the traditional parties were ill-equipped to cope with. No doubt all advanced states have had to cope with varying degrees of inflation and the problems of reconciling increasing welfare demands with politically acceptable taxation levels, thus making electoral popularity more and more elusive for both governments and oppositions. But we have to ask whether these are causes rather than symptoms. Why has it become more difficult for established parties to accommodate new demands? Why can parties with long-cultivated mass bases no longer depend on their members' blind loyalty to see them through hard times? Where is the ballot fodder of yesteryear?

We can only speculate. It is possible that changes in the social structure – in type of occupation, in home-ownership and 'consumerism', in educational and geographical mobility, have helped to break down those homogeneous sub-cultures that instilled and reinforced political loyalties of almost religious intensity. It is possible that the convergence of party programmes, and the reduction of the party struggle to competing claims of administrative competence, have, by suggesting that the stakes are marginal rather than fundamental, removed many of the spurs to political faith and political activism. It is very likely that changed methods of propaganda and persuasion – the rise of television, the decline of the local meeting – have made the voter more of a private individual and less of a group actor.

What we can assert is that all the evidence points towards a lessening in the intensity of party loyalty, so that however much individuals may continue to 'identify' with this or that party, they are more and more willing to act inconsistently with this identification. In the recent referenda in Norway (on the Common Market) and Italy (on divorce) large numbers of electors defied the instructions of their parties in a way that would almost certainly not have happened fifteen years ago. In America not only do fewer people identify with either of the major parties, but there has been a startling and continuous rise in ticket-splitting since the 1950s.[1] We do not know how many people hesitated before casting their vote in 1974. Of the admittedly small *Sunday Times* panel, 41 per cent changed their minds at least once during the campaign.[2] Britain is therefore in line with most other Western democracies. That the changes in some of these democracies contrast with

[1] Sundquist, J. L., *Dynamics of the Party System. Alignment and Realignment of Political Parties in the United States* (Washington D.C., 1973), pp. 340–50.
[2] See note 8, *supra*.

those in Britain – the tendency in France and West Germany, for instance, being towards fewer parties – seems less important than some observers have suggested,[1] when we bear in mind that the common factor in all countries is volatility and a greater willingness to realign.

That leaves two questions to be asked about aspects of the British representative system that I emphasize in the main text – the class basis of electoral choice and the preference for a clear-cut, bi-polar party alternative.[2] The occasion for the election, a dispute between the government and the trade unions, might have been designed to polarize voters on class lines, but the evidence whether it did so is inconclusive. The proportion of electors agreeing 'that there is a class struggle in this country' rose steadily from December 1973; of Labour voters 74 per cent thought so, of Conservatives 48 per cent.[3] On the other hand, survey evidence of voting by social class does not indicate strong polarization. NOP's 'Portrait of the Electorate' showed the following alignment compared with the previous election:

Percentage Charges of Party Support by Class, 1970–1974 in per cent

	Con.	Lab.	Lib.
Class AB	—12	0	+11
Class C1	— 7	—10	+18
Class C2	— 4	—10	+15
Class DE	— 8	— 5	+13

and ORC showed a similar pattern[4]

	Con.	Lab.	Lib.
Class AB	—11	0	+ 9
Class C1	— 9	— 5	+14
Class C2	— 6	— 7	+12
Class DE	— 5	— 8	+13

It is obvious that in an election in which one-quarter of the votes did not go to the class parties there was a strong counter-current at work as well: the pressure to make a rational choice about the next government against the pressure to reaffirm acquired loyalties.

To suggest that the high vote for minor parties was in itself a repudiation of the two-party system is again to assume that the electorate has a collective mind; it was, at best, a repudiation of the two

[1] Crewe, I. 'Do Butler and Stokes Really Explain Political Change in Britain?', *European Journal of Political Research*, II (March 1974) pp. 50–1. The reduction in the number of parties in France and Germany can certainly be attributed to the personalization of executive office. There is no uniform trend towards fewer parties in Western countries.

[2] Pp. 102 ff; 60–1.

[3] Gallup Poll, *Daily Telegraph*, 21 February, 1974.

[4] NOP *Political Bulletin* Feb. 1974; ORC, *Changes in Voting Behaviour,* 1970–1974 (mimeo.) cf. pp. 104, 109.

main parties. The reluctance, not merely of the main parties but of the Liberals, too, to arrive at a formal coalition arrangement underlined the instinctive dislike of British politicians for this form of government, as well as their lack of skill in operating it. Since the February election was not run as a contest between single-party and shared government, we cannot read any specific preference into the result. But the Liberal Party has subsequently made participation in a coalition and the formation of a national government part of its official policy, and the form of government may therefore be a specific issue in a subsequent election. If, on those conditions, the Liberals held or increased their following, we should have to revise, at least for the time being. Disraeli's dictum that 'England does not love coalitions'.

CONTENTS

I

Parliament and Democracy

'IN democratic states,' wrote Aristotle, 'the people (i.e. demos) is sovereign.'[1] Yet it is one thing to possess a legal right, another to exercise it effectively. In Britain we have a Parliament, and parliamentary elections, as instruments for expressing popular opinion democratically. But the day-to-day business of legislation and policy-making, even the organization of the political parties which canalize opinion, is delegated to a small number of representatives elected for that purpose. Clearly there is a point at which democratic purpose and representative institutions may clash; the two not only have widely divergent historical origins, but may have purposes inconsistent with each other. Representation need not be democratic and democracies need not be parliamentary.

REPRESENTATION WITHOUT DEMOCRACY

Parliaments are a legacy of the feudal Middle Ages. Mediaeval monarchs could not expect to rule as autocrats or despots. They were expected to seek the advice of the 'estates of the realm', each of which had defined functions and status, both in relation to each other and in relation to the monarch. Because of poor communications, if for no other reason, monarchs depended on the goodwill of local notables for administration, the dispensing of justice, the raising of soldiers and the collection of taxes. Those whose help was indispensable to the monarch were in turn able to insist that the law be not changed, nor taxes levied, without their consent. In England the parliaments which date from the second half of the thirteenth century were representative in two distinct ways, by interest and by territory.

The interests represented in Parliament were the Lords Spiritual (archbishops, bishops and mitred abbots), the Lords Temporal, a category whose definition was uncertain at least until the Tudors, and the Commons. Within the Commons representation was divided between counties and boroughs. Because members of the House of Commons

---

[1] Aristotle, *Politics* (tr. E. Barker) (Oxford, 1948), p. 128.

sat on behalf of communities, not interests or individuals, there was no attempt to equate representation with either population or the size of the electorate. Each county sent two knights, each borough two burgesses. The only exception was the City of London which sent four. Within each county the franchise belonged, from 1430, to all freeholders whose tenements had an annual value of 40 shillings. Within the boroughs it varied widely. Neither system was changed until the Reform Act of 1832. By the accession of Henry VIII (1509) the House of Lords numbered about 100, with spiritual peers slightly in the majority. In the Commons 37 counties were represented by 74 members and 110 boroughs by 222 members.[1]

Parliament, like so many other British institutions, nowadays serves purposes far removed from those for which it was originally intended. Yet vestiges of these purposes remain. We still have a House of Lords and a House of Commons. A peer of the realm may not vote in a parliamentary election. A clergyman of the Established Church may not sit in the House of Commons. Each belongs to an 'estate' already represented elsewhere.

But a reminder of the feudal origins of parliamentary representation is not merely of antiquarian interest. Extreme democrats claim that only 'the people' as a whole, undistracted by class interests or party divisions, should exercise sovereignty; doctrinaire liberals that only individual citizens can be properly represented. But mediaeval social theory viewed society 'corporatively' and 'pluralistically'. Each individual belonged in turn to a larger grouping according to his function, occupation or class. Each of these groupings had legitimate, though limited, rights and privileges within society, thus ensuring the cohesion and stability of the whole. This mediaeval corporatist ideal has again become fashionable in the last hundred years and has attracted social reformers who see in it a remedy for the materialism and class warfare of modern industrial society. On the Left it has been the basis for syndicalists and Guild Socialists, who feel that a 'workers' state', with all that this implies in centralization and bureaucracy, is a contradiction in terms. On the Right, where social cohesion and the maintenance (or revival) of traditions are valued more, it has been the basis of a number of Papal encyclicals and of some experiments by Fascist régimes.

Such views are nevertheless a long way from those which dominate the parliamentary and electoral politics of modern Britain. Only during the last three hundred years, since the Restoration of Charles II, has the public discussion about parliament and representation been conducted in a vocabulary whose meanings we readily understand.

In the eighteenth century, under the influence of Whig ideas, it was

[1] Neale, Sir J. E., *The Elizabethan House of Commons* (London, 1949), pp. 140-1.

considered proper and desirable that representation should be by
interest, even if these interests were no longer the corporations and
estates of mediaeval society. The 'balanced constitution' of the eighteenth century was, in the eyes of its advocates, a balance of the country's
most important interests, 'the great peers, the leading landed gentlemen,
the opulent merchants and manufacturers, the substantial yeomanry',
as Edmund Burke enumerated them.[1] An even more eloquent panegyric
of the old system came from Sir Robert Inglis in 1832, during the debate
on the Reform Bill. He saw Parliament as

'the only constituent body that ever existed, which comprehends within itself, those who can urge the wants and defend the claims of the
landed, the commercial and the professional classes of the country; those
who are bound to uphold the prerogatives of the Crown, the privileges
of the nobility, the interests of the lower classes, . . . the rights of the
distant dependencies, of the East Indies, of the West Indies, of the
colonies, of the great corporations.'[2]

All representation of interests presupposes that some interests are more
important than others. The Duke of Wellington noted with approval
that 'the representation of the people at present contains a larger body of
the property of the country, in which the landed interests have a pre-
ponderating influence'.[3] Between 1660 and 1832 Parliament did indeed
represent landed property *par excellence*. But it was not merely property
collectively, it was also individual property that was represented. According to Namier the great families and the Crown between them were able,
in 1760, to nominate nearly half the House of Commons.[4] The Duke of
Newcastle alone 'returned' seven members.

From the end of the eighteenth century onwards this system was
subject to criticism from two sources. There were, firstly, those who
denied that the balance of interests represented in Parliament corres-
ponded with the balance of interests in the country. The land and, to a
limited degree, commerce had spokesmen in Parliament. Manufacturing
industry had virtually none. Manchester, Birmingham, Leeds and
Glasgow did not return a single member. On these grounds alone at
least a radical redistribution of constituencies was demanded. But
objections went further. The whole idea that only well-established
corporate interest should have a voice in Parliament was being

[1] Burke, E., 'Thoughts on the Cause of the Present Discontents', *Works*
[Oxford World's Classics], Vol. II (Oxford, 1906), p. 38.
[2] Beer, S. H., *Modern British Politics* (2nd edn, London, 1969), p. 19.
[3] Jennings, Sir I., *Party Politics*, Vol. I: *Appeal to the People* (Cambridge,
1960), p. 10.
[4] Namier, Sir L. B., *The Structure of Politics at the Accession of George III*
(2nd edn, London, 1957), pp. 148-9.

questioned. In its place arose the demand that since it was individual citizens who voted in elections, they should be represented as individuals. It was nonsensical that a taxpayer in one borough should have a free say in who became his MP, while a similar taxpayer in another borough was deprived of it. The logical end of this line of argument was universal suffrage. Under the impact of the American and French revolutions, but spurred also by such domestic events as the attempt to unseat John Wilkes after his election as MP for Middlesex, radical propagandists and radical associations began increasingly to demand suffrage reform. Joseph Priestley, Richard Price and above all Tom Paine based their arguments on human equality and natural rights.[1] Yet one did not have to accept the revolutionary implications of these doctrines in order to advocate 'freer' representation. It was simply necessary to argue that each man was the best guardian of his own interest. Each man should therefore be free to make his political choice without the intervention of patrons and unhampered by the accidental survival of anomalies. This argument belonged to the Utilitarian school, particularly James Mill and Jeremy Bentham. Because it was based on enlightened self-interest rather than radical egalitarianism it was less dangerous to the established order.

Both Bentham and the elder Mill favoured universal suffrage, but this was by no means a necessary consequence of the individualist approach. All that was necessary was that every elector, once the qualifications for the franchise had been consistently defined, should make his personal unfettered choice. There was no inherent reason why the franchise should not be restricted to taxpayers, property owners, heads of families, or men over 30 – to persons, that is, who could be expected to behave in a sober, responsible way – as long as the categories were defined by rational argument rather than historical accident.

When reform did come, it made concessions to each of these criticisms of the old order, but the concession was in each case incomplete. The Reform Act of 1832 did two things: it redistributed constituences, and it extended the right to vote. In redistributing constituencies the Act met the criticism that the country's main interests were unfairly represented. Scotland, Ireland and the North of England gained seats, the South of England lost. Cornwall went down from 42 to 13 seats, Wiltshire from 34 to 18. Lancashire went up from 14 to 28, Staffordshire from 10 to 17. Beyond that there was no attempt to make constituencies of equal size. There were still thirty boroughs with electorates below 300 and twelve with electorates over 5,000.

In dealing with the franchise the Act moved decisively towards

---

[1] cf. Priestley, J., *Essay on the First Principles of Government* (1768); Price, R., *Observations on the Nature of Civil Liberty* (1776); Paine, T., *Common Sense* (1776), and *The Rights of Man* (1792).

individualism. There had already been an important step in this direction in 1828–9, when Catholics and Dissenters were at last given the same political rights (including the right to sit in Parliament) as members of the Church of England.[1] Now the franchise in all counties and all boroughs was equalized. In the boroughs the right to vote was given to every householder who occupied a house of at least £10 rental value; in the counties three further categories of copyholders, leaseholders and tenants-at-will were added to the existing forty-shilling freeholders. In some ways the new franchise was more difficult to defend than the old. The old, however eccentric, was at least part of the British way of life. The new invented an arbitrary and not necessarily equitable dividing-line. Sir Robert Peel, leading the Tory opposition to the Bill, asked

'. . . if it be a question of right, why . . . limit the franchise to particular districts and particular classes? Why confine the privilege of voting to those who rent a house at 10 *l.* a year? The law knows no distinction in this respect between the contributors to the support of the state.'

Why exclude 'all that class of society which is above pauperism and below the arbitrary and impassable line of 10 *l.* rental which you have selected?'[2]

Why indeed?

In 1832 British parliamentary representation, feudal and corporative in origin, took an irreversible, but incomplete, step towards democracy, with its urban classical roots.

DEMOCRACY WITHOUT REPRESENTATION

Not only the idea of democracy, but the word itself, came to us from the city-states of classical Greece. But Aristotle's definition of democratic states, that in them 'the people is sovereign', leaves two important questions unsolved. The first is: are 'the people' simply a collection of all the individuals in a state, or are they a cohesive group with common interests and common desires? The second is: how is popular sovereignty to be expressed? Should the whole body of citizens take all the important administrative and judicial decisions, or should these be delegated? And if delegated, how?

Those who advocate pure or direct democracy reply that the people are indeed a collectivity with a will of their own, and that the expression of this will must be protected against two enemies – either self-seeking individuals among the people, or elected representatives who develop autocratic habits. If the people tolerate factions among themselves, or

---

[1] But Jews were excluded until 1858, and atheists until 1888.
[2] 3 March 1831. *H. C. Debates,* 3rd series, Vol. II, 1345–6.

B

delegate their collective sovereign power to individuals, then there is a danger that this power will slip out of their hands altogether. Among modern political theorists Jean-Jacques Rousseau is the foremost exponent of this doctrine:

'Sovereignty, being no more than the exercise of the general will, can never be *alienated*, and . . . the sovereign, who is a collective being only, can be represented by no one but himself . . .

'For the same reason that sovereignty is inalienable, so, too, it is *indivisible*. Either the will is general or it is not. Either it is the will of the whole body of the People, or it is the will merely of one section. Sovereignty cannot be *represented*, for the same reason that it cannot be alienated. It consists essentially of the general will, and will cannot be represented . . . The Deputies of the People are not, nor can they be, its representatives. They can only be its Commissioners. They can make no definite decisions. Laws which the People have not ratified in their own person are null and void.'[1]

The argument is simple: those who have the power to make major decisions on behalf of the people, even if freely elected to such positions of power, inevitably become masters, perhaps even tyrants. Parliaments, therefore, can never be democratic and Rousseau had nothing but contempt for the Englishman's 'freedom':

'The English people think that they are free, but in this belief they are profoundly wrong. They are free only when they are electing members of Parliament. Once the election has been completed, they revert to a condition of slavery: they are nothing.'[2]

One further consequence follows. If the people's interest is to be opposed to that of individuals it must also be opposed to that of factions. Partisanship belongs to the parliamentary game; partisanship is the expression of special, and therefore selfish, interests. 'If, then, the general will is to be truly expressed [according to Rousseau] it is essential that there be no subsidiary groups within the state.'[3] No parliaments, no parties. That, necessarily, is the slogan of all extreme democrats. No power may be interposed between the will of the people and the making of policy. The slogan is valid only if we share two of the extreme democrat's basic assumptions. The first is that all élites and all oligarchies are hostile to the public interest; the second that there can

[1] Rousseau, J.-J., *The Social Contract* [Oxford World's Classics] (Oxford, 1947), pp. 269, 271, 372–3.
[2] *Ibid.*, p. 373.
[3] *Ibid.*, p. 275.

never be any serious dispute as to where the interests of the people lie. The need to take political power out of the hands of 'the interests' or organised minorities, and restore it to 'the people' has been a constant refrain in radical and democratic propaganda over the past two hundred years. It took overtly anti-parliamentary forms most frequently in those states which were least accustomed to the workings of a representative system. Nearly a century after Rousseau the French Socialist, Victor Considérant, thundered:

'If the people delegate their sovereignty, they resign it. The people no longer govern themselves; they are governed . . . Then, people, resign your sovereignty! I guarantee you a fate the opposite of Saturn's: your sovereignty will be devoured by your daughter, the Delegation.'[1]

Similar themes recur in Spain, Italy and Russia. In Britain, too, the tendency to equate the will of the people with the public interest was widespread. The Radical J. A. Roebuck, attacking the opponents of working-class suffrage in 1859, claimed

'The majority of a country can have no interest inimical to the interests of the country. If you give power to a minority, that minority may have interests at variance with the interests of the country; but the majority cannot – if they understand their own interests.'[2]

These doctrines, or at least their relevance to modern life, have not lacked critics. The first and most obvious line of attack is that direct participatory democracy may be fine in a Greek city-state or a rural Swiss canton, but is inapplicable to modern states with fifty or a hundred million inhabitants. To that some anarchists and federalists reply that this merely proves the need to decentralize power and to reduce the size of the unit of administration. It is, indeed, worth noting that the whole idea of a community based on direct self-government is agrarian or at any rate pre-industrial, and that in Western Europe the appeal of such theories has declined since the mid-nineteenth century. In industrial civilization division of labour is the criterion of modernity in both economic and political processes.

There are, however, three weightier objections to doctrines of primitive democracy. The first is theoretical and it concerns the very nature and definability of such concepts as 'the people'. This objection

[1] Considérant, V., *La Solution ou le Gouvernement Direct du Peuple* (Paris, 1850). Quoted by Michels, R., *Political Parties. A Sociological Study of the Oligarchical Tendencies of Modern Democracy* (intr. Lipset, S. M.) (New York, 1962), p. 75.
[2] Quoted by Beer, *op, cit.*, p. 42 n.

is discussed later in the book.[1] The second is technical and is in its essence the subject of a significant admission by Rousseau himself:

'If we take the term in its strict meaning, no true democracy has ever existed, nor ever will. It is against the natural order that a large number should rule and a small number be ruled. It is inconceivable that the people should be in permanent session for the administration of public affairs, and it is clear that commissions could not be set up for that purpose without the form of the administration being thereby changed.'[2]

The most important objection, however, is the third. This challenges not the feasibility of direct democracy, but its desirability. Just as some denounce representative institutions because these interpose an élite between the people and the exercise of power, so others welcome such institutions for precisely this reason. All forms of parliamentary representation modify or qualify the degree to which the wishes or opinions of the governed can influence the policies of the governors. There is, however, an enormous range within which a representative body *can* assert its autonomy.

REPRESENTATIVE DEMOCRACY

The basic characteristics of democracy have not changed since they were defined by Aristotle:

'The law declares equality to mean that the poor are to count no more than the rich: neither is to be sovereign, and both are to be on a level . . . A constitution of this kind is bound to be a democracy; for the people are the majority, and the will of the majority is sovereign.'[3]

This definition leaves untouched the question of representative institutions. Extreme democrats reject all representation as being incompatible with popular sovereignty; in the context of nineteenth-century Britain, however, it was the composition, rather than the idea of Parliament itself, that was attacked. Democracy meant, in effect, parliamentary government with universal suffrage and majority rule. Thus the People's Charter, drawn up in 1838 by Radicals dissatisfied with the First Reform Act, made six demands:

manhood suffrage
secret ballot

---

[1] See below, pp. 141–2.
[2] Rousseau, *op, cit.*, p. 331.
[3] Aristotle, *op. cit.*, p. 197.

payment for members of parliament
abolition of the property qualification for members
equal-sized constituencies
annual elections.

The Chartists seemed to their contemporaries dangerous revolutionaries, but had the Charter been enacted, Rousseau would still have regarded Englishmen as slaves. On the one hand nineteenth-century democrats, whether Radicals like the Chartists, or Utilitarians like Bentham and the elder Mill, were individualists. They were convinced that every sane, adult citizen had the right to a say in the country's government, and to be elected as the representative of his fellow-citizens. At the same time there was a populist element in their thought. Universal suffrage would enfranchise not only every individual, but 'the people', the under-privileged many, collectively. Individual rights were equated with popular sovereignty at the expense of considerable conceptual confusion.[1] When, after the Reform Act of 1884, the majority of adult males had the vote in Britain, Joseph Chamberlain exclaimed, 'At last we have a Government of the people and by the people.'[2] We are back at Roebuck's insistence that the interests of the majority and the interests of the nation necessarily coincide.

In the twentieth century such self-confident over-simplifications are treated with disdain, and the weaknesses of the classical individualist and populistic standpoints are generally accepted.[3] There remains one rather more intractable problem. Granted some degree of majority suffrage, how does this affect the position of the individual legislator? Which deserves higher priority – the will of the people, or the MP with a mind of his own?

THE DEMOCRATIC REPRESENTATIVE

Tom Paine, at the end of the eighteenth century, was fully aware of the dilemma and in no doubt as to how it should be resolved. So that

'*the elected* might never form to themselves an interest separate from the electors, prudence will point out the propriety of having elections often;

---

[1] The two concepts tend also to be confused in R. A. Dahl's otherwise admirable *A Preface to Democratic Theory* (Chicago, 1956), especially p. 45. Dahl regards the majoritarian principle as the most extreme form of democracy, classifying it as 'populistic' (pp. 34–5), but he fails to make the important distinction between extreme populists, who oppose all mediation by representative institutions, and those majoritarians who accept parliamentary forms and who are therefore closer to Dahl's notion of 'limited government'.

[2] Beer, *op. cit.*, p. 41.

[3] See below, pp. 140–2.

because as the *elected* might by that means return and mix again with the general body of the *electors* in a few months, their fidelity to the public will be secured by the prudent reflection of not making a rod for themselves.'[1]

It was for the same reason that the Chartists demanded annual Parliaments. There were, however, other views on the extent to which Parliament as a body, and the individual member of it, should be bound by the views and instructions of the electorate. Parliament consisted of the King's advisers. Through Parliament, 'the grand inquest of the nation', grievances might be aired and requests made known. Parliament might participate in the responsibility of governing and might even in the course of time seize the major share of 'carrying on the King's government'; but it needed to do so in the light of the national interest and its own sense of responsibility, not as an unquestioning reflector of the popular mood.

This notion appealed most easily to Tories, to whom national unity and the dignity of the state, personified by the monarch, came paramount. But while the Whigs attached greater importance to Parliament than the Tories, and less to the Crown, they agreed that members of Parliament were responsible primarily to their own consciences. One of them in 1734 declared

'After we are chosen and have taken our seats in the house, we have no longer any dependence on the electors, at least in so far as regards our behaviour here. Their whole power is then devolved upon us, and we are in every question that comes before this House, to regard only the public good in general, and to determine them according to our own judgments.'[2]

It was not merely Parliament collectively, but the individual MP also, who was considered autonomous. The classical claim on behalf of the independent parliamentarian was that made by Edmund Burke to the electors of Bristol after the declaration of the poll in 1774:

'Parliament is not a *congress* of ambassadors from different and hostile interests; . . . but parliament is a *deliberative* assembly of *one* nation, with *one* interest, that of the whole . . . You choose a member indeed; but when you have chosen him, he is not member of Bristol, but he is a member of *parliament* . . .

[1] Birch, A. H. *Representative and Responsible Government. An Essay on the British Constitution* (London, 1964), p. 42.
[2] *Ibid.*, p. 29.

'Certainly, gentlemen, it ought to be the happiness and glory of a representative to live in the strictest union, the closest correspondence, the most unreserved communication with his constituents . . . It is his duty to sacrifice his repose, his pleasures, his satisfactions to theirs. But his unbiased opinion, his enlightened conscience, he ought not to sacrifice to you; to any man, or to any set of men living. These he does not derive from your pleasure; no, nor from the law and the constitution. They are a trust from Providence, for the abuse of which he is deeply answerable. Your representative owes you, not his industry only, but his judgment; and he betrays, instead of serving you, if he sacrifices it to your opinion.'[1]

Such statements, like any other clear-cut attempt at imposing rigorous principle on British constitutional conventions, ignore the compromises and ambiguities of the political market-place. And it may also be said that such lofty, even arrogant, claims to independence are irrelevant in our days of universal suffrage. Yet the notion that 'any set of men living' should be the dictators of an MP's behaviour remains repulsive – at any rate if that set of men are not themselves MPs. When Mr Frank Cousins resigned from the Cabinet in July 1966, and resumed his post as General Secretary of the Transport and General Workers' Union, the union's general council asked him to resign from Parliament. A Liberal MP, quoting Burke's 1774 speech, claimed that the union's action was an attempt to 'control or limit [Mr Cousins'] complete freedom of action in Parliament', The Speaker rejected the complaint but only because it had not been raised at the earliest opportunity. He did not pronounce on its merits.[2]

Nor were eighteenth-century claims to independence strictly accurate, since at least half the members of the House of Commons were not 'elected' at all. They were nominated by a patron, and the practice was certainly not an eighteenth-century innovation. The system of patronage did, however, contribute towards making the House of Commons a national forum, as opposed to 'a congress of ambassadors'. While MPs could not avoid speaking and voting for specific economic interests, they could in many cases avoid the concentration on parochial issues which a numerous electorate might have forced on them. There was little pressure on the MP to be a native or a resident of the constituency he sat for. The fifteenth-century statute requiring knights and baronets to be 'dwelling and resident' was soon ignored, though not formally

---

[1] Burke, E., 'Speech to the Electors of Bristol, on his being declared by the Sheriffs, duly elected one of the Representatives in Parliament for that City, on Thursday, the 3rd of November, 1774', Works, Vol. II, pp. 164–5.
[2] The Times, 20 July 1966.

repealed until 1774.[1] According to Sir John Neale, at least 164 out of 341 borough members of the 1584 House of Commons were 'outsiders'.[2] Patrons could use their power to advance a brilliant protégé with no local connections. Hampden, the elder and younger Pitt, Fox, Burke, Canning and Gladstone all owed the beginnings of their careers to such 'pocket' or 'rotten' boroughs.

With the extension of the franchise, the question of the member's independence became more, not less acute. Just as Paine and the other radicals saw in the electorate's control over the member a guarantee of democracy, so the more moderate Liberals saw in a strong, independent Parliament a protection against mob rule. To ensure good government, those who compose Parliament must be different from, and better than, the general run of men. They must *not* be representative of the electorate in the sense of being its mirror-image in intellect and social composition – otherwise it could not, in James Madison's phrase, 'refine and enlarge the public view'.[3] How can this be made to happen? It is possible that the bulk of the electorate actually prefers to be ruled by its betters. Nations where that happens were classified by Walter Bagehot as 'deferential':

'It has been thought strange, but there *are* nations in which the numerous unwiser part wishes to be ruled by the less numerous wiser part. The numerical majority – whether by custom or by choice is immaterial – is ready, is eager to delegate its power of choosing its ruler to a certain select minority. It abdicates in favour of its *élite*, and consents to obey whoever that *élite* may confide in . . .
England is the type of deferential countries.[4]

'The mass of the old electors [he wrote some years later, after the Second Reform Act] did not analyse very much: they liked to have one of their 'betters' represent them; if he was rich they respected him much; and if he was a lord they liked him the better. The issue put before these electors was, Which of two rich people will you choose?'[5]

Much has been made of the alleged political deference of the British. Bagehot thought that it was to wealth, social station and public ceremony. More serious-minded Liberals felt that it ought to be to intellect.

[1] Porritt, E. and A. G., *The Unreformed House of Commons. Parliamentary Representation Before 1832* (Cambridge, 1903), Vol. I, p. 122.

[2] Neale, *op. cit.*, endpaper, p. 31.

[3] Hamilton, A., Madison, J. and Jay, J., *The Federalist Papers* No. 10 [Mentor Edition] (New York, 1961), p. 82. (Hereafter referred to as *The Federalist*.)

[4] Bagehot, W., *The English Constitution* (introd. R. H. S. Crossman) (London, 1963), p. 247.

[5] *Ibid.*, p. 271.

James Mill, while advocating universal suffrage, was 'perfectly confident' that

'the opinions of that class of the people, who are below the middle rank, are formed and their minds are directed by that intelligent and virtuous rank who come the most immediately into contact with them . . . The vast majority would be sure to be guided by their advice and example.'[1]

His son, John Stuart Mill, was even more adamant:

'It is so important that the electors should choose as their representatives wiser men than themselves, and should consent to be governed by that superior wisdom . . . that it seems impossible to lay down for the elector any positive rule of duty . . . Individuals, and peoples who are acutely sensible of the value of superior wisdom, are likely to recognize it, where it exists, by other signs than thinking exactly as they do.'

To ensure this, the franchise would have to be weighted in favour of an *élite*, not indeed of money or land, but 'of authenticated superiority of education'.[2]

This is, however, not the only way of minimizing the impact of democracy on parliament. Another is to allow a reasonably long interval between elections. Only in this way, according to J. S. Mill, can a legislator demonstrate that he need not be 'a mere obedient voter and advocate of their opinions, by which he can render himself in the eyes of his constituents a desirable and creditable representative'.[3] Only in this way, wrote Madison at the time of the constitutional debate in America, can a legislator acquire any expertise. This

'can only be attained, or at least thoroughly attained, by actual experience of the station which requires the use of it. The period of service ought, therefore, to bear some proportion to the extent of practical knowledge requisite to the due performance of the service.'[4]

A third way of stabilizing a democratically elected parliament is to counter-balance it with a second chamber. Such a chamber may take a form that is irrelevant to this discussion: a hereditary House of Lords or (as in Canada) an appointed Senate stand or fall by *not* being democratic. But even an elected second chamber may fulfil a stabilizing purpose if its size, electoral base and term of service differ from those of the lower house. This is what the authors of the *Federalist* had in mind

[1] Mill, J., *An Essay on Government* (Cambridge, 1937), p. 72.
[2] Mill, J. S., *Representative Government* [Everyman Library] (London, 1910), pp. 319, 320.
[3] *ibid.*, p. 313.
[4] *The Federalist* No. 53, p. 333.

when they proposed a Senate of the kind which was eventually set up in the United States:

'Every new election in the states is found to change one half of the representatives. From this change of men must proceed a change of opinions; and from a change of opinions a change of measures. But a continual change even of good measures is inconsistent with every rule of prudence and every prospect of success . . .

'Another defect to be supplied by a senate lies in a want of due acquaintance with the objects and principles of legislation. It is not possible that an assembly of men called for the most part from pursuits of a private nature, continued in appointment for a short time . . . should, if left wholly to themselves, escape a variety of important errors in the exercise of their legislative trust . . .

'A good government implies two things: first, fidelity to the object of government, which is the happiness of the people; secondly, a knowlege of the means by which that object can be best attained.'[1]

THE POLITICIAN AS PROFESSIONAL

Madison was not alone in his demand for expertise in politics, and in his apprehension that excessive democracy would bring bad government. Liberals and Conservatives alike, during the nineteenth century, feared the irruption of the masses into politics. They did so because they accepted the arguments and the vocabulary of the Radicals who talked of 'the will of the people' or 'the will of the majority'. Men like Alexis de Tocqueville, J. S. Mill or Matthew Arnold did not like the prospect of having to live under the 'tyranny of the majority' and wished, by constructing appropriate institutions, to avoid this fate. But they agreed with the Radicals in thinking that 'the people' or 'the majority' were real entities with definable qualities; one had to be an ultra-sceptical reactionary to regard such concepts as absurd or nonsensical. Experience since then has shown that these concepts are not very useful in analysing the political process, for reasons to be more fully discussed below.

More immediately relevant are the reasons why the coming of universal suffrage has disappointed many of the hopes of the early democrats, and failed to confirm the worst fears of their Liberal and Conservative contemporaries, 'All professions,' wrote Bernard Shaw, 'are conspiracies against the laity.' To the democrat it is essential that justice, the administration, the social services, the making of laws, should be as accessible as possible to the ordinary citizen and should work in his interests. To ensure this, their workings should be supervised by

[1] ibid., No, 62, pp. 379–80.

laymen, and many devices, from juries to parent-teacher associations, exist for this purpose. Pre-democratic conventions – the ceremonial of the Law Courts and of Parliament, the often incomprehensible jargon of statutes and white papers, the Establishment in-jokes which pervade the more literate branches of the mass media – are all obstacles to this popular control, but they are not the most serious. Radical democrats made a great mistake when they supposed that the mysteries of government had been invented solely as a plot to keep the people in ignorance. The misapprehension was a widespread one, and even Lenin believed that after the revolution management and administration would be within the grasp of 'any literate person'.[1]

Within six months he was disillusioned,[2] and for a very elementary reason. The more modern a society, the more advanced its economy, the more specialized and sophisticated becomes the business of running it. The possession of any skill gives the possessor power over those who lack it; this is most directly and obviously true when the skill itself is in the use of political power. The observation of this fact led Robert Michels to formulate his 'iron law of oligarchy':

'It is organization which gives birth to the dominion of the elected over the electors, of the mandatories over the mandators, of the delegates over the delegators. *Who says organization, says oligarchy.*

'By a universally applicable social law, every organ of the collectivity, brought into existence through the need for the division of labour, creates for itself, as soon as it becomes consolidated, interests peculiar to itself. The existence of these special interests involves a necessary conflict with the interests of the collectivity. Nay, more, social strata fulfilling peculiar functions tend to become isolated, to produce organs fitted for the defence of their own peculiar interests. In the long run they tend to undergo transformation into distinct classes . . .

'According to this view, the government, or if the phrase be preferred, the state, cannot be anything other than the organization of a minority . . . The majority is thus permanently incapable of self-government; . . . always and necessarily there springs from the masses a new organized minority which raises itself to the rank of a governing class. Thus the majority of human beings . . . must be content to constitute the pedestal of an oligarchy.'[3]

This thesis has been seminal to much of modern political anslysis,

[1] Lenin, V. I., 'Can the Bolsheviks Retain State Power?' (September, 1917), *Selected Works* (Moscow, 1960), Vol. II, pp. 438–9.
[2] Lenin, V. I., 'The Immediate Tasks of the Soviet Government' (April, 1918), *op. cit.*, Vol. II, pp. 725, 727; 'Left-Wing Communism: An Infantile Disorder' (1920), *op. cit.*, Vol. III, p. 438.
[3] Michels, *op. cit.*, pp. 353–4, 365.

even if Michels' statement of it is extreme. The empirical evidence is overwhelmingly in favour of the existence of what the Italian sociologist Gaetano Mosca christened 'the political class', though the ease with which one may join that class, or rise within it, varies greatly from one country to another. All the pressures of twentieth-century life operate towards professionalism and expertise. Most British Members of Parliament are 'professional' politicians in the sense that they have decided to make politics their career (and have to decide this at a fairly early age); and in the sense that parliamentary politics has become a full-time occupation. This is deplored by some on the Right, who have a gentlemanly aversion to making a living out of public service, and by some on the Left who see the professional as too remote from the common man whom he is supposed to represent. The current debate on how to make the House of Commons more professional and expert illustrates this cleavage. Especially within the Labour Party there is a tendency for traditional Left-wingers, like Michael Foot and John Mendelson, to oppose greater committee powers, for they see the floor of the House as the one place where indignant public opinion could make an impact on government.[1]

In present-day discussion about British parliamentary institutions we do not read much about the need to defend legislators against the importunities of the demos. The century of the common man, has not brought the common man much closer to the places where the big decisions are made. It is the alternative danger seen by Madison that causes concern, that

'men of factious tempers, of local prejudices, or of sinister designs, may by intrigue, by corruption or by other means, first obtain the suffrages, and then betray the interests of the people',[2]

or, less melodramatically, that elected representatives, at all levels of organization, are out of touch with those who voted for them.

No legislature has ever accurately reflected the social composition of the electorate. In their social origins and previous occupations legislators differ from party to party and from country to country, but in every party and every country the professional and managerial classes are over-represented at the expense of manual workers. 'Whether one likes it or not', a recent observer has written,

'politics is a middle-class job and the training appropriate for middle-

---

[1] The left-right correlation is by no means complete on this subject. Age is also an important factor: younger members on both sides are more 'efficiency minded'.

[2] *The Federalist* No. 10, p. 82.

class jobs is also a training for politics. The dice are loaded by the present structure of society as well as by the natural conditions which govern the job of politics in any society.'[1]

Yet the dice are not hopelessly loaded. 'The people may not really govern themselves,' Professor V. O. Key has written, 'but they can stir up a deafening commotion if they dislike the way they are governed.'[2] It does not follow that all democracy and all elections are a farce, simply because Members of Parliament are not invariably the direct executors of their constituents' wishes, or because they are able for lengthy periods to act largely as they please. To regard all oligarchies and all élites as *ex hypothesi* incompatible with democracy is to become the prisoner of one's own dogmatic definitions.

WHO REPRESENTS WHOM?

The debate about political representation is old: in the Western world it goes back 2,500 years. Of the major contributions that have been made to it, two at least are not relevant to contemporary Britain. Direct democracy on the Athenian or Swiss model is out, at least on the national level. So is the type of limited, corporate representation which prevailed from the thirteenth to the eighteenth centuries. Universal suffrage has come to stay. Debate has therefore been effectively narrowed to a small, connected range of issues: what are the roles and mutual relationships of public opinion on the one hand and an élite of political leaders on the other? What are the assumptions about representation and election on which the parliamentary system of a particular country rests?

In Britain these assumptions are twofold. On the one hand Parliament is not the only representative body in this country. There are local councils; and there are any number of organizations to speak on behalf of special interests – trade unions, professional associations, churches, political parties, groups of do-gooders. Many people indeed feel that these subordinate groups are more effective than Parliament in promoting their particular claims. On the other hand Parliament is the only institution representative of the whole nation. This was so even before universal suffrage; eighteenth-century Tories and Whigs agreed that members sat for one national constituency, not a collection of parochial ones. It is even more strongly the case now that every adult citizen has the vote, even if some decline to make use of it.

[1] Blondel, J., Voters, *Parties and Leaders. The Social Fabric of British Politics* (London, 1963), p. 133.
[2] Key, V. O. jr., *Politics, Parties and Pressure Groups* (5th edn, New York, 1964), p. 6.

There is, however, a major difficulty in calling Parliament collectively, or its members individually, *representatives* of the electorate. A representative is clearly under *some* obligation to his elector, has *some* responsibility towards him and acts to *some* extent with his consent. There are, in any system, widely differing notions as to how close these links ought to be; there may even be sharply divergent estimates of how close they actually are. The nature and the strength of the links depend in any system on two important factors. These are (a) the assumptions prevailing in society about morality and conventions in public life – what might be called the 'political culture' of the country concerned; and (b) the relevant political institutions. In some cases the institutions may be specifically fashioned to enable the system to work in a particular way (without necessarily achieving this); in other cases the fact that an institution has been long established and works reasonably well may in turn affect the political habits of the population. A number of basic questions therefore arise before we can know who represents whom in a given state:

How many and how deep are the divisions of interest or ideology among the population?

For how long have they been habituated to parliamentary institutions?

What is the electoral system in force?

How are parliamentary candidates selected?

How many political parties are there and what is their accepted role?

How effective are parties in influencing or transmitting public opinion?

How great is the power of pressure groups, and what is their relationship with parties and MPs?

These are the questions that the remaining chapters will examine. Out of them should emerge some idea of how democratic, and how representative, our electoral system manages to be.

II

Parties and the Electoral System

In 1832 the British electoral system changed from an historic to a rational basis. The right to vote and, to a lesser extent, the distribution of constituencies were now derived not from tradition but from first principles. All subsequent changes are merely logical extensions of the principles of 1832, as the opponents of that reform had foreseen. This is true despite the fact that the substantive difference between 1833 and 1967 is much greater than that between 1831 and 1833.

ONE MAN, ONE VOTE

Before 1832 the qualification for the vote in the boroughs had been corporative: because it was, in theory, the community that was represented, the franchise could, and did, vary from one community to the next. After 1832 it was individualistic, and all demands for further reform, beginning with those of the Chartists, were for greater concessions in the direction of individualism. With the Second Reform Act of 1867 all householders, and all lodgers paying more than £10 in rent, were enfranchised in the boroughs. The Third Reform Act of 1884 extended the same qualification to the county constituencies. By 1885 58–60 per cent of the adult male population was entitled to vote.[1] Universal male adult suffrage was not achieved until 1918, when women over 30 also gained the right to vote. In 1928 women, like men, became entitled to vote at the age of 21. In 1969 the voting age was lowered to 18 for both sexes.

A major concession to individualism came with the Ballot Act of 1872. The secret ballot had been consistently demanded by the Radicals and had almost been included in the 1831 draft of the First Reform Bill.[2]

---

[1] Blewett, N., 'The Franchise in the United Kingdom, 1885–1939', *Past and Present* 32 (Dec., 1965), p. 30.

[2] Butler, J. R. M., *The Passing of the Great Reform Bill* (London, 1914), p. 180.

Although it involved an important principle concerning the freedom of individual choice, its immediate effect outside Ireland should not be exaggerated. The power to intimidate voters was probably declining, at any rate in the towns, and in the counties ingrained habits of deference could not be instantaneously wiped out by statute. The Ballot Act was also intended to curb the bribery of electors. In this it was less effective. Only the Corrupt and Illegal Practices Act of 1883, which stiffened penalties, limited candidates' expenses and obliged them to appoint an agent, made British elections relatively clean.

It was not until 1948 that the principle of 'one man, one vote' finally triumphed, for until that date some electors had been entitled to cast more than one vote. There were two qualifications entitling a person to plural voting. The first was the possession of business premises in a constituency where the elector was not already resident. In 1918 the minimum rateable value of such property was fixed at £10 for men and £5 for women. The second was the possession of a university degree. James I had in 1603 created separate constituencies for the Universities of Oxford and Cambridge, in which any MA was entitled to vote. In the course of the nineteenth century the same principle was extended to Trinity College, Dublin, the Scottish universities and the newly-founded universities in England and Ireland. In 1948 there were twelve university members.

Both the business and the university vote undoubtedly favoured the Conservative party at the expense of Liberals and Labour, but the extent has probably been exaggerated. Between the wars the number of business electors amounted to between 1 and 1½ per cent of the whole; the number of university electors to about half that.[1] Before 1918 there was no limit to the number of votes a properly qualified person might cast. After 1918 no one could cast more than one vote in addition to his residential vote. A business elector had to vote in person in a constituency which might be far from his home; university electors could vote by post, but the registers tended to be unreliable. At general elections between 1922 and 1945 the Conservatives probably owed an average of not less than seven and not more than eleven seats to business voters.[2] Of the twelve university seats eight or nine were generally held by Conservatives or Conservative-minded Independents. At no election since 1918 did plural voting decide which party gained a majority. It has been argued that but for the abolition of plural voting the Labour Party might not have gained its overall majority of six in 1950. But it is equally arguable that whatever benefit Labour derived

[1] Butler, D. E., *The Electoral System in Britain since 1918* (Oxford, 1963), p. 147.
[2] *ibid.*, p. 148.

from its 1948 legislation was cancelled by another of its provisions, namely the postal vote.[1]

Parallel with the demand for 'one man, one vote' was the demand for 'one vote, one value'. That meant in the first place an equalization of constituencies. All that the 1832 redistribution had done was to alter the balance between the agricultural and the industrial interests: there had been no counting of heads. The redistribution which accompanied the Second Reform Act laid down a minimum population for borough representation. All boroughs below 5,000 were disfranchised, those between 5,000 and 10,000 were to have only one member, and the five largest boroughs were to go up from two to three (although, in an attempt to produce some kind of proportional representation, each elector was to have only two votes.) The redistribution of 1885 abolished all boroughs with less than 15,000 inhabitants and reduced all those with less than 50,000 to one member. The counties and most of the larger towns were subdivided into single-member constituencies. Only 24 of the two-member boroughs survived this reorganization and in 1948 the remaining twelve were abolished. The principle that Parliament represented individuals at last triumphed over that of the representation of communities. Even then the principle of equalized constituencies was not yet accepted, though the disparities were greatly reduced. In England the largest constituency was now fourteen times the smallest, compared with thirty-five times in 1865.[2]

It was not until the redistribution of 1918 that one can speak of tolerably equal constituencies; not until 1944 that permanent machinery was set up for periodic revision by the creation of Boundary Commissions, and that the number of qualified electors, not the total population, was to determine the size of the constituency. The Commissions were to report every three to seven years, to establish an 'electoral quota' by dividing the total electorate by the number of seats available, and to recommend electorates 'as near the electoral quota as is practicable', while respecting local government boundaries and avoiding inconveniences of size and shape. The Commissioners made their first report in 1948, the second in 1954. But many local councils, party officials and MPs felt that such frequent disruption was more of a nuisance than a benefit, and the interval between redistributions is now not less than ten and not more than fifteen years. The next set of proposals was therefore presented in 1969. But the Labour Home Secretary, Mr Callaghan, persuaded the House of Commons to reject them, ostensibly on the grounds that a review of local government boundaries was imminent, but almost certainly because he feared that the proposed changes, like those of 1948, would harm Labour by reducing the number

[1] See below, p. 93.
[2] *Whitaker's Almanack*, 1875, pp. 90–2; *ibid.*, 1885, pp. 121–9.

c

of city centre seats.[1] That the 1954 boundaries were badly out of date is high-lighted by the following examples of extreme growth and shrinkage:

	1953	1969
	electorates	
Hitchin	58,666	99,377
Manchester Exchange	55,607	18,643
Billericay	53,050	113,452
Birmingham Ladywood	51,719	18,309

One of the first acts of the newly-elected Conservative government in 1970 was to put the new boundaries into force, yet these, too, may prove to be unsatisfactory by the time of a 1974 or 1975 general election. Since they are based on 1965 electorates they take no account of the rapid movement of the population since then, nor of the uneven distribution of 18- to 21-year-old electors.

There is, however, a second disparity in constituency sizes which is sanctioned by statute. Northern Ireland, which has had its own parliament since 1922, is deliberately under-represented at Westminster; Scotland and Wales are deliberately over-represented. In 1955 the number of electors per MP in the different parts of the United Kingdom were

England	56,347
Wales	50,034
Scotland	47,717
Northern Ireland	72,713

If the seats in Great Britain (i.e. excluding Northern Ireland) had been allocated according to the same quota. England would have had 12 more seats (523 instead of 511), Wales 3 fewer (33 instead of 36) and Scotland 9 fewer (62 instead of 71). In part the over-representation of Scotland and Wales is a concession to national sentiment, but it is also true that it would be difficult to amalgamate the remoter mountain and island constituencies in order to ensure mathematical justice. These anomalies notwithstanding, the regional distribution of constituencies over the last 140 years illuminates the main shifts of population and economic power:[2]

---

[1] For a discussion of the probable effects, see Pulzer, P. G. J., 'Redistribution: Need Labour Lose?' *Socialist Commentary*, September 1967, pp. 20–3; *Nuffield 1970*, pp. 414–15.

[2] Taken from Jennings, Sir I., *op. cit.*, Vol. I, pp. 26, 31, 37; Boundary Commission for England: Second Periodical Report, 1969, Cmnd. 4084; for Scotland, Cmnd. 4085; for Wales, Cmnd. 4086; for Northern Ireland, Cmnd. 4087.

	1831	1885	1918	1955	1971
Northern counties	72	154	171	167	165
Eastern counties	50	36	27	26	25
Midlands	101	90	92	107	114
London and Home Counties	48	99	126	136	132
South and West	211	77	69	75	80
Wales and Monmouth	27	34	35	36	36
Scotland	45	70	71	71	71
Ireland	99	101	101	12	12
Universities	5	9	15	—	—
	658	670	707	630	635

The magnetic strength of the South-East emerges most clearly, as does the nineteenth-century rise of the North. In this century the stagnation of the North, the boom of the Midlands and the slow recovery of the agricultural South stand out. The share of Scotland, Wales and Ireland (Northern Ireland only, after 1922) has, of course, been artificaly frozen.

The Reform of 1832 is significant because it marked the first breach in the traditional doctrine of representation by community and interest and the first major step towards an individualist doctrine. The reforms of 1944 and 1948 are significant because they mark the final steps in this direction. All double voting was abolished, and with it went the last remnants of 'corporative' representation – that of university graduates and proprietors of business premises. Parliament accepted the principle that constituences should not only be made, but kept, equal; in the interests of equality the minuscule constituency of the City of London, which had survived all other redistributions, went. Of its 10,800 electors, three-fifths[1] were business voters. Its *raison d'être*, apart from sentiment, was therefore the representation of a special interest, and its retention on these grounds had been urged by such corporatively-minded Conservatives as L. S. Amery.[2]

But the reform which gave to British electoral politics its present shape is that of 1883–5. It was then that the right to vote passed from a minority to the majority, that the greatest inequalities among constituencies were eliminated, and corruption all but suppressed. From the 1820s to the 1880s electoral reform was the outstanding political issue; after 1885, the violence of the suffragettes notwithstanding, this was no longer so. A wide suffrage, combined with single-member constituencies, also helped to give the party structure the shape we know today; indeed, to the modern debate about representation and electoral systems party is central.

[1] 1945 electorate: total, 10,830; business, 6,608.
[2] Quoted by Butler, *op. cit.*, p. 73.

THE FUNCTION OF THE PARTY

'The . . . proposition, that each is the only safe guardian of his own rights and interests [wrote J. S. Mill] is one of those elementary maxims of prudence, which every person, capable of conducting his affairs, implicitly acts upon, wherever he himself is interested.'[1]

That is one half of the Liberal doctrine of representation. The other half is that the MP himself must follow his own conscience, receiving neither instructions nor subsidies from governments, private patrons or parties. As an ideal it was widespread for most of the nineteenth century; as a description of reality it was never very convincing. Nevertheless, it had its uses, and the need to pay lip-service to the principle of disinterestedness led to changes in parliamentary procedure which made it more difficult for members to speak or vote on measures from which they stood to gain personally. Interests could no longer be furthered as informally or crudely as in the eighteenth century, nor opinion so easily controlled. But interest and opinion there continued to be. Nor were they necessarily those of individuals only. Large groups or classes of men might share an interest or opinion and combine to promote it. In other words, interest and opinion were furthered by party. Few political systems, and no parliamentary system, can work without party. No one has yet discovered how to give effect to George Washington's warning, in his Farewell Address, against 'the spirit of party'. But party systems differ widely and they may be differentiated by several criteria: by the internal organization of the parties, by the number of parties in competition, by the long term relative strengths of these parties and by the functions they perform in the legislature. These criteria cannot be clearly separated from each other; in particular, the function of parties in a given system must depend on the number of competitors.

As regards the number of parties, it is usual to distinguish between single-party, two-party and multi-party system. The single-party system, because it offers no opportunity for competition, is necessarily authoritarian, though it may vary in this respect from Kemal Atatürk's People's Republican party, which monopolized Turkish politics from 1923 to 1946, to the Nazi party. A two-party system is one in which each of the main competitors sets out to gain an absolute parliamentary majority and so form a government unaided. This arrangement is quite consistent with the existence of other, minor groupings; indeed, in Anglo-

[1] Mill, J. S., *Representative Government*, p. 208.

Saxon countries, normally considered archetypal for the two-party system, such minor parties are universal.[1]

Multi-partism predominates in most parliamentary systems, both on the continent of Europe and in certain extensions of continental political practice – in Israel, for example, and in most Latin American republics. So widespread is it that one observer had suggested that it, rather than the classical, Anglo-Saxon two-party arrangement, should be regarded as the 'norm'.[2] If, however, we look at parties in the light of our other criteria, viz. their relative strengths and their roles in the legislature, we find that the multi-party category is too wide to be satisfactory. We need in the first place to distinguish between the moderate plurality of parties that is usual in most of present-day northern and western Europe, and the extreme fragmentation of, for instance, Weimar Germany. We need also to distinguish between situations in which none of the fairly large number of parties can, by itself, dominate the political scene (as in Finland, Holland or Switzerland, where the largest party rarely gets over 30 per cent of the vote); those where one party is overwhelmingly stronger than any of the others (as in Sweden, Italy or Israel), so that it becomes virtually impossible to form a government without it; and those where two leading contenders tower above the rest (as in the West Germany, Austria or Belgium). Lastly we need to consider what the ideological distance is between the various parties – how ready they are to co-operate with each other, and to work within the established parliamentary system.

This will still leave a fundamental distinction between two-party and multi-party systems, and this is to be sought in the origins of the parties.

British parties have their origin within Parliament, and became important through Parliament's victory in its struggle for supremacy against the King. Once it was established – as it was in the Revolution of 1688 – that Parliament could dispose of the crown, and that no revenue could be raised without its consent, it followed that Parliament possessed a general veto over the monarch's policy. Parliament had begun in the thirteenth century as a consultative body; by the beginning of the eighteenth its members had the power to decide whether they supported or opposed the Administration of the day. Party, however loosely organized, thereby became an instrument of government, and

---

[1] Between 1920 and 1968 there have only once been fewer than six candidates in US presidential elections. In Britain the following parties, in addition to the Liberals, have put up more than one candidate since 1959: Communists, Scottish National, Plaid Cymru, Irish Republican, Republican Labour, Independent Labour Party, Socialist Party of Great Britain, New Liberal, British National Party, Union Movement, Radical Alliance, National Front, Democratic Party.

[2] Epstein, L. D., *Political Parties in Western Democracies* (New York, 1967), pp. 56–7, 70.

the dividing line between parties was the question of support for the government. That, in essence, is why historically there have been two main parties in British politics. Party allegiance did not have to rest on principle. It could be dictated by personal prejudice, family connection or financial interest. Parties certainly did not require a mass of organized adherents: until the end of the nineteenth century they were what Max Weber would have classified as 'cadre parties' (*Honoratiorenpartei*) as opposed to 'mass parties'.[1] Policy was made *ad hoc* by the parliamentary leaders; candidates, if not nominated by patrons, were self-appointed; constituency organization, in so far as it existed, was in the hands of a few local notables. By the end of the eighteenth century party had developed sufficiently to inspire Burke's definition of it: 'Party is a body of men united, for promoting, by their joint endeavour, the national interest, upon some particular principle in which they are all agreed.'[2] Party is not contrasted here with the national interest, it is equated with it. A party should be able, for a limited period, to take over the running of the state and, for the time being, to be identified with it.

As a description of party in his own day Burke's words are unrealistic. Some of the odium of faction or conspiracy still hung about the word. Nor did a neat division into 'government' or 'opposition' exist, in the way that Burke's prescription implies, for then a party must either be promoting the national interest in office, or challenging those who are. As long as the monarch was still actively engaged in politics, opposition could entail disloyalty, if not treason, and the process of legitimation was a slow one. 'The Opposition' as a collective noun began to be used in the 1730s, and the convention that supporters and opponents of the government should sit on different benches facing each other, arose, as far as we can tell, at the same time.[3] It was not until 1826 that the phrase 'His Majesty's Opposition' was first used, and then in a spirit of badinage.[4] It was only after the First Reform Act, when the Crown was deprived of the parliamentary patronage which it had enjoyed through the so-called Treasury boroughs, that a genuinely neutral monarch could be served, in alternation, by one of two competing bodies of men.

A party of the Anglo-Saxon type is primarily an instrument of self-government, even under a restricted franchise. Multi-party systems presuppose a sharp distinction between party and state. In most continental European states, where there is no long-standing tradition of parliamentarism, but instead one of bureaucratic absolutism, there may

[1] Weber, M. *Economy and Society* (New York, 1968), pp. 1130–3.
[2] Burke, E., 'Thoughts on the Cause of the Present Discontents', *Works*, Vol. II, p. 82.
[3] Foord, A. S., *His Majesty's Opposition* (Oxford, 1964), pp. 155–8.
[4] *ibid.*, p. 1.

even be a sense of the underlying hostility between them. The separation between the 'unofficial' party and the 'official' state is emphasized by the nineteenth-century Swiss jurist Johann Caspar Bluntschli:

'Party is, as the word itself implies, only part of a greater whole, never the whole itself . . . It must never identify itself with this whole, with the people or the state . . .

'Parties are not state institutions, . . . not members of the state organism, but free social associations whose formations depend upon a changing membership united for common political action by a definite conviction.'[1]

Benjamin Constant in 1816 defined party in the continental sense even more succinctly: 'A party is a group of men professing the same principle.'[2] What is absent is Burke's reference to the national interest – not because the leaders of continental parties necessarily lack patriotism but simply because the party is not seen as a suitable instrument for promoting it.

The function of a party in a multi-party system is, quite literally, to 'represent'. The emphasis may be on an ethnic grouping, an economic class, or some philosophical imperative. Where deeply-held religious controversies or long-established ethnic differences cut across each other, or across the recognized economic dividing lines, multi-partism is inescapable. Sometimes the fragmentation of loyalties can be extreme. In the parliament of the multi-national Habsburg Empire there were, on the eve of the First World War, twenty-eight political parties, ranging from Slovene Clericals to Czech Agrarians; in the various successor-states which emerged from the collapse of that Empire only the Communist parties attempted to embrace more than one nationality, religion, class or region. Even within Weimar Germany, which was ethnically homogeneous and administratively fairly centralized, regional and occupational particularism flourished. What is one to make of the Bavarian Farmers' League, The Württemberg Wine-growers' and Farmers' Union – or for that matter the People's Bloc of Inflation Victims or the party of the Vital Interests of Celibates? These are clearly not instruments of self-government. They are, rather, instruments for securing concessions from the state on behalf of a particular interest, or preventing encroachments by the state on the prerogatives of that interest. Because the interest represented is almost always a minority of the social whole, or because it is concerned with speaking

---

[1] Bluntschli, J. C., *Lehre vom modernen Staat* (Stuttgart, 1875–6), pp. 499, 504. Quoted by Arendt, H., *The Origins of Totalitarianism* (2nd edn, London, 1958), pp. 253–5.
[2] Duverger, *Political Parties* (London, 1954), p. xiv.

only on a limited range of subjects,[1] government by coalition becomes the norm. Both the party leaders and the electors understand this. Thus Abraham Kuyper, who organized the more fundamentalist wing of Dutch Calvinists into the Anti-Revolutionary Party at the end of the nineteenth century, warned his followers:

'More than a quarter of the Chamber we can never win; in this situation all the clamour for a ministry of our own can make no other impression on insiders or outsiders than foolhardiness. .... It is easy to blind ourselves to the question where to find men prepared and able to solve the big questions which our policy, based on our principles, faces.'[2]

'Majoritarian' parties (in Duverger's terminology),[3] serve a different purpose in parliamentary politics from non-majoritarian ones. In two-party systems there is a direct connection between electoral choice and the formation of a government. In multi-party systems cabinets are constituted not as the direct outcome of an electoral verdict, but as the result of bargaining among the elected. Even major parties in multi-party systems do not set out to gain absolute parliamentary majorities, though they may from time to time succeed in doing so.[4] And even then, either because the parties concerned are not psychologically ready for sole governmental responsibility, or because they would not be trusted to use their monopoly in moderation, coalitions may continue even though there is no arithmetical need for them. In contrast, in an Anglo-Saxon state, single-party minority government is preferred to a coalition when an election does not produce an absolute majority.[5]

While majoritarian parties can be distinguished clearly from others in terms of historical origin and original purpose, present-day practice allows a good deal of overlap. Whatever the party system, every party

---

[1] Since most people belong to more than one social category, they have some choice in the 'interest party' they can support. In a given state, where the majority of the population are Catholics, the party devoted to the maintenance of Catholic interests may yet remain in a minority, because some Catholics prefer to give priority to the protection of their interests as wage-earners, businessmen, or recipients of fixed pensions.

[2] Quoted by Daalder, H., 'The Netherlands', in Dahl, R. A., (ed.) *Political Oppositions in Western Democracies* (New Haven, 1966), pp. 216–17.

[3] Duverger, *op. cit.,* p. 283.

[4] Absolute majorities have in recent times been enjoyed by the Swedish Social Democrats (1940–4, 1968–70), the Norwegian Labour Party (1945–61), the Italian Christian Democrats (1948–53), the Belgian Christian-Social Party (1950–4), the Austrian People's Party (1945–9 and 1966–70), the West German Christian Democrats (1953–61) and in Ireland by Fianna Fail (1933–43, 1944–8, 1957–71 and since 1969).

[5] e.g. in Britain: 1892–5, 1910–15, 1924, 1929–31; in Canada: 1921–6, 1957–8, 1962–8.

likes to build up a loyal, dependable following, and most parties have, from time to time, to devote themselves to the business of governing.

The Conservative and Labour parties in this country, Republicans and Democrats in the USA to a rather lesser extent, do have definable principles, even if not doctrinaire ideologies, and each of these parties has some supporters who are loyal to it for doctrinaire rather than pragmatic reasons. Similarly, even a non-majoritarian party can hardly ignore the national interest. It is always tempting to persuade others, and not too difficult to persuade oneself, that what is good for oneself is good for one's country; that a prosperous agriculture, or full employment or Church supervision of schooling, or toleration for Anabaptists, are in the national interest. Moreover, the coalition government, once constituted, cannot restrict itself to debating the ethics of divorce or the validity of historical materialism. Everyday problems of economics, defence and foreign policy cannot be ignored. The election manifesto must contain at least some reference to the party's intentions in these fields beside the recitation of its immutable principles, and its fate at the polls can, after all, depend on its administrative performance.

In practice, therefore, where fragmentation is not extreme, and where each of the parties is committed to working within the system, a bipolar scheme of responsible party government may emerge. This seems to have happened during the 1960s in Norway and Denmark, where the various anti-Socialist parties have combined to provide an alternative government to the previously hegemonial Social Democratic/Labour parties, and in West Germany and Austria, where a pattern of major-party alternation has supplanted the earlier coalition-mindedness. The emergence of this type of bi-polarity does not require a reduction in the number of parties; it does, however, require a transformation in the parties' character, from being purely representative of one or two well-defined interests, to becoming broadly-based, pragmatically-minded bodies headed by potential governmental teams.[1]

An outstanding example of the way in which differing concepts of the role of party can co-exist is the Labour Party in this country. The Labour Party was intended by its founders to be the representative of a sectional interest whose claims, they felt, had been ignored by the other parties. Its purpose was defined by Keir Hardie in 1900 as 'promoting legislation in the direct interest of labour', and the 1906 manifesto of the Labour Representation Committee began: 'This election is to decide

---

[1] This point is discussed further by Kirchheimer, O., 'The Transformation of the Western European Party System', in La Palombara, J. and Weiner, M., *Political Parties and Political Development* (Princeton, 1966), pp. 177–200; Pulzer, P. G. J., 'The German Party System in the Sixties', *Political Studies* XVIII (March, 1971).

whether or not Labour is to be fairly represented in Parliament'.[1] The emphasis is clearly on a party of minority status operating on a limited range of issues – not surprisingly, for the example that inspired Hardie and his colleagues was the success of the Irish Nationalist Party under Parnell, equally a sectional party.[2] At the same time it must be obvious that the sectional interest which the party was to represent constituted the majority of the nation, thus permitting the sectional party to become at the same time a majoritarian party. This is in fact what happened, though the process changed the character of the party. But there is no evidence that in the early days any of the party's leaders thought in terms of eventually replacing one of the established groupings in the two-party game.

THE TWO-PARTY GAME

Before a two-party system of the British kind can operate successfully, three conditions need to be fulfilled: historical continuity, social homogeneity and political consensus. To what extent do they exist in Britain, and why?

Historical Continuity. A two-party system can operate most easily when parties originate among politicians within the legislature, rather than among the disfranchised outside it. The notion that it was the function of the legislature to support an Administration in office was – as we have seen – familiar by the end of the seventeenth century. The dichotomy between a 'government' and an 'opposition' party, each ready to assume the running of the country, was familiar by the beginning of the nineteenth century. Indeed, it seems to have been taken for granted that two was the correct number of parties for the proper functioning of a parliamentary system. George W. Cooke, in his *History of Party*, published in 1836, defined his subject as 'the principles and practice of the two classes of statesmen . . . which alternately govern a mighty Empire'.[3] The American scholar, A. L. Lowell, was equally certain sixty years later that

'The normal condition of the parliamentary system, . . . among people sufficiently free from prejudices to group themselves naturally, and possessing enough experience to know that the practicable and attain-

---

[1] Bealey, F. and Pelling, H., *Labour and Politics, 1900–1906. A History of the Labour Representation Committee* (London, 1958), pp. 28, 264.
[2] Pelling, H., *The Origins of the Labour Party* (2nd edn, Oxford, 1965), p. 55.
[3] Cooke, G. W., *The History of Party. From the Rise of the Whig and Tory Factions in the Reign of Charles II to the Passing of the Reform Bill* (London, 1837), p. v.

able and not the ideal is the true aim, is a division into two parties, each
of which is ready to take office whenever the other loses its majority . . .
'A division into two parties is not only the normal result of the
parliamentary system, but also an essential condition of its success.'[1]

Lowell later modified his views and it cannot, indeed, be categorically
maintained that the triumph of Parliament over the Crown *need* have
brought about bi-polarity. But it remains true that the notion of responsibility for government entered into party thinking at an early stage. The
idea that 'the King's government must be carried on' and the idea of
popular representation in Parliament are therefore not in contradiction
to each other in this country, they are complementary. L. S. Amery,
who has given us the clearest statement of the Tory view of the constitution in modern times, emphasizes the force of political habit rather
than that of political institutions when he says:

'Our whole political life, in fact, turns round the issue of government . . .
'The two-party system is a natural concomitant of a political tradition
in which government, as such, is the first consideration, and in which the
views and preferences of voters or of members of Parliament are
continuously limited to the simple alternative of "for" or "against". It is
indeed only under the conditions created by such a tradition that there
can be any stability in a government dependent from day to day on the
support of a majority in Parliament.'[2]

When, therefore, the right to vote was extended in the nineteenth
century, the newly enfranchised could accept the idea that they were
voting not merely for representatives of their special interests – they
were doing that as well, of course – but also for an administration.
Butler and Stokes have shown that the majority of the electorate have at
least a partial understanding of the principles of responsible party
government, including the need for a formed opposition to act as a
control on the administration, and a periodical alternation of power to
make the control credible:

'The norms of party control held by the electorate, especially the wide
acceptance of the desirability of turnover in office, help to explain why
actual transfers of power are so easily accepted.'[3]

.   .   .   .   .

[1] Lowell, A. L., *Governments and Parties in Continental Europe* (Boston–New
York, 1896), Vol. I, pp. 71–2.
[2] Amery, L. S., *Thoughts on the Constitution* (Oxford, 1947), pp. 16–17.
[3] Butler, D. E. and Stokes, D., *Political Change in Britain: Forces Shaping
Electoral Choice* (London, 1969), pp. 33–4, 431–6; quotation from p. 436.

The two-party framework, which had evolved to suit the needs of aristocratic and oligarchic government, has thus survived into the age of mass suffrage. But it might not have survived if the transformation had been less gradual. Had universal suffrage been grafted onto the British constitution in 1832, the shock might have been too great. As it was, none of the Reform Acts up to 1918 was so cataclysmic in its immediate effects that the two existing parties were unable to absorb new divisions of opinion as they arose – industry *versus* agriculture, Church *versus* chapel, democratization *versus* hierarchy, labour *versus* capital. Gradualness of change is essential for historical continuity, though it cannot by itself guarantee it. But the mass electorate of modern times did not merely inherit parliamentary government; it also inherited a united nation-state and a monarchic dynasty in which the question of succession had long been settled beyond dispute. Any traditional controversies that there might be about the form of the state – monarchy or republic, unitary or federal structure – were dead. London has for centuries been accepted as the capital, in contrast with the metropolitan rivalries of major cities in Germany or Russia. The combination of these factors sufficed to ensure historical continuity, and the historical continuity made it much easier for social homogeneity and political consensus to predominate.

Social Homogeneity. Homogeneity is a relative term, and a subjective one. Much of the recent comment on the British social structure has emphasized the strength of class divisions and class-consciousness, the status-ratings based not merely on occupation, but on region and accent, the inequalities of educational opportunity, and many other aspects all of which would seem to contradict the thesis of homogeneity. But against them must be measured the unifying factors.

Firstly, of the major industrial states, Britain is by far the oldest. This means that we are, and have been for the best part of a century, an overwhelmingly urban nation; more than that, a nation of large city-dwellers. Nearly two-fifths of the population live in the eight major conurbations. Large cities break down regional peculiarities and the differences of character and tradition that flourish in agricultural or sparsely-populated countries: the conditions and preoccupations of life are much the same in Bristol and Bradford. The vast majority of us are employed in industry, or in services indirectly connected with industry: only 4 per cent are directly employed in agriculture. Moreover, most farms are large-scale enterprises, making the conditions of work similar to those in industry. Britain lacks a peasant class, and peasants are a powerful force against homogeneity because of their hostility to administrative intrusion, their resentment of industry and city ways and their geographical and cultural isolation, often leading to political separatism.

Secondly, because national unity has been so long established, and because population is so concentrated, regional separatism counts for little. Of course, a Lancastrian or a Cornishman may be proud of his county's attributes; much sentiment and prejudice, as well as some truth, is talked about the differences between North and South, but these differences hardly undermine the sense of national allegiance. In Scotland and Wales national sentiment is stronger and spurted power-fully in the 1960s. But Scotland and Wales between them amount to only one-seventh of the population of Great Britain, the number of people who speak Gaelic or Welsh is declining and the number who speak no English at all is now negligible. It may well be that it is their numerical inferiority rather than their similarity to the English that gives the Celtic nations in the United Kingdom so little influence;[1] whatever the cause, the political effect is the same.

Thirdly, cultural unity is further strengthened by the absence of notable religious cleavages. In matters of religious observance Britain is a largely indifferent country. In so far as it is not, it is an over-whelmingly Protestant country. Protestants are, it is true, divided into the Church of England on the one hand and the Nonconformist (or Free) Churches on the other – Methodists, Baptists, Congregationalists, Quakers, Presbyterians (though the Presbyterians are, in Scotland, the Established Church). Throughout the eighteenth and nineteenth centuries the differences between Church and chapel were one of the major causes of religious cleavage. These could be vehement: as late as 1902 some Nonconformists went to prison rather than pay rates which would be used to subsidize Anglican schools. But though Nonconformists for long suffered discrimination and contempt they were not, after 1688, persecuted. Religious passions, even at their height, were not as fierce as they tend to be in Catholic countries.

Regional, linguistic and denominational differences all have their effects on political conflict and party allegiance,[2] but the conflicts take place in a framework of co-existence and are not fought out to the death. There has, it is true, been one major exception to this rule in the last 200 years. In Ireland a Catholic peasant community, with a strong sense of national identity, created a separatist movement and its own sectional political party. Perhaps it was a matter of luck that the Irish dispute was solved without doing more damage to our constitutional framework, and it remains true that the politics of Northern Ireland to this day show a

---

[1] As argued in Richard Rose's ingenious paper, *The United Kingdom as a Multi-National State,* University of Strathclyde Survey Research Centre, Occasional Paper 6 (Glasgow, 1970).

[2] Examined in detail in Chapter IV.

degree of sectarian bitterness generally lacking in Britain. But it is now a fact that British political homogeneity had survived the Irish Question.

Of all the cleavages in British society, by far the most important is that of class. Class-consciousness is the biggest single determinant of both social and political behaviour. Yet this, too, needs to be seen in perspective. In the first place, the British have acquired their reputation for class consciousness in part because it is the *only* major dividing line in British society. We lack the linguistic conflicts of Canada or Belgium, the strong regional peculiarities of the USA or Spain, the Protestant-Catholic divisions of Holland, Germany or Switzerland, the conflicts between supporters and opponents of the Church in countries such as France or Italy, which are, nominally, overwhelmingly Catholic. That leaves only class, with all its rich variations – education, occupation, residence, accent, vocabulary. But precisely because class differences are relatively undistracted by religious or ethnic minority problems, because the class conflict is a nation-wide one, class is itself a factor making for national unity, As a result, the major political issues which divide opinion are felt equally strongly throughout the country. What affects voters in Dorset also affects voters in Northumberland. Class could undermine national unity only if conflicts assumed revolutionary intensity, and this has for a long time not been so. True there is a separate working-class 'sub-culture' with its own social customs, values and entertainments, though even it is being slowly undermined by the mass media.[1] But this sub-culture stops short of alienation from the political system. For all the prevalence of 'us/them' dichotomies, most working men do not feel that because they are working men they are second-class citizens and need, for self-protection, to inhabit a separate world. No political movement has tried, like the Social Democratic Party of Germany, or the Communist parties of Italy and France, to envelop their whole social and cultural existence in a self-contained catacomb.

The social homogeneity of Britain is relative: all that can be said of it is that it is greater than in most other countries. It is politically important, because it is essential to the functioning of the two-party system, for without it the necessary political consensus could not exist.

Political Consensus. 'Consensus' is a fashionable and much abused word. It can, for instance, mean widespread agreement on the importance of a particular issue or on a particular policy. It was said that President Johnson tried to achieve a 'national consensus' on US policy in Vietnam, or on such domestic issues as civil rights and the anti-poverty

---

[1] cf. Hoggart, R., *The Uses of Literacy* (London, 1957); Jackson, B. and Marsden, D., *Education and the Working Class* (London, 1962); Runciman, W. G., *Relative Deprivation and Social Justice. A Study of Attitudes to Social Inequality in Twentieth-Century England* (London, 1966).

programme. Or that successive British Prime Ministers have tried to create a consensus on trade union legislation, or on entering the Common Market. This implies little more than bi-partisanship or supra-partisan-ship: an attempt to gain support for a particular line of action from those who are normally indifferent to politics, or who normally support the opposing party. It implies also that any dissentient from the consensus policy appears peculiar, idiosyncratic, even suspect. Consensus of this kind need not arise out of a normally conciliatory political atmosphere. Indeed the manufacture of a specific consensus, say over an aggressive foreign policy, may be a device for uniting an otherwise highly frag-mented or fissiparous community.

Endemic, as opposed to epidemic, consensus does, however, require a normally conciliatory atmosphere. This is a consensus about 'how' rather than 'what'. Both sides, followers as well as leaders, must be prepared to accept alternation in power, and the legitimacy of the decisions which their opponents make when in office. Most discussion of how strong this consensus is in Britain has tended to be subjective and impressionistic, though the circumstantial evidence that there has been no serious threat of revolution or civil war for more than a century does tempt one to argue from the effect to the cause. There is, however, some recent survey evidence which confirms these impressions. A comparative survey conducted in five countries during 1959–60 revealed the following differences in attitudes to politics:[1]

1. Presented with nine attributes of their nation, respondents were asked which of them they felt proud of. On 'governmental and political institutions' the replies were

	%	Order of preference
USA	85	1
UK	46	1
Germany	7	6
Italy	3	5
Mexico	30	1

2. Asked whether they felt free to discuss politics with others, they replied

	With anyone	With a few	No/Don't know
USA	29	34	37
UK	29	35	36
Germany	23	14	63
Italy	22	15	62
Mexico	19	22	56

[1] Almond, G. A. and Verba, S., *The Civic Culture. Political Attitudes and Democracy in Five Nations* (Abridged edn, Boston-Toronto, 1965), pp. 64, 82, 80, 97.

3. The proportion of respondents who refused to reveal how they had voted was

	%
USA	2
UK	2
Germany	16
Italy	32
Mexico	1

4. Asked whether they would be displeased if a son or daughter married a supporter of the major opposing political party, there replied in the affirmative

	Right-wing parent %	Left-wing parent %
USA	4	4
UK	12	3
Germany	19	8
Italy	58	14
Mexico	22	24

Survey evidence also shows that most people in Britain accept the idea that a political party must govern, as well as represent. The qualities they seek in a party leader are those that one would associate with executive responsibility – 'strong leader', 'strong enough to make unwelcome decisions';[1] even when they are asked to volunteer the qualities they most like or dislike in specific party leaders, respondents rate executive ability almost equally with personal integrity and well above all other characteristics, such as education, physical appearance or their stand on policy issues.[2] The relative popularity of the parties also depends heavily on the administrative competence of the government of the day, especially in managing the economy.[3] This might seem too obvious to mention – but it is obvious only in a political system governed by majoritarian parties.

It follows from what has been said that a party operating in a system of alternating power must be comprehensive in its appeal and following. Majoritarian parties are not only coalitions of individual interests which left to themselves, could never hope for a share of political power; they

[1] Abrams, M., Rose, R. and Hinden, R., *Must Labour Lose?* (Harmondsworth, 1960), p. 25.

[2] Butler and Stokes, *op. cit.*, pp. 378–80.

[3] Butler and Stokes, *op. cit.*, 182–3, 389–418. For an elaborate attempt to correlate opinion poll fluctuation with economic trends, see Goodhart, C. A. E. and Bhansali, R. J., 'Political Economy', *Political Studies* XVIII (March, 1970).

are also, to some extent, competitors for the good-will of some of these interests – farmers, owner-occupiers, old-age pensioners and so on. In this sense both the Labour and Conservative parties are comprehensive parties, though both may sometimes stress ideological or sectarian themes for internal party consumption. So is the Liberal party which, whatever its present numerical weakness, nevertheless has majoritarian aspirations. All other parties which contest British elections are, significantly, single-issue or at least single-ideology parties.[1]

Any attempt, therefore, to turn a comprehensive party into a sectarian or ideological one will be disastrous for the party concerned. In Britain this applied to the Labour Party in 1960 when, at the Scarborough conference, a motion committing the party to unilateral nuclear disarmament was passed. In the eyes of many, and certainly of those opposed to unilateralism, this turned a party which has survived by virtue of being different things to different people, into a vehicle for pressing an extreme view on a single issue. It happened in the USA in 1964 when Senator Goldwater, an extreme conservative, was adopted as presidential candidate for the Republican Party. One liberal American commentator went so far as to comment

'[Goldwater] has broken the usual rules of political conduct by treating a major party as a 'front organization . . . He has altered the character of the party by committing it firmly to an ideology . . . If he is successful, whether elected or not, in consolidating this party coup, he will have brought about a realignment of the parties that will put the democratic process in this country into jeopardy . . .

'The achievement of the Democratic party over the past thirty years has been testimony to the effect of the consensual ethos . . . Naturally the constant task of accommodating broad differences under the same roof has regularly led to the blurring of issues, to a great deal of juggling and about-facing by the skilled professionals. It has also led to a built-in pattern of hypocrisy. But the American political party is based on the understanding that in politics hypocrisy is a minor vice and a major virtue; its other name is tact.'[2]

Above all, both majoritarian parties must be loyal to the parliamentary system, something which is not required of all the contestants under multi-partism. A multi-party system can accommodate a Communist party which regularly polls between 20 and 25 per cent of the total, as in France, Italy or Finland; it could even have accommodated a Nazi party which polled, at the height of its support, 37 per cent of the total,

---

[1] See above, p. 37.
[2] Hofstadter, R., 'Goldwater and his Party', *Encounter* 133 (Oct., 1964), pp. 2, 3–4.

D

had the remaining parties been agreed on giving priority to the preservation of the Republic. A two-party system clearly cannot accommodate such a party.

'ONE VOTE, ONE VALUE'

The principle of 'one man, one vote' is now part of the electoral law of the land. The critics of our electoral system, however, complain that it does not provide 'one vote, one value'. This is not merely because constituencies continue to be of unequal size, despite the efforts of the Boundary Commissioners, but because the distribution of seats in parliament is not proportionate to the votes cast for the various parties. It is even possible for one major party to get fewer votes than the other, but more seats, as in 1951:[1]

Party	% of votes	No. of seats	% of seats	Votes per seat
Labour	48·8	295	47·3	47,521
Conservative	48·0	321	51·4	42,734
Liberal	2·5	6	1·0	121,759
Others	0·7	2	0·3	99,484

Even when this exceptional anomaly does not occur, it is usual for the minor parties to be under-represented at the expense of the major ones, as in 1959:

	% of votes	No. of seats	% of seats	Votes per seat
Labour	43·8	258	41·0	47,347
Conservative	49·4	365	58·0	37,671
Liberal	5·9	6	1·0	273,085
Other	0·8	—		

Votes, it is clear, do not have equal values. The objections to this are twofold, but the distinction between them is often blurred. There is, on the one hand, the individualistic argument: it is unfair that a Labour supporter's vote should (as in 1951 or 1959) be worth less than a Conservative supporter's. It is unfair that a Scottish or Welsh elector's vote should be worth more than an Englishman's or Ulsterman's.[2] It is unfair that a vote cast in Billericay (electorate: 123,000) should be worth

---

[1] Labour's lead in votes at this election was exaggerated by the unopposed return of four Conservatives in very safe Ulster seats. Had these been contested Labour would probably still have been slightly ahead, but by 100,000 rather than 230,000 votes.

[2] See above, p. 34.

less than a quarter of a vote cast in the Western Isles (electorate: 23,000). It is unreasonable that all those who voted for an unsuccessful candidate should be deprived of a representative of their choice. On the other hand there is the argument based on collective representation, on the premise that the legislature should be a 'mirror' of national opinion. According to this view, Liberals, Communists or Scottish Nationalists should sit in the House of Commons in exactly the proportions to which votes are cast for them in the country. This pre-supposes that parties and legislatures exist for purposes which we associate with continental multi-party systems – for the representation of interests rather than the formation of a government.

A 'mirror' parliament of this kind can emerge only under a system of proportional representation. This, in turn, raises the larger question: does the electoral system influence the number and size of parties? Or more specifically: would the adoption of a different electoral system change the face of British politics?

It is often argued that proportional representation leads to multi-partism, and the single-member simple-majority constituency to a two-party system. The experiences of Anglo-Saxon countries on the one hand, and most continental European states on the other, are cited as proof. Yet the evidence as to causality is far from conclusive. It is more likely that the desire for sectional representation inspires the demand for proportional justice, not that the proportional system causes the proliferation of parties.[1] What the proportional system does do is to discourage a reduction in the number of parties. Where the social structure is stable, the number and relative strengths of the parties remains stable, as the charts illustrating the party histories of Sweden and Switzerland demonstrate (Figure II.1). Where the social structure is unstable, parliamentary chaos may indeed ensue. In Germany in 1930, the year in which Hitler made his first big breakthrough, no fewer than 35 party groups contested the elections. This fragmentation undoubtedly further weakened the fragile democracy of the Weimar Republic, but it was merely one symptom of the disintegration of German society under the impact of inflation and unemployment. Nothing could be more facile than to suppose that the rise of Hitler could have been halted by the importation of the British electoral system.

That changes in the electoral system may seriously affect the composition of the legislature, without greatly changing the electors' loyalties, is shown by two widely disparate examples, France and Guyana. French multi-partism is often attributed to proportional

[1] For the argument that proportional representation causes multi-partism, see Duverger, *op. cit.*, pp. 216–55; Schattschneider, E. E., *Party Government* (New York, 1942) pp. 64–85; Hermens, F. A., *Democracy or Anarchy? A Study of Proportional Representation* (Notre Dame, 1941), passim.

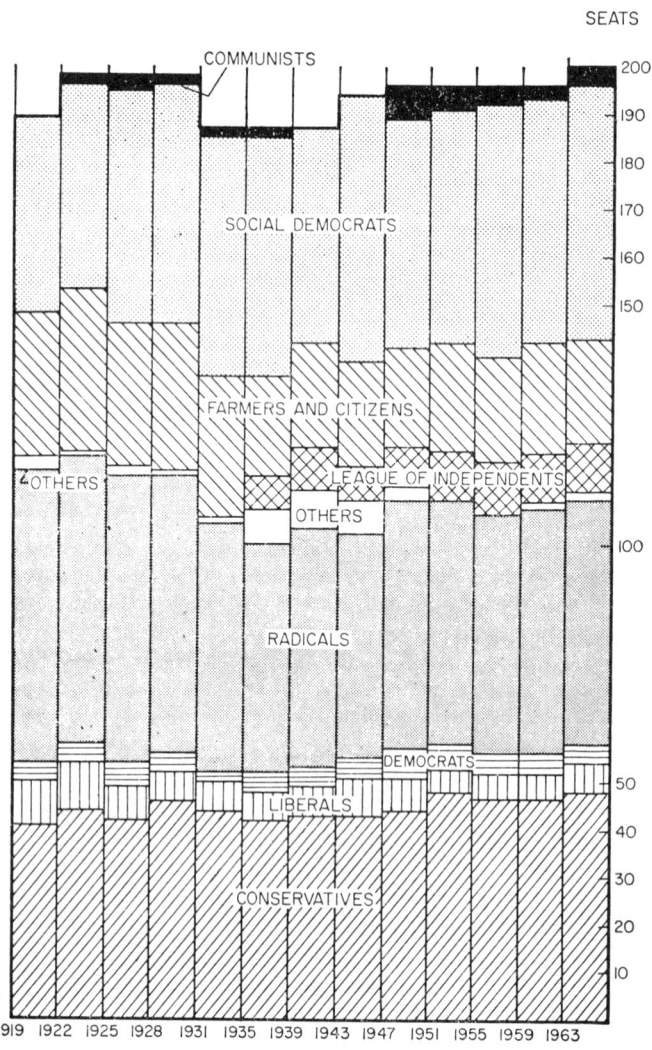

FIGURE II. I(a): Multi-party system in a stable society (a) Switzerland

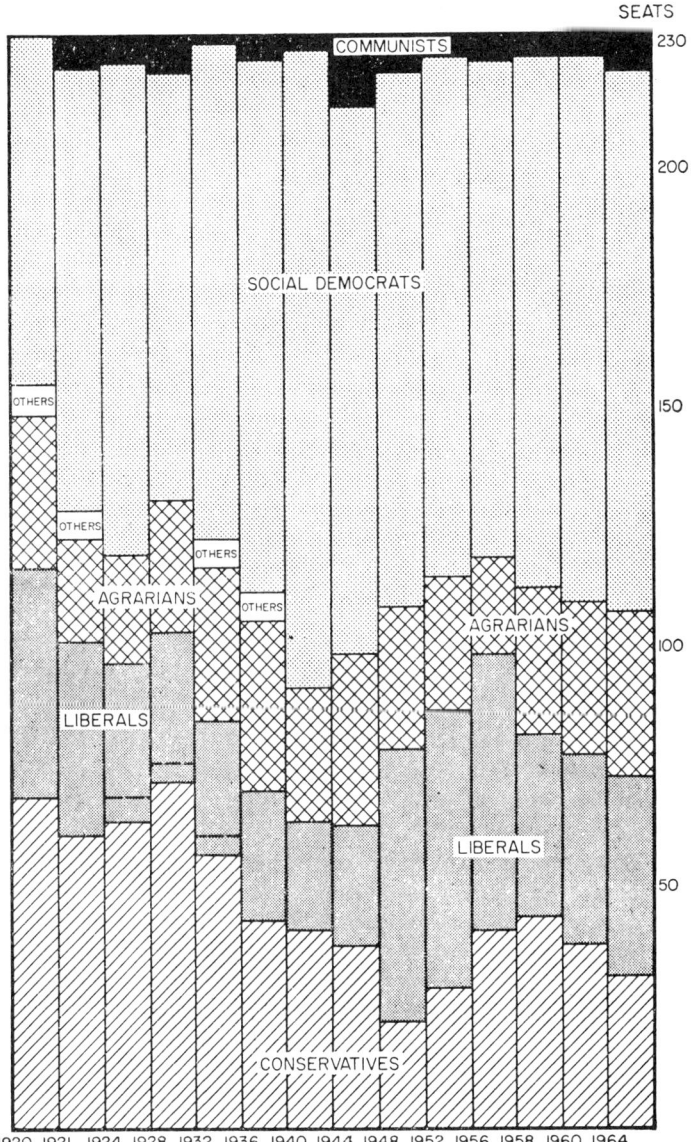

FIGURE II. I(b): Multi-party system in a stable society (b) Sweden

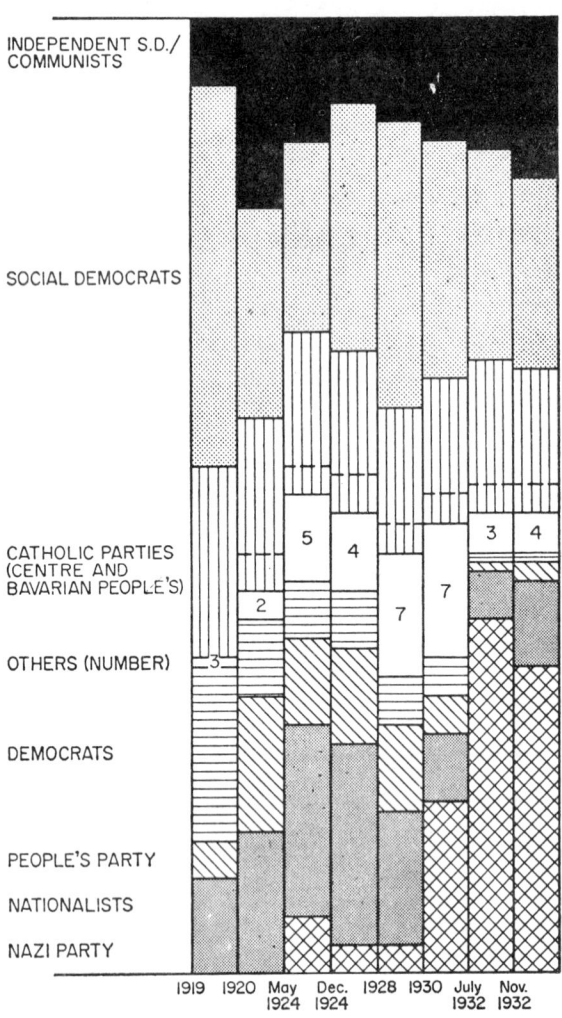

FIGURE II. I(c): Multi-party system in an unstable society: Germany
(in per cent of total vote)

representation, yet for most of her democratic history France has not operated under this system. From 1875 to 1885, from 1889 to 1919 and from 1928 to 1940 there were single-member constituencies, with a second ballot where no absolute majority had emerged. From 1885 to 1889 there were multi-member constituencies, again with a second ballot where no list had secured an absolute majority. From 1919 to 1927 there was a list system with modified proportionality. Only between 1945 and 1951 was there strict proportional representation by lists. Between 1951 and 1958 lists could combine and obtain all the seats in a constituency if they gained a majority. Under the Fifth Republic since 1958 there have again been single-member constituencies with two ballots.[1] The effect of these changes on voter allegiance and parliamentary strengths may be seen in the example of the Communist Party, which has most to gain from pure proportional representation and most to lose from any system that puts a premium on the ability to form alliances.

French Communist Party. Votes and Seats

	Votes	% of total	No. of seats
1946 (Nov.)	5,431,000	28·2	181
1951	4,934,000	25·9	101
1956	5,427,000	25·6	150
1958	3,870,000*	18·9*	10
1962	3,992,000*	21·8*	41
1967	5,030,000*	22·5*	73
1968	4,435,000*	20·0*	34

(votes for metropolitan France only. *Figures from 1962 onward relate to first ballot.)

Support for the party, which is based on class-consciousness, is affected remarkably little by the exigencies of electoral tactics. It lost 82 seats in 1951 because the anti-Communist parties formed alliances; it regained 50 of these in 1956 because the anti-Communists failed to ally. General de Gaulle's electoral appeal deprived it of a quarter of its support in 1958, but his new electoral system deprived it of almost all its seats. Since then its fortunes have depended less on fluctuations in its own voting strength than on the willingness of other anti-Gaullist parties to vote for them at the second ballot: this was high in 1967, and relatively low in 1962 and 1968.

In Guyana (at that time the colony of British Guiana) the British government in 1963 substituted proportional representation for single-member constituencies. The purpose of the exercise was to prevent the People's Progressive Party of Dr Cheddi Jagan from gaining an absolute

[1] Campbell, P. W., *French Electoral Systems and Elections since 1789* (2nd edn, London, 1966).

majority, and in this it was successful. The change in the electoral system made a decisive difference to the composition of the Legislative Assembly, but very little to the number of votes given to the various parties.

Votes and Seats in Guyana

Party	1961 % of votes	Seats	1964 % of votes	Seats
People's Progressive	42·1	20	45·9	24
People's National Congress	41·0	11	40·5	22
United Force	16·3	4	12·4	7
		35		53

Again, there is nothing surprising here. Political loyalties in Guyana are rooted in ethnic community ties and it takes more than a change in rules to shift them.

If the reasons that have been given above for the evolution of the two-party system in Britain are correct – historical continuity, social homogeneity, political consensus – then we do not need the electoral system as an explanation. At the same time, even if it is true that our two parties have evolved for reasons that have nothing to do with the single-member constituency there is no doubt that this system has made it easier for the main parties to maintain their ascendancy. It is the single-member straight-majority system which makes it possible for one or the other party to enjoy a working majority in the House of Commons without necessarily having an absolute majority of the country's votes. Indeed the relationship between votes and seats is almost as predictable in Britain as in countries with proportional representation. Generally speaking, in accordance with the 'cube law'[1] if votes are cast in the proportion of A:B, seats are won in the proportion of $A^3:B^3$

THE EFFECTS OF PROPORTIONAL REPRESENTATION

Many remedies have been proposed for the injustices of the British electoral system. Only two of them have been seriously discussed. The first is that of the alternative vote. Its purpose is to ensure that within

[1] Kendall, M. G. and Stuart, A., 'The Law of Cubic Proportions in Election Results', *British Journal of Sociology* I (Sept., 1950); D. E. Butler, *op. cit.*, p. 195. As a rough guide the cubic law has turned out to be valid, provided that both the major parties fight most of the constituencies and there are no gross inequities in constituency boundaries. For exceptions to, and qualifications of, the law, see below, p. 120.

the single-member constituency the elected representative should at least be representative of the majority;[1] its effect is therefore the same as the second ballot. Instead of marking a cross on the ballot paper against the one candidate he wishes to see elected, the elector marks the candidates 1, 2, 3 (and so on depending on the number of candidates). If, at the first count, no candidate achieves an absolute majority, the candidate with the lowest number of votes is eliminated and his votes transferred according to the preferences indicated – and so on, until one of the candidates has achieved an absolute majority.

The alternative vote very nearly became law in this country. In 1931 the minority Labour government, which depended on Liberal support, sponsored a bill to introduce it. The bill passed the House of Commons, but the fall of the government ended its career. The alternative vote can undoubtedly give minorities greater influence in that it offers them bargaining power, though it may be objected that this bargaining power goes, in Sir Winston Churchill's words, to 'the most worthless votes given for the most worthless candidates'.[2] It does not, however, give the losing major party greater representation. Calculations of its possible effect in Britain must rest on assumptions about how Liberal voters would have expressed their further preferences. Dr David Butler has calculated that at almost every election since 1918 it would have further exaggerated the majority of the winning party, except in 1950, when it might have led to a Conservative, as opposed to a Labour victory.[3] Even in 1964 it would probably have slightly increased Labour's overall lead of four.[4]

The second important proposal for reform is the single transferable

---

[1] In 1929 more than half the members (315 out of 615) were elected by a minority of votes, but the number has been as low as 33 (1931) and 37 (1951 and 1955). In 1945 33·4 per cent sufficed to elect the Conservative member for Caithness and Sutherland. Other low winning votes since the war have been:

1970	Ross and Cromarty (Conservative)	33·2%
1962	South Dorset (Labour) (by-election)	33·5%
1970	Cardigan (Labour)	33·5%
1970	Pembroke (Conservative)	34·7%
1964	Huddersfield West (Labour)	35·8%
1945	Merioneth (Liberal)	35·9%
1945	Orkney and Zetland (Conservative)	36·0%
1964	Caithness and Sutherland (Liberal)	36·1%

In all, twenty-six constituencies have been won by candidates polling below 40 per cent, nine of them more than once.

[2] 2 June 1931. H. C. Debates, 5th Series, Vol. 253, 106. Quoted by Lakeman, E. How Democracies Vote: A Study of Majority and Proportional Electoral Systems (London, 1970), p. 70.

[3] Butler, op. cit., pp. 192–4.

[4] Steed, M., 'Alternative Vote and the Speaker's Conference', New Outlook 49 (Nov., 1965), p. 11.

vote, which the House of Commons rejected by only seven votes in 1917. This is a form of proportional representation, based on multi-member constituencies, but does not tie the voter to the list of a single party. Instead, by enabling him to indicate an order of preference for all the candidates, he can, if he wants to, vote for Independents, or candidates of more than one party, as well as discriminating among the candidates of any one party.[1] This system is currently in force in Eire, Malta and in Australia for the Commonwealth Senate. In Britain it was used for electing University members of Parliament between 1918 and 1945, and has been used for electing the House of Laity and the Church Assembly. The Liberal Party advocates STV (single transferable vote) for parliamentary elections. They are presumably in favour of it because they hope to benefit from it, while opponents of the change argue that all proportional representation leads to multi-partism and therefore weak government. All discussion must be hypothetical, but there are three main hypotheses which have to be tested:

1. *That the change in the electoral system will have no appreciable effect on people's voting habits.* If this is valid, then the Conservatives would probably still have gained absolute parliamentary majorities in 1955 and 1959, and Labour in 1945. Calculation for the other post-war elections must involve some guess-work. A certain amount depends on how the multi-member constituencies are drawn up, and some allowance must be made for the fact that the Liberals would probably fight more seats. Two different estimates for the 1966 election are

Estimated Party Strengths in 1966
under Single Transferable Vote

		(1)		(2)	
	% of vote	Seats	% of total	Seats	% of total
Labour	47·9	320	50·8	328	52·0
Conservative	41·9	265	42·0	265	42·0
Liberal	8·5	39	6·2	33	5·3
Other	1·7	6	1·0	4	0·7

(1) Estimated by M. Steed, in D. E. Butler and A. S. King, *The British General Election* of 1966, p. 293.
(2) Estimated in *Representation* No. 23, April, 1966, p. 4.

This, however, is the least plausible of the three hypotheses. It is much more likely that a change in the electoral system will lead to some change in voting habits.

2. *That the change in the electoral system will benefit the smaller parties.*

[1] For a lucid exposition of how STV works, see Lakeman, *op. cit.*, pp. 105–40.

This supposes that electors are at the moment deterred from supporting the party of their first choice by the assumption that its candidate stands no chance of success.[1] A good deal of electoral propaganda is based on the validity of this assumption. In 1964 and 1966 Liberal posters bore the slogan 'If you think like a Liberal, vote like a Liberal'; in 1950 a Conservative poster (showing a torn ballot paper) read, 'A vote for the Liberal is a vote wasted'. Gallup Poll have periodically asked electors whether they would vote Liberal if they thought the Liberals would get a majority. Between 30 and 35 per cent usually answer 'yes'; in 1962, just after the Orpington by-election, 46 per cent said 'yes'.[2] The trouble is that this question refers to an extremely hypothetical situation. It assumes a situation in which the Liberal Party *nationally* is a challenger for power (as it last was in 1929), rather than to one in which the Liberal was *locally* in a winning position. Before this could happen there would have to be a major realignment of party forces, brought about by other factors than electoral reform. One can only say that if the change to proportional representation encouraged voting for minor parties, then absolute majorities in the House of Commons would indeed became the exception rather than the rule. Whether Britain would, as a result, be worse governed, is an altogether different question; the advocates of STV are bound to argue that it would not.

3. *That the change in electoral system will be detrimental to the smaller parties.* This seems, on the face of it, contrary to all accepted ideas. Yet if it is true that people in this country vote for a government rather than primarily for the representation of an ideology or an interest, then parties capable of forming a government single-handedly will be even better off under STV. At present the major parties gain from the 'wasted vote' argument in marginal seats, but lose by it in safe seats. For in a safe Conservative seat it is the Labour votes that are principally wasted, and there is a strong incentive to cast them instead for a minor party with a wider local appeal – Liberal, Welsh Party or Scottish Nationalist. In the constituencies where Liberals increased their share of the poll between 1959 and 1964, they did so principally at the expense of the minority party.[3] The thirteen seats which the Liberals have gained at by-elections or general elections since 1958 include only one which could also have been gained by the other major party (viz. Caithness and Sutherland);

[1] This assumption underlies most hypothetical calculations, including the latest one by Butler, D., Stevens, A. and Stokes, D., 'The Strength of the Liberals under Alternative Electoral Systems', *Parliamentary Affairs* XX (Spring, 1969).
[2] Gallup Political Index, September, 1962, p. 164; Butler and Stokes, *op. cit.,* p. 320, n. 1; Lakeman, *op. cit.,* pp. 246–54.
[3] Berrington, H. B., 'The General Election of 1964', *Journal of the Royal Statistical Society,* Series A, Vol. CXXVIII (1965), pp. 42–5.

the other twelve were all, from a two-party point of view, safe seats.[1] Of the eleven other seats in which the Liberals have, since 1959, come to within 10 per cent of the winning candidate, only three are marginal.[2] The rise in support for the Liberal Party during the fifties and early sixties was restricted entirely to safe seats. There the Liberal vote rose by 4·1 per cent between 1950 and 1966; in marginals it declined by 0·3 per cent. Comparing the Liberal performances in the two types of seat Mr Michael Steed concludes that 'nearly a third of the Liberal vote can be squeezed into voting for another party'.[3] One could go further and argue that once the Liberal, or any other minor, party had crossed local credibility threshold – especially at a by-election when the fate of the government is not at stake – it could do appreciably better than under proportional representation. Some at least of the success of the Scottish National Party between 1966 and 1968 might be explained in this way.[4]

But what happens under STV, when every seat is a marginal one? For those who want the maximum representation of minority views, no vote will be wasted. For those essentially involved in a plebiscite between ministerial teams, every minority vote will be wasted.

THE FUTURE OF THE PARTIES

It is easy to exaggerate the continuity and consistency with which a two-party system has operated in this country. Even in the nineteenth and twentieth centuries the two-party pattern has periodically broken up – 1846–66, 1885–95, 1918–31 – only to reappear in a new form. The reason for this resilience is that politicians and voters alike see party not only as the representative of sectional interests and beliefs, but also as an instrument of government. Both politicians and voters believe, rightly or wrongly, that this task of government is best entrusted to a single party with an absolute parliamentary majority. These beliefs prevail because of the way in which the British constitution has developed. They are not the consequence of the simple-majority system of election, nor of single-member constituencies, which did not become general until 1885. What is true is that this method of electing members of parliament

---

[1] Torrington (1958), N. Devon (1959), Orpington (1962), Bodmin, Inverness, Ross and Cromarty (1964), Roxburgh, Selkirk and Peebles (1965), Cheadle, N. Cornwall, Aberdeenshire West, Colne Valley (1966), Birmingham Ladywood (1969).

[2] Safe Con.: Banff, Blackpool N., Chippenham, W. Derbyshire, Tiverton, Worcester. Safe Lab.: Paisley, Merioneth. Marginal: High Peak, Leicester N-E, Rochdale. Seats previously held by Liberals, but lost by less than 10 per cent are excluded.

[3] *Nuffield 1966*, p. 285.

[4] McLean, I. S., 'The Rise and Fall of the Scottish National Party', *Political Studies* XVIII (Sept., 1970), pp. 369–70.

exaggerates the gap between the parties, and thus makes single-party government possible. If it is the exigencies of government and the firmness of traditional loyalties that determine the number of parties, there is no reason to suppose that this country will depart from the pattern of major party alternation in the foreseeable future. Nothing is more dangerous than to mistake the temporary discomfiture of one of the major parties for the break-down of two-party competition.[1] Even a change in the electoral system need not bring about a major revision – indeed, as we have seen, it could possibly strengthen the hold that the major parties have. What can change, of course, and what has changed after every one of the realignments in the past, is the names, composition and aims of the contestants. It is one thing to forecast, for the long term, a continuance of two-party competition, quite another to assume that the parties themselves are therefore immune from major change.

[1] As tended to happen during the Labour Party's troubles in 1959–61, e.g. 'What is at issue is the survival of the Labour Party as we know it' (Abrams and Rose, *op. cit.*, p. 59); 'It is hard to escape the conclusion . . . that the government of the country will remain in the hands of the Conservatives for the foreseeable future' (Mackintosh, J. P., *The British Cabinet,* 1st edn, London, 1961, p. 488); 'If . . . the present lines of development could be developed into the future, the next ten years would probably see a gradual decline in the fortunes of the Labour Party' (Jennings, Sir I., *Party Politics,* Vol. II: *The Growth of the Parties,* Cambridge, 1961, p. 379); 'If we must find a parallel with Labour's misfortunes, it is not with its own earlier history, but with the decline of the Liberals between the wars' (Beer, S. H., 'Democratic One-Party Government in Britain?' *Political Quarterly* XXXII (Apr.–June, 1961), p. 115.)

III

Members and Parties

POLITICAL parties, once they are established as part of the mechanism of parliamentary government, serve two main purposes. On the one hand they are a means of mobilizing electoral support for the measures being debated by the 'political class'; on the other, they are a means by which popular demands and popular grievances can be translated into official policy. The two purposes are complementary though they can involve serious clashes of interest.

THE EVOLUTION OF CONSTITUENCY ORGANIZATION

Before 1832, party bonds rested on individual links between notables. Elections took place once every seven years; contests were few;[1] voters were easily bribed. As for autonomous associations by groups of citizens of the kind that became common towards the end of the eighteenth century – for instance, the Society for Supporting the Bill of Rights (1769), the Yorkshire Association (1779) or the Society of the Friends of the People (1792) – these were clearly suspect as subversive.

After 1832 electoral organization demanded some extension of party machinery. Only in 1918 was the duty of drawing up registers of electors handed to local authorities; until then the biggest task of election managers and agents was to ensure that eligible electors were registered. The Tories set about centralizing the task of registration through the Carlton Club founded in 1832. The Radicals followed suit in 1836 with the Reform Club. But the habits of electioneering were not changed overnight by the Reform Act and contests remained the exception, not the rule. In 1835 there were contests in only 174 out of 401 constituencies.[2] As late as 1868 there were unopposed returns in

---

[1] In 1761 there were 48, in 1780, 80 (Namier, Sir L., *The Structure of Politics at the Accession of George III*, p. 159; Christie, I. R., *The End of North's Ministry, 1780–2*, pp. 54–57.)

[2] Gash, N., *Politics in the Age of Peel. A Study in the Technique of Parliamentary Representation, 1830–50* (London, 1953), p. 441.

210 out of 487 constituencies, in 1880, 110 (145 and 93 respectively if one excludes Ireland).[1] Nor were the parties in Parliament any more coherent. Not until 1867 did the party in power issue whips for the majority of divisions in the House of Commons; not until after 1918 was this usual for the opposition party.[2] Modern party discipline certainly did not exist before 1867 and cannot really be dated earlier than the 1880s.[3] Voluntary associations flourished more easily than before 1832, led by the Chartists (1838) and the Anti-Corn Law League (1839). Groups like these tried to put pressure on Parliament through their voting power, as well as by petitions and demonstrations. But, large or small, they were, unlike the parties, devoted to the achievement of a single objective and they steered clear of direct links with the established parties. Mass membership of parties, as opposed to agitational groups, was unknown.

What changed the nature of party organization both inside and outside Parliament was the reform of 1867. There were now over two million electors, and no constituencies with fewer than 5,000 inhabitants. Informality in politics was no longer possible. The impetus to further organization came from both above and below. The established party leaders found it more necessary to mobilize opinion, not merely with machines but with policies. To the newly enfranchized it was obvious that the vote should be used to remedy their grievances.

Not surprisingly, the Conservatives were more successful in organizing from above, the Liberals from below; nor is it surprising that the Conservatives were once more first off the mark. The interests which the Conservatives existed to defend – land, aristocracy, Church, monarchy – formed a more coherent amalgam than the uneasy 'Liberal' coalition of Whigs, capitalists and Radicals, and they were more seriously threatened by the advance of democracy. Moreover, the Conservatives had a more self-confident and clear-cut view of the proper relation between leaders and followers. Working-men were to be invited to confide in the natural leaders of society, but not to dictate to them. The National Union of Conservative and Constitutional Associations, which evolved between 1867 and 1885 under the lead of John E. Gorst and Lord Randolph Churchill, was intended to be a 'handmaiden'.[4] Except during the brief period of Lord Randolph Churchill's ascendancy (1883-6) it has never

---

[1] Hanham, H. J., *Elections and Party Management. Politics in the Time of Disraeli and Gladstone* (London, 1959), p. 197.

[2] Beer, *Modern British Politics*, p. 263.

[3] *ibid.*, pp. 257, 262. See also Lowell, A. L., *The Government of England* (New York, 1908), Vol. I, p. 317, Vol. II, pp. 79–80; and Berrington, H. B., 'Partisanship and Dissidence in the Nineteenth-Century House of Commons', *Parliamentary Affairs* XXI (Autumn, 1967), pp. 344–5, 348.

[4] McKenzie, R. T., *British Political Parties. The Distribution of Power within the Conservative and Labour Parties* (2nd edn, London, 1963), p. 146.

claimed to be a policy-making body, though its views could not always be ignored. Until 1965 the party's leader graced its annual conference only on the final day. 'Tory Democracy' as Lord Randolph christened his policy, referred to the relationship between the new mass electorate and the traditional party leadership, not primarily to a policy of social reform, though it followed that some programmatic attractions were needed to ensure the loyalty of the masses.

The Liberals were in a more difficult position. Like the Whigs after 1832, they were divided into those who desired no further reform and agreed with the Tories on the need to protect parliament from mob control, and those Radicals for whom the final political objective was the subordination of the representative to the voter. To establish constituency organizations was therefore to risk playing into the hands of the Radicals. This is indeed what happened. Constituency organization arose naturally enough through the need to mobilize Liberal supporters in the large cities. This was especially urgent in three-member boroughs where each elector had only two votes[1] and where Liberal votes had to be evenly spread among the three candidates to ensure a clean sweep. This is what the Birmingham 'caucus' under Joseph Chamberlain and Francis Schnadhorst first achieved. But the large cities were also the strongholds of Radicalism. The purpose of the National Liberal Federation, which was founded in 1877 under the auspices of the caucus, was not merely to extend organizational efficiency; it was, according to Chamberlain, 'that the people at large should be taken into the counsels of the party'. The invitation to the first conference stressed 'the direct participation of all members of the party in the formation and direction of policy'.[2] Even in the Liberal Party the Federation never formally gained the constitutional right to make policy, although its influence, especially in the 1880s and 1890s, was much greater than that ever achieved by the National Union.

The Labour Party, entirely a product of the age of mass participation in politics, had indeed constituency organizations long before it became in the conventional sense, a national party. The Labour Representation Committee, as it was known from 1900 to 1906, was a confederate body to which trade unions and socialist societies belonged collectively. By 1906 there were a hundred local LRCs with the responsibility of nominating candidates;[3] elsewhere the task rested on the Trades Council, a body in which the local trade union branches came together. As the purpose of the Labour Representation Committees was to challenge the established duopoly of Conservatives and Liberals, constituency organization was the first need. It was only in 1918 that Labour turned

[1] See above, p. 33.
[2] Beer, op. cit., p. 52,
[3] McKenzie, op. cit., p. 468.

itself into a national political party, with local party branches to which individuals, not merely members of affiliated societies, could belong. When it came to deciding the relationship between the rank-and-file and the parliamentary party, Labour's kinship with Radicalism became obvious. Labour was committed to the representation of a particular interest and, after the adoption of a Socialist programme in 1918, a particular policy. Labour MPs were consequently delegates on behalf of a class and a doctrine, not parliamentarians in the eighteenth-century style. Unlike the Conservatives and Liberals, Labour had no tradition of leadership by social superiors, and the whole temperament of Labour supporters was hostile to the idea that their leaders, once elected, could know better than their followers where their true interests lay. Independence could only be an excuse for betrayal. This is the origin of the unhappy conflict for supremacy between the party conference and the parliamentary party which has bedevilled Labour's history.[1]

In the mid-twentieth century the constituency party is an integral part of the national party organization. Disputes arise from time to time concerning individual branches and there are no doubt the normal tensions that exist between generals and officers in the field. *De facto* the constituency branches of all three parties are handmaidens, though they are handmaidens enjoying a good deal of autonomy and discretion. Their main duties are to nominate parliamentary candidates, to collect money, to canvass supporters and get them to the poll, and to distribute propaganda in support of the party's policy. The whole of their activity is therefore dominated by elections, whether parliamentary or municipal; and municipal elections, however importantly they may loom to local functionaries, are seen by headquarters in London as a way of lubricating the general election machinery.

SELECTING THE CANDIDATE

'Adoption is hell for the candidate, pure joy for those that select him. The choice of a candidate is for the constituency party worker the reward of many years of hard, unglamorous work. It is a pleasure to be savoured. Whereas he would normally "look up to" his candidate, and will tend if not to praise at least to justify him, it is at the selection conference that he comes briefly into his own. Then it is "they" who are the suppliants, he who calls the tune.'

These are the words of a former Conservative MP in an article rather ungraciously entitled, *Government by Greengrocer*.[2] They apply with

---

[1] See below, pp. 149–51.
[2] Critchley, J., 'Government by Greengrocer' ('Candidates: How They Pick Them') *New Statesman*, 5 February 1965.

E

equal force to the Labour Party. With one major qualification, local parties are free to hire and fire as they choose, even if the freedom of choice is in practice often limited.

That party headquarters should be involved in the selection process at all is a symptom of the move from oligarchical to mass politics. Approval by the leadership became a condition in the Conservative Party in 1874.[1] The present machinery dates from 1935 when the Standing Advisory Committee on Candidates (SACC) was set up. Apart from specifying selection procedure, SACC draws up the 'List of Approved Candidates', which local associations are urged, but not required to consult and it has a power of veto over anyone selected.[2] Only one major change has been made since then. Up to 1948 it was open to any candidate or MP to offer to pay his own election expenses and to make generous annual subscriptions. This had the obvious consequence of making it easy for rich men to buy good seats and of barring poor, talented aspirants. But it had the additional disadvantage of branding the Conservatives as the rich man's party, and of weakening the organization where it did not have to bother with fund-raising. Since 1949 constituency associations have had to meet all election expenses out of members' subscriptions. Donations are limited to £25 per year for candidates and £50 per year for MPs, and must not be made a condition of selection.[3]

The Labour Party, because of its loose organization, was in no position to impose control over candidates before 1918. All that had been required was a signed pledge to accept the constitution of the party, to obey the decisions of the parliamentary party, and to abstain from campaigning under different party labels or in opposition to other Labour candidates.[4] Even this was dropped in 1911 when doubts arose as to is legality. The present 'Model Rules' date in their essence from 1929–30. Transport House, the party headquarters, maintains two lists of candidates: List A contains the names of those who have been sponsored by a trade union affiliated to the party and approved by the National Executive Committee (NEC) of the party. List B contains the names of other individuals who wish to be considered. As in the Conservative Party, a Constituency Labour Party (CLP) is not required to consult either list, but individuals cannot simply present themselves. They need to be nominated by a body affiliated to the CLP, such as a trade union, a ward committee or a co-operative society. Selection is also

[1] Beer, *op. cit.*, p. 258.
[2] Ranney, A., *Pathways to Parliament. Candidate Selection in Britain* (London, 1965), pp. 21–4, 26–7.
[3] *ibid.*, p. 53.
[4] McKenzie, *op. cit.*, p. 474 n.

subject to approval by the NEC; again, as in the Conservative Party, inclusion in List B is not in itself a guarantee of this. In its financial arrangements the Labour Party had fewer safeguards against dependence on patrons than the Conservatives. Though individuals are now limited to donating £50 a year, a union sponsoring a candidate may (but by no means always does) contribute generously within the maxima laid down in 1957.[1] Between 1945 and 1959 some 220 constituencies received grants from unions and 45 from the Co-operative movement.[2]

What do the residual central powers amount to? Neither party headquarters wants to buy trouble. The leaders of both parties know that they lead heterogeneous coalitions of sometimes highly sensitive groupings on whom, in the last resort, the coherence of the party's organization depends. All public quarrels are bad publicity. Action is therefore taken only when inaction is the greater evil.

Since the war only one Conservative candidate has been disavowed by the SACC – Mr Andrew Fountaine, candidate for Chorley in 1950, who had made an anti-Semitic speech at a party conference and has since become president of the racialist British National Party. Only one constituency association has been disaffiliated. No member of Parliament has been expelled from the party, which would have disqualified him from readoption, none has been even deprived of the party whip, though some have voluntarily resigned it. In 1959 Sir David Robertson, MP for Caithness and Sutherland, who had resigned the Conservative whip retained the de facto support of his association. Neither he nor Mr Fountaine was opposed by an 'official' London-sponsored candidate.

The Labour Party has greater ideological difficulties and needs to guard against infiltration from the far Left as well as deviation towards the Right. In the 1945–50 parliament five MPs (four on the Left, one on the Right) were expelled from the party, of whom one (Mr Konni Zilliacus) worked his passage back. The various MPs who have lost the parliamentary whip, were all readmitted in time for the subsequent general election. The NEC has since the war withheld approval from five candidates adopted by constituencies, four of them left-wingers. Two of them have subsequently reappeared as (unsuccessful) candidates in other constituencies. What is not known is how many names have been kept off the B List. Up until 1960 scrutiny of the list was very lax.

The almost automatic right of a sitting member to readoption has

[1] Harrison, M., *Trade Unions and the Labour Party Since 1945* (London, 1960), pp. 80–8.
[2] *ibid.*, p. 81.

long been an axiom of British politics. Yet constituencies do from time to time try to unseat their incumbents, generally for personal failings – neglect of duties, old age, possibly drunkenness or a lapse from sexual decorum. Professor Ranney has calculated that between 1945 and 1964 known attempts to enforce retirement totalled eighteen for the Conservatives and sixteen for Labour. In each party twelve of the attempts were successful.[1] Here, too, the constituencies meet little resistance from party headquarters unless there are obviously procedural irregularities or blatant challenges to the authority of the national leadership. Thus Transport House has twice successfully resisted the attempts of left-wing CLPs to get rid of MPs who were judged too 'loyal' to the leadership.[2] The two Labour MPs whom constituencies refused to re-adopt in 1970 managed to counter-attack. One, the 83-year-old Mr S. O. Davies, (Merthyr Tydfil), stood as an Independent against the official candidate and defeated him by nearly two-to-one – the first success of its kind for twenty-five years. The other, Mrs Margaret McKay (Clapham) a flamboyant and controversial supporter of the Arab cause, did not contest the election but, with her case in mind, the 1970 Labour conference created a right of appeal to the NEC for dismissed MPs. The only other MP denied renomination was Mr George Currie (North Down), an Ulster Unionist who became the victim of the tensions of Northern Irish politics.

On the face of it, these powers of selection and rejection would seem to make local party branches anything other than 'handmaidens'. After all, if Harold Wilson or Edward Heath had failed to convince their constituency selection committees they might today not be leading their parties. The real situation is rather less melodramatic. Most constituency parties rely on party headquarters to supply them with aspirants. Even if the final choice is made locally, the supply of suitable nominees can, to some extent, be rigged. A person who is both able and ambitious can count on being selected sooner or later; so can anyone whose party is determined to see him in Parliament. At by-elections, as opposed to general elections, both party headquarters take greater care over selection procedure – indeed the Labour Party has special powers to do so – partly because an isolated by-election attracts more publicity than any one single contest in a general election, partly also because front-benchers defeated at the preceding general election may be looking for a way back. But since previous parliamentary experience is one of the qualities a selection committee values most highly, few prominent party members need be in the wilderness for long. Indeed, upward

[1] Ranney, *op. cit.*, p. 74, 181.
[2] Mrs Bessie Braddock (Liverpool, Exchange) and Miss Elaine Burton (Coventry South), both in 1955.

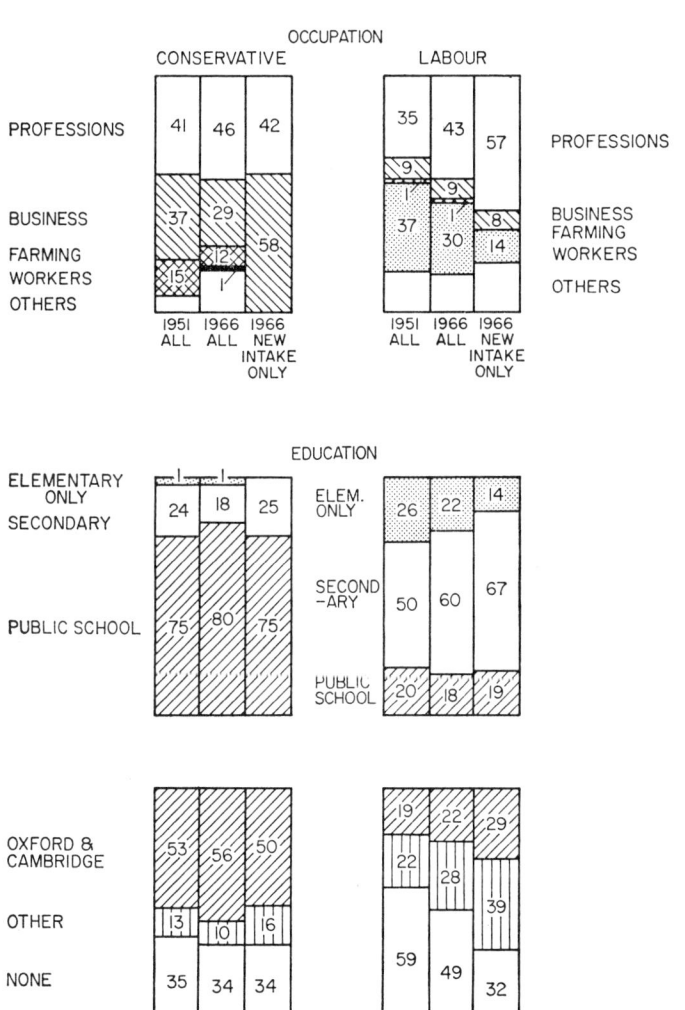

FIGURE III. 1: Background of MPs 1951 and 1966 by (a) Occupation (b) Education (in per cent)

mobility, whereby long-serving members graduate from marginal to safe seats, is a familiar feature of both parties.

'He who can make nominations is the owner of the party' wrote one American scholar.[1] But the centralization of the British system of government and of British political sentiment has led to a degree of party cohesiveness which makes localism count for much less in British than in American government. Local parties acquiesce in tactful central leadership not out of self-sacrifice but because they are in fundamental agreement with the leadership about the national role of the party. There is only one respect in which they exercise a moulding influence: they do, to a considerable extent, determine the social composition of the parliamentary parties.

IS THERE A POLITICAL CLASS?

Whatever else MPs may be representative of, it is not the social composition of their constituents, nor even the social composition of their own voting supporters. We have already noted that this is common form in parliamentary democracies, and indicated the reasons for this. The professionalism of politics means that it attracts predominantly upper- and middle-class people, those who have enjoyed higher education and have managerial or administrative experience. It attracts, in particular, members of the 'talking' and 'communicating' professions – lawyers, teachers, journalists, advertisers. But in addition to that, a country's political system inevitably reflects its social values and class attitudes: it is not surprising that those who find their way into Parliament have those attributes – whether of education or of occupation – which also make them leaders of society in other respects. A comparison of the backgrounds of Labour and Conservative MPs in 1951 and 1970 shows that there have not been any startling changes. Those that have taken place are towards greater similarity between the major parties and further away from social representativeness.

Education, which in Britain designates both skill and status, is perhaps the best single criterion for judging how far the two major parties differ from each other, and how far from the population at large. In both parties, educational standards have been rising, and this is reflected in the increasing share of the professions – among Conservatives at the expense of farmers and businessmen, among Labour at the expense of workers.[2] Among Conservatives the change has been slower: for a time the preference for educated men had the paradoxical result of increasing the public-school contingent:

[1] Schattschneider, E. E., *Party Government*, p. 64.
[2] *Nuffield 1951*, p. 41; *Nuffield 1966*, pp. 208–10.

Educational Background of Conservative
MPs, 1945–70

Year	All public schools	%	Eton only	%	Harrow only	%
1945	142	66	57	27	13	6
1951	240	75	76	24	23	7
1955	260	76	78	23	20	6
1959	263	72	73	20	20	5½
1964	229	76	68	22	17	5½
1966	216	85	54	22	14	5½
1970	243	73	59	18	14	4

In one sense the percentages for the 1960s are misleading; public-school men in general, and Etonians in particular, sit for the safest seats and get adopted for the most winnable ones. (As late as 1970 only fifteen of the eighty-two Conservative candidates from Eton, Harrow and Winchester failed to get elected.)[1] Like trade-unionists on the Labour side, therefore, they suffer least when the party does badly.

Even among university graduates, who have been gaining in both parties, clear differences remain. Labour is distinctly a red-brick party – at least in absolute numbers, though not necessarily in terms of getting the more winnable seats. In the Conservative Party, on the other hand,

Success of University-educated Candidates, 1950–70

	Conservative	%	Labour	%
1950 'Oxbridge'	156	75	55	56
Other	29	27	74	48
1955 'Oxbridge'	182	72	46	49
Other	36	40	65	39
1959 'Oxbridge'	181	69	46	43
Other	35	40	55	40
1964 'Oxbridge'	155	61	60	49
Other	33	32	74	47
1966 'Oxbridge'	144	54	83	59
Other	26	27	103	54
1970 'Oxbridge'	170	71	72	59
Other	38	32	82	37

[1] 1966: public school, successful 204, unsuccessful 205; state school, successful 49, unsuccessful 103.
1970: public school, successful 243, unsuccessful 135; state school, successful 83, unsuccessful 155; (*Nuffield 1966* p. 208; *Nuffield 1970*, p. 301).

graduates of Oxford and Cambridge are not only more numerous, they have a better chance of adoption in a winnable seat.[1]

The influx of graduates and professional men into the Labour benches has been the biggest single change in the social composition of Parliament since the decline of the aristocratic element in the nineteenth century. It has taken place almost entirely since 1964 and its impact has been even more sudden than a comparison of the total parliamentary contingents (Table III.1) would suggest. Of the 72 *new* Labour MPs in 1966,[2] 68 per cent were university graduates, compared with 42 per cent in the 1964 parliament; 14 per cent were workers compared with 32 per cent for their predecessors.[3] The rather smaller 1970 intake shows similar proportions, with only six working-men (eleven per cent) among the 54 newcomers.[4] The complaint that 'we could do with many more MPs of the artisan/craftsman type', made by the Labour Party's national agent[5] is not one previously heard from that source.

In the Conservative Party change has come more slowly. In their continuing predilection for a public-school business or professional man, preferably Church of England, Conservative constituency associations maintain their most successful and significant defiance of Central Office wishes. At any rate in the county constituencies it is important that the candidate should live locally, after selection even if not before[6]; even more important that the aspirant should be a 'gentleman':

'The first "player" to be adopted for a county seat [according to Julian Critchley] was Mr John Biffen, ... a village schoolboy who got to Cambridge, he defeated, having been a National Service lance-corporal, a colonel and two majors to win the nomination.'[7]

Ever since the organizational reforms of the 1940s Central Office has been urging selection committees to adopt more trade unionists, more women, more Jews and Catholics. The party conference endorses this principle. Do local parties know their job better than the party leaders

[1] Ross, J. F. S., *Elections and Electors. Studies in Democratic Representation* (London, 1955), pp. 415–17; *Nuffield 1950*, pp. 46–7; *Nuffield 1951*, p. 39; *Nuffield 1955*, p. 42 *Nuffield 1959*, p. 128; *Nuffield 1964*, p. 237; *Nuffield 1966*, p. 208; *Nuffield 1970;* p. 301.

[2] Including by-election victors, 1964–6.

[3] *Nuffield 1966*, p. 201

[4] *Nuffield 1970*, p. 302

[5] *Sunday Times*, 3 January 1971.

[6] Mr Christopher Soames, a Conservative ex-Cabinet minister who lost his seat in 1966, declined an invitation to be short-listed for a by-election in Honiton (Devon) on the grounds that he was not prepared to 'uproot his family'. (*The Times*, 12 January 1967).

[7] At a by-election in 1961 (Critchley, *loc. cit.*). But Mr Critchley forgot about Mr Ray Mawby, an electrician who has sat for Totnes since 1955.

in this respect? The answer is that they are trying to do different jobs. Presumably nobody in Central Office imagines that the tide could be turned in the crucial marginals by adopting more Jewish lady shop stewards instead of retired colonial administrators. What they are concerned with is a *nationally* balanced ticket that will rid the party of the stigma of exclusiveness and privilege. Constituency parties, on the other hand, act from the perspective of local conditions, and from their own – perhaps highly misleading – impressions of what will please their own voluntary helpers. For a long time they not only failed to respond to pleas from London; until the mid-sixties the chances of 'minority' groups steadily declined. In 1951 there were 23 women candidates; in 1959, 27; and in 1966, 21. In 1951 there were 15 workers; in 1959, 13; and in 1966, 6.[1] Catholics, on balance, do as well in the Conservative Party as in the Labour Party. Nonconformists are more numerous and more successful on the Left, as they have traditionally been.[2] The only three Jews to sit on the Conservative benches between 1945 and 1970 were all baronets. In this respect the party had become more exclusive than at the beginning of the century: in 1900, out of 12 Jewish MPs 8 were Conservatives.[3] The 1970 intake reversed these trends. For the first time there are more Conservative women MPs (15) than Labour (10); the nine Jewish Conservative MPs are also a record. The 'professional' contingent is not noticeably larger, but it is broader: teachers and journalists have been gaining at the expense of the Bar and the armed services. And with two working-men in Parliament since 1964 the Conservatives are well on the way to the target set by Sir Stafford Northcote in the heyday of Tory democracy.[4]

Within the Labour Party the problem of social balance is the reverse. Nothing was more natural in the party's early days than that the great majority of its candidates should be working-class and union-sponsored. It did not follow, however, that this was the ideal arrangement once Labour became a national party with aspirations to forming a government. Though Labour has always had a number of aristocratic and intellectual sympathizers, the predominantly 'cloth cap' image was considered a deterrent to recruiting followers outside the traditionally militant industries. A further trouble was that MPs who entered

---

[1] *Nuffield 1951*, pp. 38, 41; *Nuffield 1959*, pp. 126–7; *Nuffield 1966*, pp. 207, 209.

[2] *Nuffield 1951*, p. 38; *Nuffield 1955*, p. 41; *Nuffield 1959*, p. 129; *Nuffield 1964*, p. 238; *Nuffield 1966*, p. 209.

[3] Halévy, E., *History of the English People in the Nineteenth Century*, Vol. VI (2nd edn, London, 1952), p. 65.

[4] He wrote to the Chief Whip in 1885 that he would be 'very glad to have two or three Conservative Working-Men in Parliament'. Viscount Chilston, *Chief Whip: The Political Life and Times of Aretas Akers–Douglas, First Viscount Chilston* (London, 1961), p. 176.

Parliament through union sponsorship were not always of very high calibre, mainly because unions needed their most talented officials for full-time administration. Few prominent union leaders have sat in Labour cabinets; the most outstanding recent exceptions, Ernest Bevin and Frank Cousins, were recruited from outside Parliament. When Mr Richard Crossman complained in 1957 that only four trade union MPs were fit for cabinet office he evoked much protest but no refutation.[1]

Since the 1920s the number of union-sponsored candidatures has fluctuated fairly narrowly between 120 and 140. Because most trade union candidatures are in safe seats, the proportion of sponsored MPs in the parliamentary party varies with the party's electoral fortunes.[2]

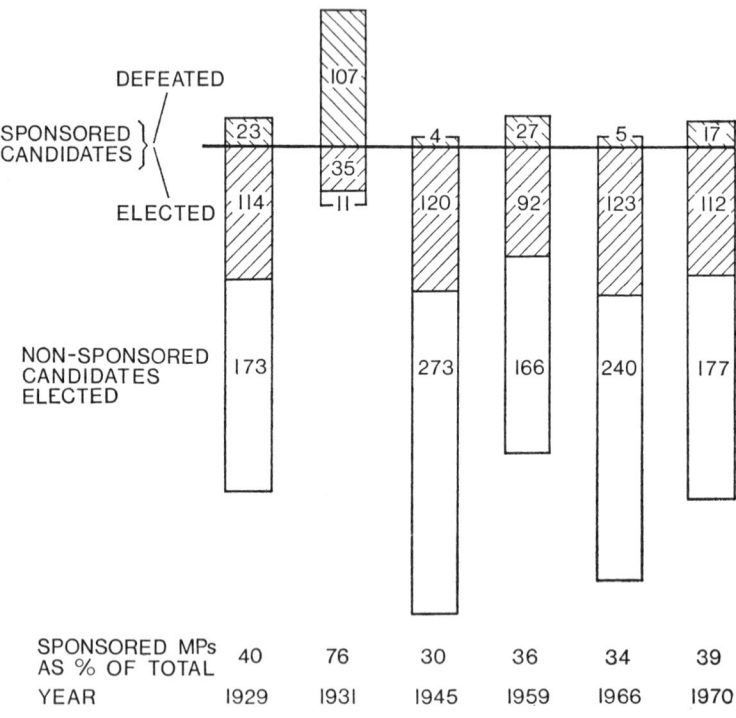

FIGURE III. 2: Trade union sponsorship of Labour Candidates

But although the number of union-sponsored MPs is as high as ever, the number of 'workers' (76) has declined and is declining. The social revolution in the Parliamentary Labour Party has left its mark even on

[1] Harrison, *op, cit.*, p. 269.
[2] *ibid.*, pp. 265-7.

union nominations. Dr Jeremy Bray (Kingswood School, Cambridge and Harvard) was sponsored by the Transport and General Workers' Union; Mr W. T. Rodgers (Quarry Bank School and Oxford) by the National Union of Municipal and General Workers.[1]

The narrow – and apparently narrowing – range from which parliamentary candidates, especially those in winnable seats, are chosen hardly entitles us to speak of a 'ruling class' in the accepted sense, or even of an oligarchy, if by oligarchy we mean a self-perpetuating clique. But it does point to the seemingly inevitable element of professionalism in modern representative politics at all levels of activity from the cabinet to the ward committee. The higher we move up the hierarchy, the more the social milieus of the parties seem to converge. With the resignation of Mr R. J. Gunter in 1968 the Wilson government lost its

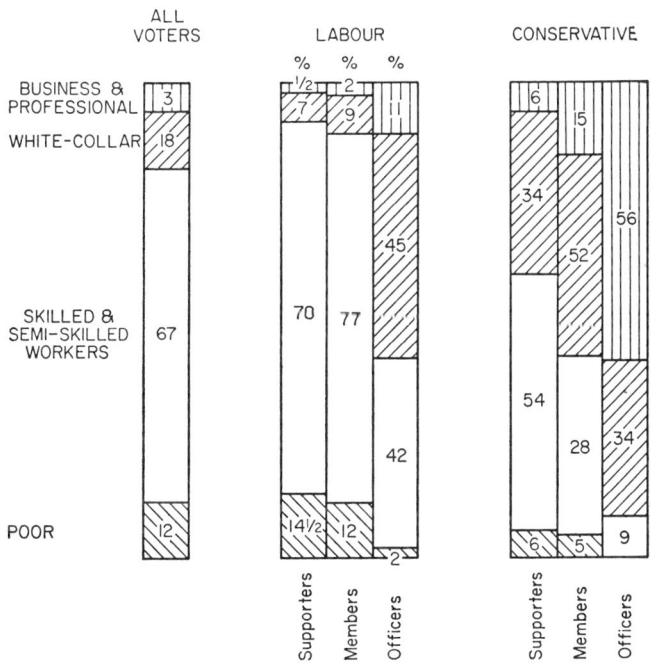

FIGURE III. 3: Supporters, Members and Officers of major Parties in Greenwich by social class (1950) [2]

[1] There is some precedent for these developments. Sidney Webb was sponsored by the Miners' Federation in 1922.
[2] Benney, M., Gray, A. P. and Pear, R. E., *How People Vote* (London, 1956), pp. 47, 51, 102–3.

penultimate proletarian. Only Mr Roy Mason, miner and LSE graduate, remained to uphold a dying tradition; Attlee's cabinet had contained eight working men, four of them miners. The Conservative Party has reciprocated by shedding its aristocracy. Mr Heath's cabinet holds only three Etonians; fifteen years ago, in Eden's cabinet, they were in a majority. Just before the 1970 election *The Times* commented that whoever won, Britain would be governed by 'fifty-year-old Oxford men, advised by senior civil servants who were up at the same time'.[1] Even the selection committees are unrepresentative in two important senses. In the first place, though the members of these committees owe their positions to supposedly democratic election by local party members, the actual management of the local party is in the vast majority of cases in the hands of a small band of devoted enthusiasts who constitute an oligarchy in the much stricter sense of the word.[2] Though nominally answerable to all local party members – often numbering many thousands – they are mostly able to act as if this were not so. Secondly, even

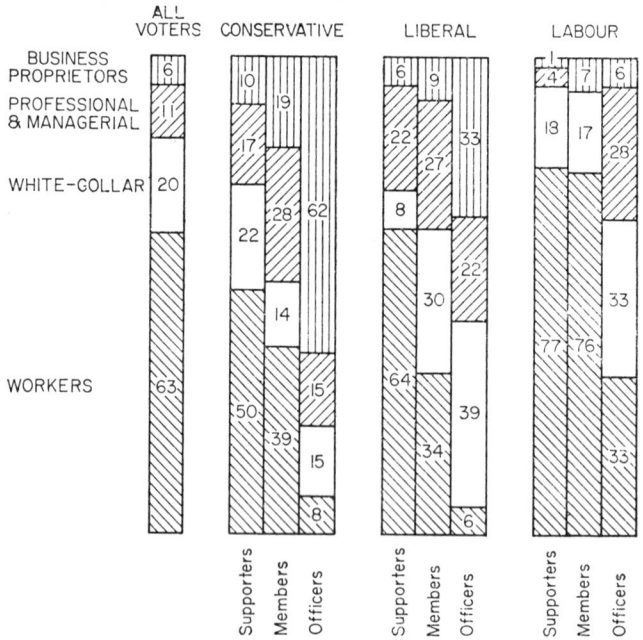

FIGURE III. 4: Supporters, Members and Officers of major Parties in Glossop (Derbyshire) by social class (1951–4)[3]

[1] *The Times*, 13 June 1970.
[2] cf. Casinelli, C. W., 'The Law of Oligarchy', *American Political Science Review* XLVII (Sept. 1953).
[3] Birch, A. H., *Small-Town Politics* (Oxford, 1959), p. 81.

if the rank-and-file members were disposed to exercise greater control they would still not comprise a cross-section of those who ultimately vote for the candidate. To a lesser extent than local party activists and to a much lesser extent than members of Parliament and, *a fortiori*, cabinet ministers, those who bother to enrol in a party at all are still an élite of sorts. Detailed studies in two widely separated boroughs bear this out overwhelmingly. (Figures III. 3, III. 4.)

The figures for both boroughs tell the same story. In all parties the higher the degree of political involvement, the greater the bias in favour of the higher social strata. The very poor are excluded from any activity except mere party membership. In the Labour Party the middle and lower middle classes gain at the expense of industrial workers; in the Conservative Party the business and professional classes gain even at the expense of white-collar workers.

Does it matter? The real importance of the selection process does not merely lie in the degree to which it limits the voter's choice. Selection amounts, in the vast majority of cases, to election. At least two-thirds of constituencies have been safe for one or other of the major parties since 1945. Seventy seats changed hands in 1964, eighty-four in 1970. Except in 1950 (when redistribution made direct comparison impossible) these have been the highest totals since the war.

CONSTITUENCY GOVERNMENT

In any election, therefore, about 90 per cent of those elected to Parliament owe their good fortune not to the discrimination of the voters, but to the smoke-filled conclaves of between 50 and 200 largely self-appointed men and women. To this state of affairs there are two obvious objections. The first is one of principle – that here are people with too much power and too little responsibility. The second is pragmatic – that the type of person who makes these important decisions is not fit to make them.

'Constituency government [wrote Bagehot] is the precise opposite of parliamentary government. It is the government of immoderate persons far removed from the scene of action, instead of the government of moderate persons close to the scene of action.'[1]

Almost a century later Mr Nigel Nicolson, reflecting on his long drawn-out quarrel with the Bournemouth East constituency association, echoed that 'the party-battle, which is at least half a pretence in Parliament, has become a grim reality outside'.[2]

[1] Bagehot, *op. cit.*, p. 161.
[2] Nicolson, N., *People and Parliament* (London, 1958), p. 169.

Those for whom party politics is the main hobby, perhaps even a passion, are surely more doctrinaire, more narrow-minded and more extremist than either casual party members or unattached voters. Their whole activity would make no sense if they lacked a conviction of the fundamental differences of principle which divide them from their opponents. This is certainly a widely held view, and the cartoonists' stereotypes of party activists are well known. Those who complain of excessive discipline in our political parties increasingly point to constituency militants rather than House of Commons whips as the villains. 'Loyalty' according to Mr Nicolson, 'is a word heard far less at Westminster than outside'.[1]

The main reason why oligarchial selection of candidates leads to less disastrous results than it might, is that this picture is largely false. True, MPs who deviate from the party line towards the centre tend to get a less friendly reception from their constituency organizations than those who deviate towards the extreme, but exceptions are numerous. At the time of Suez there were, among Conservative MPs eight principal 'anti-Suez' rebels who abstained from a vote of confidence in the government on 8 November 1956, and eight principal 'pro-Suez' rebels who resigned the whip in May, 1957, when the government abandoned the British boycott of the canal. None of the 'pro-Suez' rebels suffered any inconvenience; of the 'anti-Suez' rebels three (Sir Robert Boothby, Sir Edward Boyle, Mr William Yates) escaped unscathed, but three others (Mr Nigel Nicolson, Sir Frank Medlicott and Col. Cyril Banks) were not re-adopted by their constituencies and, in addition, subjected to varying degrees of discourtesy. The one 'pro-Suez' Labour rebel (Mr Stanley Evans) met such hostility from his local party that he also resigned his seat.[2]

Suez, it may be argued, is a special case which aroused exceptionally strong emotions, and Nigel Nicholson had compounded his difficulties with his local officials by having on an earlier occasion favoured the abolition of hanging. In contrast, of the twenty-seven 'Profumo' rebels who abstained from voting for the government on 17 June 1963, only one (Dr Donald Johnson) had serious difficulties with his constituency, although all but four of them had records of previous right-wing or centre deviations.[3] Before the 1966 election three 'liberal' Conservative MPs encountered difficulties with their associations, but overcame them. Mr Terence Higgins, Mr Richard Hornby and Mr Humphry Berkeley had all voted in favour of oil sanctions against Rhodesia and in favour

[1] ibid., p. 75.

[2] Epstein, L. D., British Politcs in the Suez Crisis (London, 1964), pp. 98–119.

[3] Rasmussen, J. S., The Relations of the Profumo Rebels with their Local Parties (Tucson, Arizona, 1966), pp. 30–40, 42, 53.

of abolishing capital punishment. Mr Berkeley had also introduced a private member's bill to legalize adult homosexuality. These three were, however, a small proportion of Conservative 'liberals'. a total of 31 Conservatives voted for oil sanctions, a total of 80 for Mr Silverman's 1965 bill on capital punishment, a total of 40 for a previous bill on homosexuality. On the other hand there was no local disapproval for any of the 55 'right wingers' who voted against oil sanctions in defiance of the party line, which was one of neutrality. In all, it is less comfortable to be a left-wing than a right-wing rebel in the Conservative Party, but even among left-wingers only a minority seem to suffer. It may be true that when Conservative candidates were deprived of their financial 'independence' in 1948 some power shifted from the MP to the caucus, but Professor McKenzie is unduly alarmist in concluding that while the leaders of the Conservative Party

'boast of the leniency and tolerance of their parliamentary discipline, they do not appear to have taken very active steps to warn their constituency zealots against exceeding their legitimate role in the political system.'[1]

The Labour Party presents a slightly different picture. Here the power of the whips is undoubtedly used more often, while the behaviour of constituency parties is less uniform. Constituency Labour Parties derive their reputation for left-wing extremism mainly from the success that 'Bevanites' have had in elections to the seven constituency seats on the National Executive Committee. It is also true that all the left-wing MPs who lost the whip in 1954 and 1961[2] continued to enjoy the confidence of their local parties. On the other hand two of the four who were expelled in 1949 received no local support[3] and three prominent critics of nationalization, Sir Hartley Shawcross and Mr Richard Stokes in the 1950s, and Mr Desmond Donnelly more recently, experienced no difficulty.[4] Only one MP was obliged to retire during the 1964 parliament – Mr William Warbey, a leading left-wing critic of the government's Viet-Nam policy. Most CLPs are subject to two conflicting pressures – on the one hand the desire to keep the Socialist faith pure, on the other loyalty to the movement and its leader. Mr Warbey's offence – and that of Conservative MPs who have made personal attacks on their leader – lies more in the act of disloyalty than in the ideological stance from which it is made.

[1] McKenzie, op. cit., p. 634.
[2] See above, p. 67.
[3] Ranney, op. cit., pp. 158–9, 182–3.
[4] Mr Donnelly has since resigned from the Labour Party on his own initiative and formed the Democratic Party, from which he has resigned to join the Conservative Party.

If the majority of those local branches in both parties which deviate from the party line lean towards the extreme rather than the centre, most branches do not lean in any direction at all. Dr Richard Rose, who has studied the resolutions submitted to party conferences between 1955 and 1960, describes almost half the resolutions as 'non-partisan' (42 per cent for Labour, 50 per cent for Conservative). Half the Conservative associations submitted fewer than two resolutions in the five-year period; in both parties fewer than one quarter of the constituencies regularly press partisan views, fewer than one-fifth extreme partisan views.[1] The popular picture of militant constituency parties being consistently defeated by trade-union block votes at Labour Party conferences is equally exaggerated. The only major issue since the war on which the party leadership has been saved by union votes was that of approving German rearmament in 1954.[2] In the crucial debates on unilateral disarmament at Scarborough and Blackpool in 1960–1 the leadership had the support of between 63 and 67 per cent of CLPs.[3]

The reasons for this comparative lack of militancy are not mysterious. For many of those who join constituency parties loyalty to the national organization is the overriding emotion. Their general political outlook was probably formed by family background and social environment rather than conscious intellectual effort. The majority of them instinctively support the party's leaders, perhaps even with strongly-felt devotion. They accept the party's programme without always fully understanding it or even very detailed knowledge of it. The routine activities of local parties – fund-raising, garden fêtes, bingo, bazaars, outings – though ultimately devoted to political ends, are in themselves non-political. It is a mistake to think that even many 'activists' are primarily, let alone exclusively, obsessed by ideological controversy. They may be no more than conscientious citizens taking on a chore for which it is difficult to find volunteers.

If the pragmatic objection to constituency government is weak, there remains that based on principle: that in the great majority of constituencies the great majority of electors have no say in who is to become their representative. The remedy that is proposed is the 'primary', a mechanism evolved in the USA as a defence against boss-dominated 'machine politics'. On three occasions primaries have in fact taken place in Britain to settle disputes about Conservative candidatures, which in each case

[1] Rose, R., 'The Policy Ideas of English Party Activists', *American Political Science Review* LVI (June, 1962), pp. 365–6; reprinted in Rose, *Studies in British Politics. A Reader in Political Sociology* (2nd edn., London, 1969), pp. 368–90.

[2] Harrison, *op. cit.*, p. 229; McKenzie, *op. cit.*, p. 502.

[3] Hindell, K. and Williams, P. M., 'Scarborough and Blackpool: An Analysis of Some Votes at the Labour Party Conferences of 1960 and 1961', *Political Quarterly* XXXIII (July, 1962), p. 331.

have confirmed the wishes of the association's executive committee.[1] One of these was in Bournemouth East and Christchurch, where the association's members voted by 3,762 to 3,671 not to readopt Nigel Nicolson, a decision which had previously been made by 298 votes to 92 at a meeting of the association and unanimously by the fifty-five member executive committee.[2] The discrepancy in these votes may seem to support the thesis that militants are more extreme than rank-and-file members;[3] whether it is valid to generalize from the unique circumstances of that episode is doubtful.

There is another difficulty. Even the large paid-up membership of the Bournemouth East Conservative Association was still a minority of the party's supporters,[4] let alone the whole electorate. In the United States a primary election can occasion a large turn-out; in one-party states (mainly the South), where the primary is effectively the election, turn-out is often higher than in the official election. This is possible because in order to participate an elector need only declare his allegiance when registering; he does not have to be a card-carrying member of a party. Some states, indeed, operate an 'open' primary, permitting any elector to vote in the primary of any one party. It is difficult to see British political parties extending this right to anyone other than full party members. The spread of the primary in the United States since the beginning of the century has undoubtedly reduced the power of some local and national oligarchs, though it has hardly transferred it 'from the politicians to the people'. It is difficult to dissent from H. J. Ford when he wrote, 'While bosses and machines may go, the boss and the machine are always with us'.[5] To which might be added that primaries, by doubling the number of campaigns, add to the cost of elections, to the advantage of the richer parties and the richer factions within them.

Candidate selection is the only segment of the British representational system in which constituency parties have played, and play, an active role. In all else, they are subordinate partners, though like many subordinates they can at times make their importance felt, In the planning of political campaigns and the determination of party policy the preponderant role goes to the national leaders.

THE CONTINUITY OF ELECTIONS

The classical argument for the infrequency of elections is that it gives

[1] Ranney, *op. cit.*, pp. 62–5.
[2] Martin, L. W., 'The Bournemouth Affair: Britain's First Primary Election', *Journal of Politics* XXII (Nov., 1960), pp. 661, 679.
[3] This is argued by McKenzie, *op. cit.*, p. 632.
[4] 1959 figures: Electorate, 60,657; voters, 46,544; Conservative voters, 29,014; membership of association, 9,724; participants in primary, 7,433.
[5] Quoted by Key, *Politics, Parties and Pressure Groups*, p. 395.

statesmen a respite from the importunities of the electorate; the five-year interval which has existed in Britain since the Parliament Act of 1911 is longer than in most parliamentary democracies. In quiet times the argument may have had some force. Parliamentary sessions were short, public interest in affairs of state limited and intermittent, the circulation of newspapers small, the outcome of elections, when they were contested, depended to a considerable extent on local conditions. This was true not merely until 1832, but largely until 1867. It was then that there began the permanent dialogue between electors and politicians. This was not merely because a mass electorate could only be reached by methods quite different from those of informal or aristocratic politics. The effect of the enfranchisement of the masses was the demand, however limited at first, for whole new areas of government activity. Once this was accepted by politicians, parliamentary sessions became longer, the subject-matter for discussion increased, mass-circulation newspapers, first published in the 1890s,[1] fed this interest, however crudely or inadequately. The political party became the two-way communication channel which it still is today: a means of justifying the actions of its leaders to the electors, and a means of discovering the wishes of the electors. There is, of course, nothing new in the actions of the government affecting the lives of the citizens. In previous centuries too, men have had to obey laws, pay taxes and fight wars. What is new is that those who govern are obliged to explain their actions (or inactivity) and to seek the citizen's approval.

The developments of the twentieth century have established the permanent dialogue even more firmly. On the one hand, the area of state activity has increased even further, thus strengthening the citizen's dependence on political events. On the other, the media of communication reach an even greater number of people. Almost everyone takes a newspaper, almost everyone has a radio or television set. Not everyone takes a deep interest in the political items; of those who do, by no means everyone acquires an accurate impression. That is beside the point. What matters is that almost every major event – the Budget, bank rate, the Trade Union Congress, a party conference, a summit trip – is accompanied by sensational publicity. Every week-end, outside the high summer, the politicians are out in force, making speeches. The long-term programme of almost every major government department – housing, education, national insurance, regional development, not to mention a war – affects most people continuously. Perhaps only a minority would voluntarily turn their minds to political events. But the majority are seldom allowed to forget them. It is the sum total of these impressions and reactions which emerges as the voter's decision; it is the

[1] *Evening News*, 1894; *Daily Mail*, 1896; *Daily Express*, 1900; *Daily Mirror*, 1904.

politicians' never-ceasing efforts to mould these reactions and impressions that constitute what Peel apprehensively foresaw as 'a perpetual vortex of agitation'.[1] Modern politics has been rightly described as a daily plebiscite.

The daily plebiscite becomes even more intense during the pre-election period. Before both the 1959 and 1964 elections, poster and newspaper advertising began in earnest some eighteen months before polling day. The uncertainty concerning the date of the election added to the suspense in each case. After the 1964 election, which resulted in an overall Labour majority of four, it was obvious that another election was at most two years off, so that from the spring of 1963 to the spring of 1966 politics and government were dominated, not to say seriously interrupted, by electoral frenzy. In the eight years from 1958 to 1966, the atmosphere of at least four-and-a-half could be accurately described as pre-electoral. But whether the parliamentary majority is four or a hundred, it remains true that party leaders need to begin planning the next election as soon as polling day is over.

CAMPAIGN MANAGEMENT

The election campaign, as an enterprise co-ordinated by party headquarters, was slow to develop. The convention that campaigns are individual constituency events – on which the greater part of British electoral law is based to this day – survived to the beginning of the century. Sir Robert Peel's address to his constituents at Tamworth in 1834 is often referred to as the first party manifesto; it was certainly approved by the whole Cabinet and enunciated general principles of policy, but it did not formally commit any Conservative candidate at the subsequent election. Until 1867 at any rate, 'agitation' was the prerogative of extra-party associations, such as the Anti-Corn Law League. The first major statesman to stump the country was Gladstone in 1876–7 and again in 1879. But he was not at that time leader of the Liberal Party, and the major effort of his 1879 campaign was restricted to his own constituency of Midlothian. His innovation caused great distaste, Queen Victoria recoiling from the 'democratic rule of that half-mad fire-brand'.[2] It was imitated by his Radical rival, Joseph Chamberlain, but not by his Conservative contemporaries, Disraeli and Salisbury, or his Liberal successor, Rosebery. Attempts by the Radicals to impose a platform on the Liberal Party were only partly successful. The 'Newcastle Programme', drawn up by the National Liberal Federation in 1891, gained only qualified acceptance from Gladstone, and the Federation never repeated even this limited success.

[1] Quoted by White, R. J., *The Conservative Tradition* (London, 1950), p. 157.
[2] Magnus, Sir P., *Gladstone. A Biography* (London, 1954), p. 270.

The Labour Party, founded in order to serve a particular purpose and based, in its earlier years, on collective leadership, had no difficulty in issuing official party manifestoes. Indeed, anything else would have been out of place. Its 1906 election address must therefore be regarded as the first of its kind in Britain. In the Conservative and Liberal parties, declarations by the leaders, though no longer directed only their own constituents, continued to function as manifestoes. As late as 1945 the Conservative election programme was entitled *Mr Churchill's Declaration of Policy to the Electors.*

Conservatism in political practice, which is common to all the parties, meant that technical innovations in campaigning were few and slow in coming. Radio was first used in 1924 and became an accepted part of electioneering. In the marathon 1945 campaign each of the main parties had ten broadcasts and the Liberals four – a saturation of the ether not attempted since. Television was first used in 1951 – on the initiative of the BBC, not of the parties[1] – when each party was allocated one programme. By 1959, when about 70 per cent of the population owned sets, television had become the main medium of political communication, with the three parties giving five, five and two broadcasts respectively. The party political programmes on television had an average audience of 21 per cent, while the sound broadcasts had one of only 3 per cent. A total of 61 per cent of the electorate – some twenty million people – claimed to have viewed at least one election programme.[2] 1959 was widely heralded as the 'TV election', though what this would imply was not clear. There was more apprehension than hope in this expectation: television offered more opportunity than any other medium for gimmickry, slickness and superficiality, and for gulling a clod-like electorate with cheap publicity tricks. These fears were not realized. Television, it turned out, had no more destroyed sane politics than it had destroyed the live theatre, professional football, the reading of novels or the art of conversation, the ruin of each of which had in turn been confidently prophesied. Indeed, the conclusion of the earliest researchers, in 1959, tended to discount the power of television to influence voting, and emphasized its educational qualities:

'There was a significant increase in political knowledge during the campaign . . . It seems . . . that the attempt to convey information does not meet with the same resistance as does the attempt to persuade, but that material designed primarily to influence opinion may also increase knowledge . . .

'Political change was neither related to the degree of exposure nor to any particular programmes or argument put forward by the parties . . .

[1] *Nuffield 1951*, p. 75.
[2] *Nuffield 1959*, pp. 92–3.

'The inter-election years become more important than the nineteen days of campaigning, however intensive, because the swing is almost entirely accounted for before the opening of the election campaign.'[1]

This assertion, summarizing the traditional wisdom on the subject, needs qualifying in a number of ways. It refers only to the balance between the main contenders and more intensive research in 1964 showed that the Liberals, who are normally 'under-exposed' profited from the extra publicity.[2] There have been similar developments in other countries: Jean Lecanuet, the last-minute Centre candidate in the French presidential election of 1965 seems to have profited equally from his television appearances.[3] The 1964 surveys revealed something else, however. The pro-Liberal movement of opinion was highest among those who were not keenly interested in politics and who were therefore stimulated by the sudden rise in the political content of their viewing diet. Also, although the switchers from one major party to another cancelled each other out, they were distinctly more aware of the themes the parties were emphasizing at the end of the campaign than at the beginning.[4]

These findings, limited though they are, enable us to answer a little more precisely than before questions on which there had been a surplus of opinion over information. In the first place, they underline the importance of television as a source of political information, especially for people with generally low interest in public affairs. In that sense, if in no other, all elections are now 'TV elections'. In the second place they show that some at least of those who change their voting intention during a campaign do so on the basis of improved information, though whether minor parties will invariably be the beneficiaries of such television exposure is another question. But the evidence of the 1964 survey does support the conclusion that these late converts to Liberalism, with their conscientious viewing habits and superior knowledge of issues 'seemed to embody some of the classic virtues of the rational democratic voter'.[5]

The experience of 1959 helped the broadcasting networks to become more enterprising, and the parties less timorous, in their attitudes to campaign coverage. In 1959 the only programmes not sponsored by the parties were *Hustings* (BBC) and *Marathon* (ITV). Popular current affairs programmes like *Gallery*, *This Week* and *What the Papers Say* were

---

[1] Trenaman, J. and McQuail, D., *Television and the Political Image* (London, 1961), pp. 232, 128.

[2] Blumler, J. G. and McQuail, D., *Television in Politics: Its Uses and Influence* (London, 1968), pp. 197–203.

[3] *Revue Française de Science Politique XVI* (Feb., 1966), p. 188.

[4] Blumler and McQuail, *op. cit.*, pp. 158–63, 207–21, 273.

[5] *ibid.*, p. 272; Milne, R. S. and Mackenzie, H. C., *Marginal Seat* (London, 1958), p. 198.

banished at a time when their relevance was greatest. Since 1964 these and similar programmes have survived, and *Election Forum*, in which the party leaders answer viewers' questions, has proved more popular than any of the parties' set pieces.[1] Because the networks are under an obligation to provide political balance, which the newspapers are not, and because both the BBC and the ITA ultimately depend on politicians' good-will, the parties have a strong say in determining what constitutes balance. Party managers tend to insist that the networks, as 'public service' media, are there to serve the politicians' views not only of what should be said, but of how – e.g. by banning confrontations of cabinet and shadow ministers – despite the well-documented public unpopularity of this stance.[2] But we must also sympathize with the politician's fear that greater freedom for the studio producer could drown what the rival candidates for government had to say – perhaps through an obsession with audience ratings, perhaps through political ignorance, perhaps from an exaggerated sense of mission as a counterweight to party propagandists.

If most of the technical improvements in television electioneering are due to the professional broadcasters, in other respects it is the parties who have been the innovators. Most leading politicians, having achieved their eminence by traditional methods, pride themselves on their instinctive ability to communicate, and their unique contact with the people's pulse. It was against these canons of intuitive campaigning that the Conservatives offended in 1957–9, by resorting for the first time to professional public relations men.[3] The firm of Colman, Prentis and Varley, which had briefly helped the party in 1949–51, was called in to plan an intensive newspaper and poster advertising campaign, in order to refurbish the party's public image after the Suez débâcle and the economic deterioration. There followed a period of publicity unprecedented in both intensity and skill. The campaign stressed consumer prosperity, opportunity for all and Labour's negative and class-ridden approach. 'Life's better with the Conservatives. Don't let Labour ruin it', was one of the most effective slogans ever coined. But the power of professional persuaders to persuade should not be exaggerated. Most propaganda is successful only if it emphasizes what people are in any case willing to believe. If the evidence of prosperity had in 1959 been less patent, or the economy had suddenly taken a turn for the worse, the themes chosen by the Conservatives and their advisers would have backfired badly. Experience in the 1964 campaign confirms this. In the first four months of that year the party spent nearly half a million pounds on

[1] *Nuffield 1964*, p. 162.
[2] Blumler and McQuail, *op. cit.*, pp. 86–103.
[3] For a detailed account of this campaign, see Lord Windlesham, *Communication and Political Power* (London, 1966), Chapter 3.

projecting the personal image of Sir Alec Douglas-Home. During that period his nop rating slumped from 58 per cent to 48 per cent.[1] And in America the much publicized 'selling of the President',[2] enabled the victorious candidate to scrape home by 0·7 per cent in 1968, having led in the polls by 15 per cent only six weeks earlier.

There were several reasons why the Conservatives were in a better position to pioneer this type of campaigning. In the first place it needs money. The Conservatives must have spent £468,000 in the 1958–9 pre-election period, compared with Labour's £103,000.[3] But Labour also had moral and aesthetic objections to commercializing politics at the expense of rational persuasion. Mr Crossman complained that the Prime Minister was being sold 'as though he were a detergent' and Mr Gaitskill thought 'the whole thing is somehow false'. When a group of advertising men with Labour sympathies offered the party their services, they were rebuffed.[4]

Labour was, however, responsible for one major innovation in the 1959 campaign. Anxious to hit the headlines in what it judged to be a predominantly hostile press, it instituted a daily press conference. In the nature of things this advantage could last for only one election: by 1964 the Conservatives and Liberals had followed suit. It was the defeat in 1959, the fourth in succession and the worst, which revolutionized Labour's attitude to campaigning, It could no longer be claimed convincingly that Labour leaders instinctively knew what the majority of the public wanted. Clearly, some of the issues raised by the party had failed to persuade: the manner in which they had been raised and failed to impress; worse still, some of the attitudes and priorities with which the party was associated, and which had once stood them in good stead, were no longer popular. Despite such objections as Mr Aneurin Bevan's that opinion polls 'took the poetry out of politics'.[5] Labour was gradually converted to the need for market research techniques.

Accordingly between 1962 and 1964 Dr Mark Abrams of *Research Services* conducted a number of surveys in marginal constituencies to discover how voters viewed the rival parties, which issues they regarded as important, and how to identify what Dr Abrams called the 'target voters'. Professional journalists and advertising men also received a much warmer welcome than before 1959 and played a larger part in designing posters and devising such slogans as 'Let's GO with Labour' with the thumbs-up symbol. It is, of course, quite possible that Labour would have won the 1964 election even if its propaganda machine had been as

[1] Rose, R., *Influencing Voters. A Study of Campaign Rationality* (London, 1967), pp. 58, 181.
[2] Maginnis, J., *The Selling of the President* (London, 1969).
[3] *Nuffield 1959*, pp. 21, 28.
[4] *ibid.*, pp. 20, 25, 27n.
[5] *Nuffield 1964*, pp. 50–1.

amateurish as in the past. No one can estimate the precise effect that Dr Abrams' findings had on the course of the campaign, but one Labour official has remarked in retrospect. 'Those polls then were prodigiously influential though of course no one will admit it now.'[1] 1964 seems, however, to have marked a temporary peak in the technical efficiency of Labour campaigning. Polls were used little between 1966 and 1970 and the pre-election advertising campaign in 1970 was ill-prepared and modest in scale. Dwindling membership and strained relations with the unions kept the party poor, but there were political as well as financial reasons that made the party leaders keep professional advisers at arm's length.

POLITICAL COMMUNICATION

Professionalism in political propaganda has clearly come to stay. In this respect Britain has merely caught up with developments in the United States and a number of continental European states. It is a consequence of technical developments; it is also a consequence of the centralization of party organization and the 'nationalization' of political opinion – trends which highly-charged propaganda machines in turn further accelerate. But all political communication flows in two directions, even if it is easier for those in command of the machine to make their points than it is for ordinary voters or party members. Opinion polls, whether published or privately sponsored, can be a weapon in the hands of the ordinary citizen, by voicing grievances and establishing priorities which the party machine is either too sluggish or too out-of-touch to convey to headquarters. A specific example of this is the question of comprehensive schools. The Conservatives had originally planned to make opposition to comprehensives a major item in their 1966 campaign, until a survey revealed that their 'target voters' were in favour of them.[2]

The irruption of the persuasion industry into politics has given rise to a rather confused debate about the ethics of such methods. That political advertising, like all advertising, is open to abuse, is undeniable. There *is* a danger that opinion could be manipulated, fears and phobias exploited and irrational sentiments generally excited by psychologically skilled 'salesmanship', though gifted demagogues in past generations have got by without the help of advertising agencies. There is, on the other hand, some hope that the possibilities of these techniques are limited. Smoothness, slickness and too-evident professionalism can evoke sales resistance. Sincerity and candour cannot be entirely simulated in a society which still respects these qualities. More than one

---

[1] *Nuffield 1966*, p. 33.
[2] *ibid.*, p. 93.

heavily researched product has been a commercial flop; more than one professionally conducted campaign has resulted in defeat.

A second, and contradictory, objection is that politicians will become all too sensitive to the whims of public opinion. Forever scanning the poll charts, they will cease to act according to their principles and consciences and simply trim to whichever point of view is currently rating fifty-one per cent. This particular objection merely re-states in a new form the central problem of democratic politics. Is the politician who consistently maintains his point of view steadfast and honest, or is he obstinate and arrogant? Is the assiduous reader of opinion polls a faithful servant of his constituents or an irresponsible weathercock? Was it magnanimous, or was it craven of the Conservative Party to soft-pedal the comprehensive school issue even though they honestly believed selective education to be better? Was it conscientious, or merely incompetent, of Sir Alec Douglas-Home to emphasize the independent nuclear deterrent in 1964 when one survey after another showed that defence policy came at the bottom of most voters' order of importance?

Professional electioneering is necessarily expensive electioneering. Characteristically, British election law is still based on the same assumptions as the Corrupt and Illegal Practices Act of 1883 which first seriously limited election expenses – namely, that it is the campaign in the constituencies, and the risk of bribery by individual candidates, which are decisive. Since the war the legal limits on campaign expenditure have scarcely kept pace with the rise in printing costs.[1] Although some candidates, especially those in marginal seats, spend suspiciously near the limit in a way that does credit to their agents' accounting skill, what surprises is that even the major parties are content to underspend by 10 to 20 per cent.

Constituency Expenditure, 1966–70[2]

Party	1966			1970		
	Total	Per candi-date	% of maxi-mum	Total	Per candi-date	% of maxi-mum
	£	£		£	£	
Conservative	480,000	766	89	590,000	949	79
Labour	450,000	726	84	530,000	848	68
Liberal	150,000	501	56	170,000	525	41
Others	50,000	338	41	110,000	424	36

[1] In 1950 limits were set at a basic allowance of £450, plus 1½d per elector in borough and 2d per elector in county constituencies. The basic allowance is now £750. (Great Britain only; N. Ireland has a lower scale.)

[2] *Nuffield 1966*, p. 203; *Nuffield 1970*, p. 333.

A few candidates, confident of their personal pull, are much more frugal. Mr Albert Evans retained South-West Islington for Labour in both 1964 and 1966 for less than £300,[1] and Mr John Parker held the much larger constituency of Dagenham for £299 in 1970.[2] Mr S. O. Davies, the victorious Independent in Merthyr Tydfil, spent less still. The danger in the 1960s, however, was not that the electors will be drowned in 'a torrent of gin and beer' (to which Gladstone attributed the Liberal defeat of 1874),[3] but that they will be suffocated by a surfeit of posters and newsprint. Labour Party expenditure on nationwide pre-election publicity trebled between 1959 and 1964, that of Conservative Party more than doubled.

Pre-election publicity expenditure, 1959–64[4]

	1959	1964
	£	£
Labour	103,000	314,000
Conservative	468,000	992,000

The early sixties seem to have marked a peak for the newly-discovered campaign techniques; since then expenditure has not escalated on the same scale. The same trends apply to the more free-booting propaganda bodies, such as the Economic League, Aims of Industry or (up to 1966), the Iron and Steel Federation. These organizations claim to be non-partisan, and their intervention is restricted to a single issue – the defence of free enterprise – but it is evident that such publicity favours the Conservatives at the expense of Labour. In 1959 they spent an estimated £1,435,000, in 1964 an estimated £1,809,000 – one-and-a-half times the total spent in all constituency campaigns. In 1970 these sums were much lower, mainly because the steel firms, who had accounted for about two-thirds the expenditure, were out of the running after nationalization, but also because even Aims of Industry had retrenched, spending £134,000 compared with £270,000 in 1964.[5] Neither these sums nor the costs of national party advertising count as 'election expenses', though if money brings any returns at all, it is this, and not the local candidate's photograph, that matters. Nor are there any proposals to limit spending on national campaigns either by parties or by private bodies. This situation restores the premium on wealth which it has been the object of legislation over the last ninety years to neutralize, but we

[1] *Nuffield 1964*, p. 228; *Nuffield 1966*, p. 203.
[2] *Nuffield 1970*, p. 334.
[3] J. Morley, *Life of Gladstone* (London, 1903), Vol. II, p. 475.
[4] *Nuffield 1959*, pp. 21, 28; *Nuffield 1964*, pp. 372, 374.
[5] Rose, *op. cit.*, pp. 106, 103; *Nuffield 1964*, p. 378; *Nuffield 1970*, p. 324.

need to remember that the sums involved are small when compared with the advertising budget of most major firms, and the cost of election campaigns in many other countries.[1]

Although the trade unions' political levy has always been strictly audited and companies are now required by law to declare donations over £100 for political purposes, the exact financial position of parties remains obscure. This is partly because there are elaborate transfer payments of locally collected money to headquarters and centrally-collected money to constituencies; partly because smaller company donations, though not tipping the national balance, may well be helpful to constituency finances; and partly because unions' and companies' political funds may flow into independent campaigns rather than party coffers. Since the war the Labour Party has derived about two-thirds of its normal central income and one-third of its constituency income from affiliation fees by trade unions; in addition the party is almost entirely dependent on union generosity for its general election fund. But this still accounts for only three-quarters of the unions' political levy.[2] More recently the Labour Party has been trying to 'live of its own', mainly by lotteries for constituency funds. The Conservative Party received £725,086 from companies during the first fifteen months of the new legal provision and a further £646,672 went to other political organizations. But since this period coincided with a special Conservative fund-raising appeal the sum may exaggerate the party's normal expectations. It amounts to about a third of the total raised by the appeal.[3] In an average year the Conservatives may expect to collect about £1 million.[4]

ARE CAMPAIGNS EFFECTIVE?

The growing centralization of campaigning means that it is the national, not the local propaganda which matters. Radio and television, advertising and newspaper reports have largely displaced the more traditional forms of electioneering. It is the slogans, quips and faux pas of the party leaders, not of the individual candidate, that set the tone of debate. The

[1] 'We finally got about five or six million dollars', according to Hubert Humphrey's 1968 campaign manager, Larry O'Brien. 'If we had finally gotten ten millions we would have licked Nixon.' White, T. H., *The Making of the President, 1968* (New York, 1969), p. 357 n.

[2] Harrison, *op. cit.*, pp. 66–7, 72, 99. Rose, *op. cit.*, pp. 254–5.

[3] Labour Party *Economic Brief*, Vol. 3, No. 1, Feb., 1970); Conservative Central Office News Service Release 252/770 (March 29, 1970); *Nuffield 1970*, p. 102.

[4] The chairman of the party's Board of Finance announced in 1971 that anticipated income would fall short, by £350,000, of the anticipated expenditure of £1,300,000 (*Daily Telegraph*, 3 April 1971).

local meeting is not dead, but it increasingly takes place at a factory gate or a shopping arcade rather than in an infant school or a dingy hall. The candidate can no longer summon his audience, he has to seek it out. An itinerant party leader can still, of course, draw a huge audience, but to the local standard-bearer a star speaker is a mixed blessing who may merely emphasize the anti-climax of his own effort. Increasingly the local candidate is merely the mouthpiece for the party's policy, not the advocate of his own personality.

The golden age of the pamphlet and the fly-sheet is over. In 1895 the Liberal Party distributed 23 million leaflets, four per elector.[1] The Labour Party's *Signposts for the Sixties*, an exceptionally well-produced document published in 1961, did well to sell a million copies.[2] In the last twenty years the output of leaflets and pamphlets by Conservative Central Office has fallen by two-thirds, although the electorate is up by a quarter.[3] (To all these figures must be added the candidates' local addresses, delivered to all electors.) Their impact is hard to measure;[4] it is probably greater inside the party – where they can educate members about new policies and provide speakers with material – than outside. Meetings, other than those with star billings, probably serve the same purpose. They raise morale and they given an impression of activity. Because they are mainly attended by the faithful they do not persuade. But the faithful are often 'opinion leaders' in their community, and the meeting equips them to pass on arguments and impressions to colleagues and neighbours.

As in quieter times the activities of the local party machine are largely administrative: their purpose is political, but their content is not. Canvassing, the hiring of halls, the addressing of envelopes and the manning of committee rooms require no ideological sophistication. They do require efficiency. The purpose of canvassing is not primarily to convert, it is partly a courtesy: if one wants a person's vote, one might at least call on him. But its main purpose is to locate supporters, especially those who might need transport on polling day, or who have moved since the register was drawn up. Whether efficient organization can win elections is disputed. For the past four elections the authors of the Nuffield studies have asked the parties to name in advance those constituencies where organisations had most improved. The results in these constituencies deviated only negligibly from the rest.[5] This is not in itself conclusive. The sample is small and parties presumably concen-

[1] Ostrogorski, M., *Democracy and the Organization of Political Parties* (London, 1902), Vol. I, p. 408.
[2] *Nuffield 1964*, p. 64.
[3] *Nuffield 1970*, p. 312.
[4] 'Who reads the leaflets, apart from the Oxford dons who write books about elections, is not known.' (Jennings, *Party Politics*, Vol. I, p. 226.)
[5] *Nuffield 1964*, p. 295; *Nuffield 1966*, p. 263.

trate their improvements in marginal seats, so that some of the improvements might cancel out. There are two other indices which suggest that organization can make a difference. They are the size of the turn-out and the size of the postal vote.

Between 1959 and 1966 there was a marked difference in turn-out between safe and marginal seats. In the country as a whole it dropped by 3 per cent from 78·8 per cent to 75·8 per cent. Between 1964 and 1966 it dropped by 1·2 per cent. But in marginal seats (i.e. those where the Conservatives had got between 47·5 per cent and 55 per cent of the major-party vote) it *rose* by 1·4 per cent; in seats which the Conservatives had held by less than 1 per cent it rose by 2·3 per cent.[1] It may be that electors in these constituencies were so conscious of their crucial role that they needed no further prodding to go out and vote. The fact that in 1970 the decline in turn-out was as great in marginal as in safe seats suggests that the exceptionally heated electioneering atmosphere of the mid-sixties may have affected some people in this way. But that can hardly be the whole explanation. The majority of those who hover between voting and abstaining are more apathetic and less well-informed than habitual voters;[2] some at least of the extra turn-out (which in a few cases bordered on the spectacular)[3] must have been due to efficient dragooning.

The postal vote provides a much more clear-cut opportunity for organizational superiority. The 1948 Act permitted the chronically sick, those who had moved and those absent on business to vote by post. In the 1964 election the average postal vote in Conservative-won seats was 1,601, in Labour-won seats 1,003. That in itself does not prove that the Conservative party is more efficient at organizing those entitled to a postal vote: evidence from other countries suggests that this facility favours more middle-class than working-class electors and is therefore a bonus to right-wing parties.[4] What is significant is that in the nine most marginally won Conservative seats in 1964 the average postal vote was 1,772.[5] In 1970 the average postal vote was 973, in the fifty most

[1] *Nuffield 1966*, p. 285. To some extent this rise in turn-out was 'technical': the 1966 register was more up-to-date than that of 1964. But this is not important What matters is the *difference* in behaviour between safe and marginal seats.

[2] See below, p. 125.

[3]
Constituency	1964 majority	1964–6 increase in turn-out
Brighton, Kemptown	Lab. 7	7·9%
Leyton	Con. 205 (by-election)	5·9%
Eton and Slough	Con. 11	5·3%
Hampstead	Con. 1,835	4·8%
Reading	Con. 10	4·2%

[4] cf. Germany: *Wirtschaft und Statistik* (Jan. 1962), p. 25; (Jan. 1966), p. 40.

[5] *Nuffield 1964*, p. 226.

marginal seats it was 1,451.[1] Postal ballots are not counted separately, but the overwhelming impression of party agents is that they help the Conservatives. On the assumption that they split 2:1 in favour of the Conservatives, they would have been decisive in at least twelve constituencies in the closely-fought 1964 election, and in at least six constituencies in all other elections.

It is one thing to dragoon, another to persuade. Canvassers and knockers-up have to go on the assumption that most people's minds are made up: an election campaign makes sense only on the assumption that some are not. It is frequently claimed that the campaign itself influences nobody: opinions are changed, if at all, in the course of a government's lifetime, not in the final hectic three weeks. As we have seen, under modern political conditions electioneering never stops. The dissolution of Parliament does not mark a beginning in the onslaught on the voters' favours, merely a change in its intensity. To that extent the voter's decision is the outcome of a host of impressions accumulated over a number of years. On the other hand opinion polls have shown some movement of opinion during all of the post-war election campaigns; except in 1955 and 1964[2] the trend was for the gap between the main parties to narrow. Old loyalties were being reasserted. Whether it was the campaign oratory or the mere proximity of polling day which had this effect cannot be proved. But if the speeches, posters and canvassers have no other effect, they at least remind people that there is an election on.

In the last resort that is the only claim that can be made on behalf of election campaigns and indeed party activity generally. They can mobilize and they can inform. They can stimulate into temporary activity those men and women for whom public affairs are not a primary and overriding concern. There is a small minority who become permanently involved in politics for a variety of personal reasons[3] and for whom political activity can become an end in itself, perhaps even an obsession. But even that larger minority who are prepared to belong to parties and lend a hand at election times have to be kept together, and sometimes even recruited, by the prospect of social or cultural activities which have little to do with the aims of the parties.[4] An election, and

---

[1] *Nuffield 1970*, p. 331. The average conceals wide variations. In Dover and Birmingham, Perry Barr, both gained by the Conservatives, the figures were respectively 3,319 and 339.

[2] In 1955 the Conservative lead increased slightly. In 1964 the various polls showed contradictory trends, roughly cancelling each other out.

[3] cf. Lane, R. E., *Political Life. Why and How People Get Involved in Politics* (2nd edn, New York, 1964); Milbrath, L. W., *Political Participation* (Chicago, 1965).

[4] cf. the claim, 'In the Young Conservatives it is not all Politics; far from it . . .', quoted by Milne and Mackenzie, *op. cit.*, p. 14. Twelve years later the

an election campaign, bring citizens into contact with the machinery of the government and with individual politicians in a way for which there are otherwise few opportunities. This participation is of great psychological importance, not only to the ordinary citizen but to the party activist and the practising politician. It is a process which does not merely legitimize the particular government that emerges from the election, but also this particular way of choosing governments and of resolving political disputes. It gives the citizen a chance to affirm his loyalties and make use of his rights; it reminds the candidate that there is a price to pay for the furtherance of his vanity or ambition. Elections are therefore a ritual, and the best testimony to its efficacy comes from states with single-party systems. Their 'elections' in which 99·9 per cent of the electorate vote for the government list are a joke for sophisticated Westerners. Yet régimes would hardly bother with them if the sole function of an election were the expression of policy choices.

---

prose style has changed, but not the message: 'A cool approach to hot ideas makes for a big, big leisure scene. Make the pace, set the style as a Young Conservative.' (1966 leaflet.)

IV

Voting
Behaviour

ALTHOUGH an election is a ritual which involves much beside the making of choices, it is also a choice; indeed, some languages have only one word for the two processes. What we think about the merits of making political choices by means of elections depends on what we think of our fellow-citizens' capacity for making choices.

Most nineteenth-century advocacy of an extended franchise rested on the assumption that voters are capable of choosing rationally, though even the most advanced liberal theorists, like James and John Stuart Mill, admitted that the least educated were least equipped to do so. At the beginning of this century Lord Bryce stipulated a more modest requirement, the 'average man',

'The man of broad common sense, mixing on equal terms with his neighbours, forming a fair unprejudiced judgment on every question, not viewy or pedantic like the man of learning, nor arrogant like the man of wealth, but seeing things in a practical, businesslike, and withal kindly spirit, pursuing happiness in his own way, and willing that everyone else should do so. Such average men make the bulk of the people, and are pretty sure to go right, because the publicity secured to the expression of opinion by speech and in print will supply them with ample materials for judging what is best for all . . .

'He may have limited knowledge and no initiative, yet he may be able to form . . . a shrewd judgment of men . . . What he lacks in knowledge he often makes up for by a sympathetic comprehension of the attitude of his fellow-men.'[1]

The foundations of such assumptions have been pretty thoroughly undermined by the progress of two modern disciplines, psychology and sociology. As a result we know much more about why people hold the political views that they do, though the implications for representational theory are by no means clear-cut.

Before we ask *why*, it is best to ask *how*. The raw material of voting

[1] Viscount Bryce, *Modern Democracies* (London, 1921), pp. 168-9.

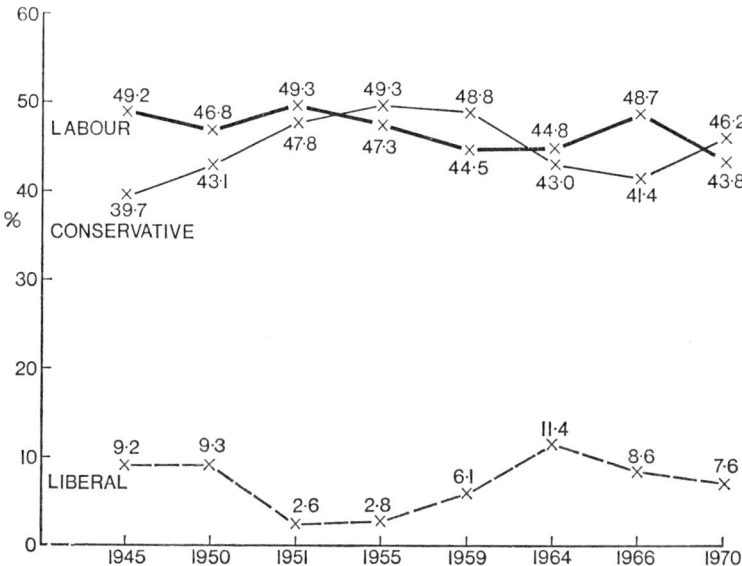

FIGURE IV. I: Percentage of total vote by Party 1945–70 (Great Britain only).

behaviour is in the voting figures (see Table on page 99). At the parliamentary level, these shifts in voting have led to great variations in representation. But then, the British electoral system is notorious for exaggerating the effects of such shifts. The chief impression which the voting figures convey is one of stability, not volatility. Figure IV.1 shows that since the war neither of the major parties has gained less than 39·7 per cent of the total vote or more than 49·3 per cent. (For the sake of simplicity Northern Ireland and the university constituencies are excluded throughout this chapter.) The contrast with the United States is striking (Figures IV.1, IV.2). Only once, in 1945, has the gap between the two main parties in Britain exceeded 7 per cent. The movement from election to election has also been small. This movement is normally measured in terms of 'net swing', which can be calculated in a variety of ways.[1] The most widely used[2] and most easily comprehensible, although

[1] See Steed, M. in *Nuffield 1964*, pp. 337–8; Berrington, H. B., 'The General Election of 1964' in *Journal of the Royal Statistical Society*, Series A, Vol. CXXVIII (1965), pp. 17–21; Rasmussen, J. S., 'The Disutility of the Swing Concept in British Psephology', *Parliamentary Affairs* XVIII (Autumn, 1965).

[2] e.g. in the Nuffield College election studies, *The Times Guide to the House of Commons*, *The Economist* and by both broadcasting networks.

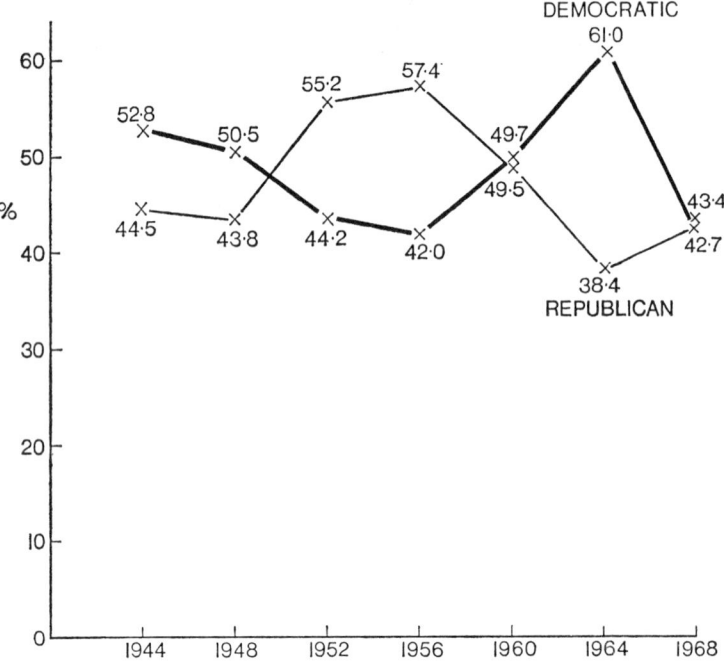

FIGURE IV. 2: Percentage of total vote by Presidential candidates in USA 1944–8.

also the crudest, is to average the percentage gain by one major party and percentage loss by the other, e.g.

Example 1 $\begin{cases} \text{Party A: } + 5\% \text{ of all votes cast} \\ \text{Party B: } - 5\% \text{ of all votes cast} \\ \text{Party Z: } \pm 0\% \text{ of all votes cast} \end{cases}$

$$\text{Swing} = 5\%$$

Example 2 $\begin{cases} \text{Party A: } + 2\% \text{ of all votes cast} \\ \text{Party B: } - 7\% \text{ of all votes cast} \\ \text{Party Z: } + 5\% \text{ of all votes cast} \end{cases}$

$$\text{Swing} = \frac{2 + 7}{2} = 4\tfrac{1}{2}\%$$

VOTES CAST IN BRITISH GENERAL ELECTIONS, 1945–70 (U.K. Totals)

	Electorate	Conservative VOTES	%	Labour VOTES	%	Liberal VOTES	%	Other VOTES	%	Turn-out %
1945*	32,836,419	9,577,667	39·8	11,632,891	48·3	2,197,101	9·1	674,703	2·8	73·3
1950	34,269,770	12,502,567	43·5	13,266,592	46·1	2,621,548	9·1	381,964	1·3	84·0
1951	34,645,573	13,717,538	48·0	13,948,605	48·8	730,556	2·5	198,969	0·7	82·5
1955	34,858,263	13,311,936	49·7	12,404,907	46·4	722,405	2·7	321,182	0·2	76·8
1959	35,397,080	13,749,830	49·4	12,215,538	43·8	1,638,571	5·9	275,304	1·0	78·8
1964	35,892,572	12,001,396	43·4	12,205,814	44·1	3,092,878	11·2	348,914	1·3	77·0
1966	35,966,975	11,418,413	41·9	13,056,951	47·9	2,327,470	8·5	456,909	1·7	75·8
1970	39,384,364	13,144,692	46·4	12,179,166	42·9	2,117,638	7·5	903,311	3·2	72·0
(Feb) 1974	39,798,899	11,963,207	38·2	11,654,726	37·3	6,063,470	19·3	1,651,633	5·2	78·9

*Voting figures adjusted to allow for double-member constituencies in which electors had two votes each, and to omit university seats.

SEATS WON IN BRITISH GENERAL ELECTIONS, 1945–70 (U.K. Totals)

	Total	Conservative	Labour	Liberal	Others	Overall Majority
1945	640	213	393	12	22	Lab. 146
1950	625	298	315	9	3	Lab. 5
1951	625	321	295	6	3	Con. 17
1955	630	345	277	6	2	Con. 60
1959	630	365	358	6	1	Con. 100
1964	630	303	317	9	1	Lab. 4
1966	630	253	363	12	2	Lab. 97
1970	630	330	287	6	7	Con. 30
(Feb) 1974	635	297	301	14	23	None

On this calculation, the purpose of which is to isolate that section of the electorate which seems to have changed its mind, the swing at post-war elections has been

1950 2·9 % to Con.
1951 1·1 % to Con.
1955 1·8 % to Con.
1959 1·1 % to Con.
1964 3·1 % to Lab.
1966 2·7 % to Lab.
1970 4·8 % to Con.

In 1951, 1955, 1966 over half the constituencies had a swing which was within 1 per cent of the national average, though in 1959, 1964 and 1970 the divergence was rather greater. This consistency is in keeping with the social and ideological homogeneity which have already been noted. Its development has accompanied – both as cause and as consequence – the rise of the modern disciplined political party, but it has become overwhelmingly true of British politics not only since the establishment of the Labour-Tory duel. Up to the First World War changes determined by local conditions and going against the tide were common. In January, 1910, when the Conservatives gained 128 seats, Liberals and their Labour allies were still able to gain thirteen seats that they had failed to capture in the landslide of 1906. The second election of that year, in December, led to virtually the same overall result,[1] but fifty-six seats changed hands. Since the war the greatest number of seats to change hands against the tide was six (in 1959); in 1950, 1951, 1966 and 1970 there were none at all. 1959 was also the only post-war election in which more than one-sixth of the seats showed swings in the opposite direction from the general trend. Only since the war have both major parties attempted to cover the entire country. 1950 was the first election in which all constituencies outside Northern Ireland were contested, with Labour candidates in every seat (except the Speaker's) in England, Scotland and Wales. It was not until 1964 that the Conservatives followed suit. The elimination of the Independent MP is also a post-war phenomenon. As late as 1945 territorial constituencies returned two Communists, one ILP and seven Independents against the opposition of the major parties. Of the Independents, four were party rebels, the other three 'genuine' non-party men. Except for the ILP members who had joined the Labour Party they were all defeated in 1950. Only in 1970 did one Independent – a party rebel – and one Scottish Nationalist succeed in getting elected. The two Nationalists, one Welsh and one Scottish, who had gained by-elections lost their seats again at the general election.

[1]

	Conservative	Liberal	Labour	Irish
January, 1910	273	275	40	82
December, 1910	272	272	42	84

We should not exaggerate the firmness of British party loyalties. Not only opinion polls but by-elections and the annual municipal elections show that the limits within which opinion can move are quite wide. Table IV.3 shows the high and low points of the parties' fortunes since 1959 as recorded by Gallup.

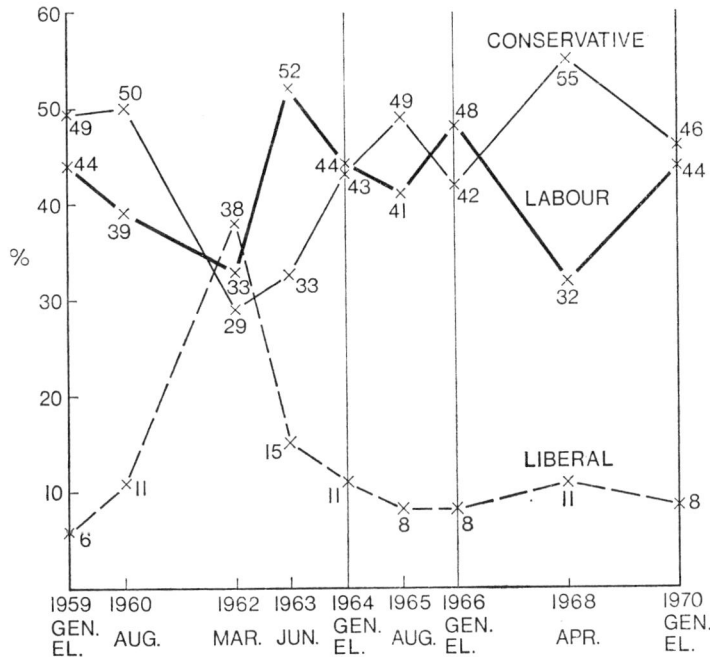

FIGURE IV. 3: Extreme Points of Opinion Poll Fluctuations, 1959–70. (Source: *Gallup Political Index*.)

Opinion polls, though accurate enough as a guide to the direction in which opinion is moving, are not so accurate that any one sample can be taken literally. The extreme points came immediately after spectacular events – Labour's defence split, the Profumo affair, devaluation – and receded fairly quickly. This shows that the number of *potentially* volatile voters is much greater than those who appear to have actually changed their minds at an election. Moreover the net 'swing' figures from election to election conceal contrary movements: movements into and out of minor parties and movements to and from abstention. The net swing to Labour between 1959 and 1964 was just over 3 per cent, but altogether 25–30 per cent of the electorate changed in one way or another between the two elections.[1] On the other hand, despite this large turn-over in allegiance and the mid-term surges by minor parties – Liberals in 1962–3, Welsh and Scottish Nationalists in 1967–8 – each general election shows a strong urge to restabilize the system.

If party loyalty is as strong as the election figures suggest, then it is clear that most electors are not, as rationalist utopians once thought, in a state of perpetual choice. On the contrary, most political allegiance seems to be a matter of habit, and it is here that the psychologists' and sociologists' explanations become relevant. What determines these habits of allegiance? Family influence, class, region, religion, sex and age all play their part. These categories are not water-tight and it is not always possible to discover which of them is an independent and which a dependent variable. But there is no doubt which of these variables has the greatest predictive power. Class is the basis of British party politics; all else is embellishment and detail.

CLASS AND PARTY

Until the middle of the nineteenth century 'connection' and local influence were as powerful as any other factors in determining party loyalty, the more so as the parties themselves had neither easily recognizable policies nor coherent internal organization. Over the last hundred years, however, class and party have increasingly coincided. Especially since the Second Reform Act of 1867, the further one went down the social scale, the more likely one was to find support for the party of the left (Liberal until 1914, Labour thereafter). For the years before the Ballot Act we can establish this from the poll-books, in which every voter's preference was recorded. True, the poll-books have a number of weaknesses. Occupational descriptions can be ambiguous – a 'cotton-spinner' may be an entrepreneur or an operative; there are few poll-books relating to the major cities; and we can, of course, discover nothing about the political preferences of the disfranchised. One of the few break-downs of major cities that we have is for Bristol, 1852:[2]

	Liberal	Conservative
Gentlemen	127	255
Service officers	5	18
Professions	30	53
Financiers	7	13
Victuallers	118	71

[1] Butler and Stokes, *op. cit.*, Ch. 12. Benewick, A. J. *et al.*, 'The Floating Voter and the Liberal View of Representation', *Political Studies* XVII (June, 1969), p. 187.

[2] Vincent, J. R., *Pollbooks: How Victorians Voted* (Cambridge, 1967), p. 16.

	Liberal	Conservative
Beer-sellers	108	32
Shoe-makers	168	11
Anglican clergy	3	56
Dissenting ministers	14	1
R.C. priest	1	0
Labourers	69	72

A comparison of the results in Cambridge in 1865 and 1868 shows the impact of the Second Reform Act:[1]

	1865		1868	
	Liberal	Conservative	Liberal	Conservative
Gentlemen and Farmers	39	67	64	91
Professions	84	135	131	195
Publicans	30	38	41	40
Servants	37	113	90	235
Labourers	6	13	289	124
Businessmen	81	53	129	72
Retailers	208	141	247	182
Craftsmen	259	191	809	393

Between the Third Reform Act (1884), which enfranchised many of the poor, and the coming of universal suffrage (1918) we can see a clearer, but still highly imperfect, correlation of class and party. According to Mr Pelling's calculation, the fifty-six most affluent constituencies were predominantly Conservative during this period, with an average 58·6 per cent Conservative vote; the eighty-nine poorest constituencies had an average Liberal (or Liberal-plus-Labour) vote of 53·2 per cent and constituencies in which mining predominated an average Liberal vote of 61·9 per cent.[2] Clearly, a large minority of the electorate did not see the party battle as a class battle during this period; local or temporary factors, the candidate's personality, issues like Ireland, religion or imperialism that cut across class lines could still weigh heavily. Political cohesion varied greatly from one industry to another. It was strong among miners, railwaymen, boot- and shoe-makers and some branches of textiles (woollens and cotton-weaving),[3] but in the early twentieth century that still meant voting Liberal, not Labour. It is only with the emergence of the Labour Party as the chief challenger to the Tories in the 1920s, and still more with the evenly balanced Conservative–Labour competition for office since 1945, that the party battle could be conducted in overtly class terms.

[1] ibid., pp. 90–3.
[2] Pelling has traced a particularly strong correlation between class and party allegiance in London and Scotland. Pelling, H., The Social Geography of British Elections, 1885–1910 (London, 1967), pp. 36, 41–2, 43, 388–9, 392, 403, 411.
[3] ibid., pp. 420–3.

All this assumes that we can measure class objectively. But can we?

Occupation and income are the most obvious criteria and to a large extent they overlap, but occupation is the more reliable of the two. The simplest course is to divide society into 'middle' and 'working' class (or manual and non-manual). The great majority of people, when asked to place themselves socially, use one of these two categories (or some fairly obvious equivalent, such as 'professional' or 'labouring') rather than any of the more refined sub-divisions that a social scientist would prefer. But simplicity is sometimes achieved at the expense of over-simplification: a division of society into two is not as easy as Marx and Engels once imagined it to be.[1] To use only two classes involves arbitrary decisions about the dividing line. This may not matter much if one simply wants to demonstrate that in general party goes with class, or to plot long-term developments in the relationship. But it becomes a serious obstacle if one wants to identify sub-groups, such as working-class Conservatives and middle-class Socialists. For this reason social investigators tend to use more elaborate scales. The first of these is an adaptation of the one used by the Registrar-General since 1911,[2] with a sub-division in the largest and most heterogeneous of the five classes, C (Routine white-collar and skilled manual). This scale is used by the Institute of Practitioners in Advertising and most market research organizations, and by all opinion polls except Gallup, which has a slightly different scale:

NOP	NPA	GALLUP	
12% AB	A Higher managerial, administrative or professional	Average + / well-to-do	6%
	B Intermediate managerial, administrative or professional	Average/upper middle and middle class	22%
22% C1	C1 Supervisory, clerical; junior managerial, administrative or professional		
37% C2	C2 Skilled manual workers	Average − /lower middle and working class	61%
29% DE	D Semi-skilled and unskilled manual workers		
	E State pensioners, casual workers	Very poor	11%

[1] 'Our epoch, the epoch of the bourgeoisie, possesses . . . this distinctive feature: it has simplified the class antagonisms. Society is more and more splitting up into two great hostile camps, into two great classes directly facing each other – bourgeoisie and proletariat.' (*Communist Manifesto*, 1848.)

[2] Stevenson, T. H. C., 'The Vital Statistics of Wealth and Poverty', *Journal of the Royal Statistical Society* XCI (1928), esp. pp. 211–12.

The third is the Hall-Jones scale which uses seven categories:

1. Professional and high administrative, e.g. surgeon, chartered accountant;
2. Managerial and executive, e.g. personnel manager, primary school headmaster;
3. Higher-grade inspectional, supervisory and other non-manual, e.g. police inspector, farm bailiff;
4. Lower-grade inspectional, supervisory and other non-manual, e.g. insurance agent, costing clerk, tobacconist;
5. Skilled manual and routine non-manual, e.g. compositor, drapery shop assistant;
6. Semi-skilled manual, e.g. assembly worker, butcher's shop assistant;
7. Unskilled manual.

This has the advantage of combining 'objective' with 'subjective' assessment, since Hall and Caradog-Jones conducted a survey to discover the status which various occupations enjoy.[1]

The most recent attempt to locate as exactly as possible the elusive dividing line between 'middle' and 'working' class has been made by Butler and Stokes who, using the market-research/registrar-general classification, found that class C1 (lower non-manual) straddled this line, both in the self-assessment of those who belonged to it and in objectively observable habits. At the top this class (telegraph operators, qualified local authority officers, secretaries and typists with subordinates, draughtsmen) 60 per cent classed themselves as 'middle'; as many as 20 per cent took a quality newspaper (*The Times, Guardian* or *Daily Telegraph*). At the bottom of the class (shop assistants, policemen, transport inspectors, lodging housekeepers) only 32 per cent classed themselves as 'middle' and only 5 per cent read a quality newspaper.[2] As Figure IV.4 shows, the drop in self-assessed status between C1a and C1b is greater than that between any other two classes, though the sharpest break in political support occurs between C1b and C2. Whether this marginal category is attributed to the broader 'middle' or 'working' classes makes a great difference to the correlation between social status and party affiliation. If it counts as middle (as is usually done, since its members are non-manual) then the two parties show degrees of class support which are almost mirror-images.

[1] Hall, J. and Jones, D. Caradog, 'Social Grading of Occupations', *British Journal of Sociology* I (March, 1950), pp. 33–4, 40. The reliability of this scale has been disputed. See Glass, D. V. (ed.), *Social Mobility in Britain*, Ch. 2, and Young, M. and Willmott, P., 'Social Grading by Manual Workers', *British Journal of Sociology* VII (Dec., 1956).

[2] Kahan, M., Butler, D. E. and Stokes, D. E., 'On the Analytical Division of Social Class', *British Journal of Sociology* XVII (June, 1966), p. 128; Butler and Stokes, *op. cit.*, pp. 69–73, 77.

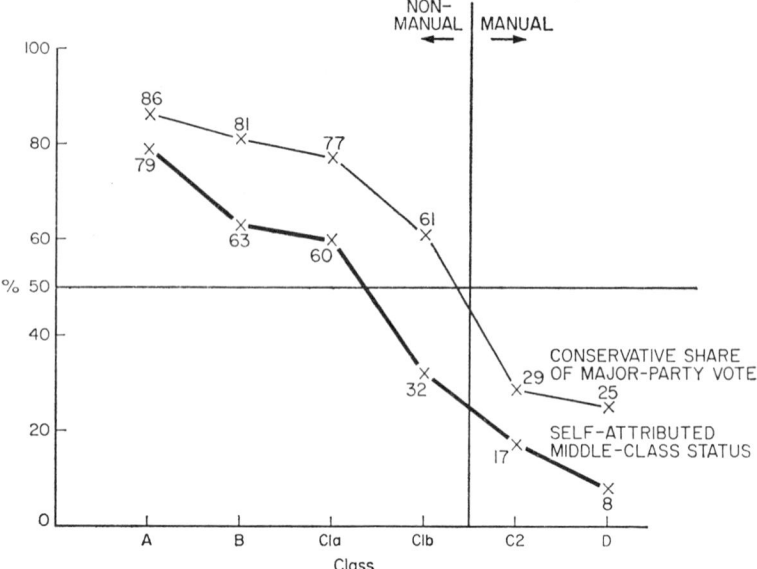

FIGURE IV. 4: Self-attributed middle-class status
and Party preference by classes (Summer, 1963).

Party support by class, counting C1b as 'middle' (summer 1963)

	Middle	Working
Conservative	77%	27%
Labour	23%	73%

If, on the other hand, it is consigned to the working class, as most of its
members seem to think it should be, the imbalance in class support
becomes considerable:[1]

Party support by class, counting C1b as 'working' (summer 1963)

	Middle	Working
Conservative	80%	32%
Labour	20%	68%

These details apart, the general picture, reinforced by the opinion
poll data in Figures IV.5 and IV.6, is a familiar one. People in manual
occupations – however defined – are, in the majority, Labour; those who
are not are, in the majority, Conservative. This 'obvious' observation
requires two qualifications. Class is by no means the only plausible
criterion for party cleavage in a modern state; it is true, however, that

[1] Kahan et al., op. cit., pp. 128–9.

British party politics are more highly class-bound than those in most other countries. A recent comparison between four Anglo-Saxon democracies (Britain, USA, Canada, Australia) showed that of the four Britain had the highest index of class voting.[1] Britain also has a higher class-voting index than most continental states, Scandinavia excepted.[2] This index is constructed by subtracting the percentage of non-manual workers voting for the party of the Left from the percentage of manual workers who do so, thus revealing the gap between the classes, e.g.

% voting for Left party

Manual:	75
Non-manual:	25
Index of class voting:	+50

A high index may therefore be achieved when most manual workers vote Left and most non-manual workers do not. A lower index may result *either* from many manual workers voting Right (e.g. Western Germany),[3] *or* from many non-manual workers voting Left (e.g. Wales),[4] an even lower or negative index when both happen (e.g. Canada).[5]

This makes the second qualification important. Class voting in Britain may be high, but it is by no means as high as it might be. Most people, asked to locate the centre of class-consciousness in Britain would probably point to the working class; and this is correct in that class-consciousness among workers is more explicit and overt than in the middle class.[6] The middle class, however, shows much greater political cohesion. In post-war elections the Labour Party has not succeeded in getting more than 20–25 per cent of the non-manual vote or 10–15 per cent of the business and professional classes. On the other hand at least a third of the working class consistently votes Conservative. Since,

---

[1] Alford, R. R., *Party and Society. The Anglo-American Democracies* (London, 1964), pp. 101–3. But there is some evidence that it is as high in New Zealand as in Britain. Robinson, A. D., 'Class Voting in New Zealand: A Comment on Alford's Comparison of Class Voting in the Anglo-American Political Systems' in Lipset, S. M. and Rokkan, S., *Party Systems and Voter Alignments: Cross-National Perspectives* (New York, 1967), pp. 94–114.

[2] Lijphart, A., 'Class Voting and Religious Voting in the European Democracies: A Preliminary Report'. Paper B–XI/2 presented at the VIIIth World Congress of the International Political Science Association (Munich, 1970), pp. 5, 14.

[3] Zölnhofer, W., 'Parteiidentifizierung in der Bundesrepublik und den Vereinigten Staaten' in Scheuch, E. K. and Wildenmann, R. (eds), *Zur Soziologie der Wahl. Kölner Zeitschrift für Soziologie und Sozialpsychologie*. Sonderheft 9 (1965), p. 153.

[4] See below, pp, 117, 119.

[5] Alford, *op. cit.*, p. 252.

[6] See below, pp. 121–2.

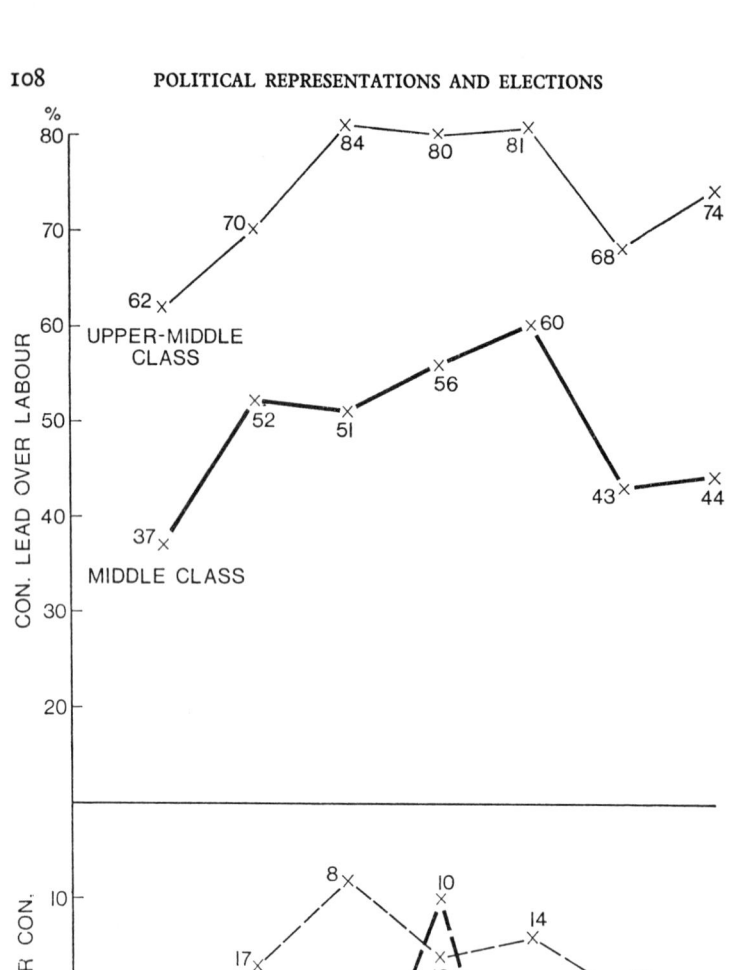

FIGURE IV. 5: Party preference by class, 1945-66 (Gallup poll).
(Source: Durant, H., 'Voting Behaviour in Britain', in Rose R. (ed.),
Studies in British Politics, 2nd edn, London, 1969, pp. 165–71.)

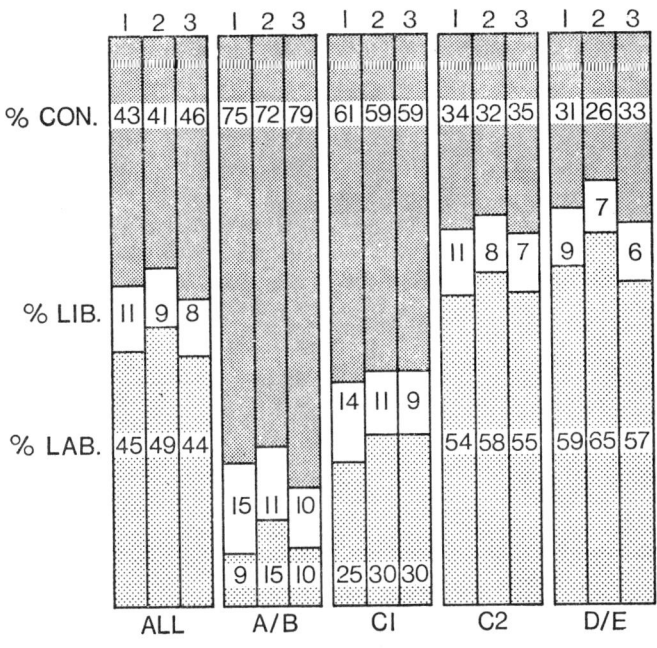

FIGURE IV. 6: Party preference by class, 1964–70 (NOP).

according to the 1961 census, two-thirds of the population are employed in manual occupations, this means that about half the Conservative vote regularly comes from the working class, but only about one-sixth of the Labour vote from the middle class. (Figure IV.7, which refers to the 1964 general election, when the two parties were evenly matched.) Class voting, I have argued, does not mean that every individual's vote can be predicted from his occupation, merely that his occupation is a better predictor than any rival characteristic. 'Pure' class voting, it is obvious would put an end to the British party system. The Conservative Party has survived the democratization of the country by its ability to gain votes of the poor. For that reason the Tory working-man has been subjected to more study than the middle-class Socialist. While some middle-class sympathy may be important to the Labour Party in providing it with leadership and local organization, and perhaps also in confirming its claim to speak for workers 'by hand or by brain', it does not have the statistical significance that working-class support has for the Conservatives.

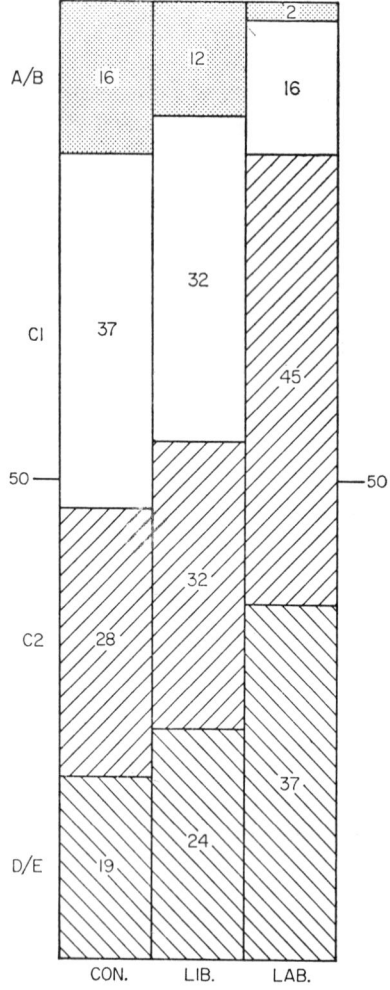

FIGURE IV. 7: Sources of support for Parties, by class (N.O.P. 1964).

What is the basis of working-class Toryism? The most important ingredient is social deference, though this may take many forms. In the nineteenth century Tory Democrats like Disraeli and Lord Randolph Churchill appealed to workers on the grounds that the Tories, unlike money-grabbing Liberal mill-owners, were true aristocrats and above the class-struggle. Factory hands who would not dream of voting for Mr Gradgrind could therefore confidently follow the Duke of Omnium. This appeal evoked, and still evokes, a response:

'The Conservatives have had more experience over the centuries. It's in the blood for them, running the country. There's more family background in the Conservatives, more of the aristocratic families, more heritage.

'They're gentlemen born. I think they're made for that sort of job.'[1]

Coupled with it is a respect for education, remembering that education is at least as much social training as intellectual qualification: 'The Conservatives are better suited to running the country. They're better educated – I think there is nothing better than to hear a public school man speak English.'[2] But equally there is respect for money and business success – as indeed there was in the nineteenth century when a great many working men were willing to follow the lead of their local Liberal or Radical employers. Today money as well as birth is associated with Conservatism: 'They are businessmen who know what they are doing. They have been brought up to rule, to take over the leadership.'[3] To some extent the snobbish attitudes implied by this deference are reflected in the Tory worker's view of himself. Conservative manual workers are more likely to attribute middle-class status to themselves than Labour manual workers.[4] But this self-promotion is not the whole explanation. As often as not deference implies a desire to maintain the existing social hierarchy, to acknowledge the superiority of 'gentlemen born'.

Deference can hardly account for the whole of working-class Conservatism. Equally important is a second category, whom McKenzie and Silver call 'secular' Conservatives[5] – predominantly younger, male, better-paid voters who happen to approve of private enterprise, value

[1] Samuel, R., 'The Deference Voter', *New Left Review* I (January, 1960), p. 11.

[2] *ibid., loc. cit.*

[3] McKenzie, R. T. and Silver, A., *Angels in Marble. Working-Class Conservatives in Urban England* (London, 1968), p. 109.

[4] Runciman, W. G., *op. cit.*, Ch. IX; also Mark, Benney and Pear, *op. cit.*, p. 188; Bealey, Blondel and MacCann, *Constituency Politics. A Study of Newcastle-under Lyme* (London, 1965), p. 176; Butler and Stokes, *op. cit.*, pp. 78–9; McKenzie and Silver, *op. cit.*, pp. 92–4.

[5] McKenzie and Silver, *op. cit.*, Ch. V.

consumer affluence or dislike trade unions.[1] They are less committed emotionally to leadership from the upper classes and take a more hard-headed and pragmatic view of Conservative capacity to govern.

Affluence may determine the form that working-class Conservatism takes; it is not, in itself, a cause of Conservatism. There is no evidence that high incomes, or the possession of consumer durables, predispose working-class voters towards the Right. The one exception is home-ownership which, at all levels of income, makes people with manual jobs feel more middle-class, and more inclined to vote Conservative than those who rent their homes.[2] There is little support for the *embourgeoise-ment* hypothesis in its crudest form – that the growth of consumer affluence makes people behave, and feel, in middle-class ways. Class identification is too firmly rooted to be overturned by the arrival of a washing-machine. However, while class and party attachments may remain fairly constant, changes in living standards notwithstanding, the intensity of these attachments may diminish. Life no longer appears as a struggle for the bare necessities; the spiritual sustenance that class solidarity gives is no longer central to social existence. This possible effect of affluence, which investigators of *embourgeoisement* have so far ignored, could be of great political importance. It almost certainly accounts for the above-average drop in turn-out in industrial constitu-encies over the last fifteen years;[3] without it we cannot account for the markedly greater volatility of the electorate. Above all, it goes hand in hand with the slow, but cumulatively significant, change in the country's occupational structure – the decline of nineteenth-century heavy indus-try and the growth of the service sector, where jobs are much less easily attributed to a dichotomous class model. The effect of such develop-ments is to make not merely Conservative but Labour commitment more 'secular'. Figures IV.10 and 11 show that over the last twenty years the Conservatives have emerged relatively weaker in the older industrial areas (North of England, Scotland, Wales) and relatively stronger in the areas of more recent expansion (Midlands, South).[4] This suggests that 'deferentials' have been replaced by secular Labour votes in the North and by secular Conservatives in the South.

RELIGION, AGE, SEX, REGION

Class is so much the most important conditioner of political allegiance that it becomes difficult to disentangle it from others. There is over-whelming evidence that women are more conservatively inclined than

[1] *ibid.*, pp. 184–9.
[2] *ibid.*, pp. 95–6; Butler and Stokes, *op. cit.*, p. 72.
[3] See below, p. 148.
[4] See below, pp. 128–9.

men,[1] as in most other countries.[2] Men have given Labour a majority
at every election since the war; women only in 1945 and 1966. If men
only had voted, it is improbable that Dr Adenauer would ever have
become Federal Chancellor of Western Germany, or that General de
Gaulle would have been re-elected to the Presidency in 1965. Sex is the
one factor which indubitably counter-balances class trends: working-
class women are more right-wing than working-class men, middle-class
women are more right-wing than middle-class men. In certain Continental European states religion, especially Catholicism, plays an important part in making women more right-wing. In Britain, where this
factor is less influential, the 'sex gap' is correspondingly smaller.

Age, too, correlates fairly closely with party preference, youth being
more left-wing than middle age or old age.[3] Yet problems of causality
arise. It may or may not be true that the older we get, the more conservative we become; in any case it has yet to be proved that this results
in vote-switching on a large scale. Some of us may rise in the social scale
as we get older, and this may lead to some conscious switching of votes.
But it is much more likely that the conservatism of old age consists of
sticking to one's chosen party, whether of the Left or of the Right. At
the same time the middle classes (who are known to be more conservative) have a higher expectation of life than the working classes, and
women (who are also known to be more conservative) than men. Is the
conservatism of the elderly a function of their age alone, or is it also a
function of their class and sex?

There is another way in which age may influence party choice. Voting
habits, at any rate in stable parliamentary democracies, tend to be formed
over a life-time; the formative process begins early – at home, at school,
in the neighbourhood and by the circumstances of the earliest elections
in which one takes part. Hence the concept of 'political generations',
whose political make-up is determined by the years in which they
reached adulthood.[4] Thus, one reason why Labour was until very
recently under-represented among older people is that they grew up, and
first voted, at a time when Labour was not yet a major party. According
to NOP the age-group most heavily pro-Labour at the 1970 general
election was 45 to 54 – men and women who first voted in 1945.[5] It is
only in the 1960s that Labour has exorcized the demographic disadvantage arising out of its recent foundation and exchanged it for a slight
advantage. One cannot, from this evidence alone, forecast Labour
electoral victories; one can say that but for the predominance of 'Labour

---

[1] *Nuffield 1966*, p. 264; *Nuffield 1970*, p. 342.
[2] Lipset, S. M., *Political Man* (London, 1960), p. 247.
[3] As for n. 1.
[4] For a thorough discussion, see Butler and Stokes, *op. cit.*, Ch. III.
[5] *Nuffield 1970*, p. 342.

H

generations' in the electorate the Conservatives would have won about fifteen more seats in 1964, 1966 and 1970.

The same difficulty in isolating causality confronts us over the influence of religion. There are valid historical reasons for associating the Church of England with Toryism, and Dissent (and Catholicism) with the Left. The Church of England is, after all, the Established Church; the alliance, at the national level, of Church and King, and at the local level of squire and parson, was bound to give it a Tory flavour. Macaulay called the Church of England 'the Tory party at prayer'.[1] Dissenters, not merely because they were, until 1829, second-class citizens, but also because of the more democratic structure of their churches and the causes dear to the Nonconformist conscience, were drawn to Liberalism. Religious affiliation could indeed infect quite a strong ideological content into political loyalty. Mr A. J. P. Taylor, himself of Nonconformist origins, is quite confident of this:

'I doubt whether anyone with an Anglican background can become a true Radical. George Lansbury came nearest to it. Yet there was always a subtle dividing line between him and the rebels round him. Gladstone tried hard, but he could never rid himself of the belief that a duke or a bishop had more political sense than Cobden or John Stuart Mill. The rule still applies in the Labour Party. Its leaders with an Anglican education seek radical ideas, but they lack radical instincts . . . Religious dissent is the only safe background for a radical.'[2]

At the same time religion can fairly easily be equated with class and occupation. Here are lists of the most strongly dissenting English counties (a) in the 1850s (b) in the 1890s.[3]

1850s	1890s
Bedford	Bedford
Cheshire	
Cornwall	Cornwall
	Cumberland
Derby	Derby
Durham	Durham
Huntingdon	
	Isle of Ely
Lancashire	

[1] At least, I think he did. The most recent historian of the Conservative Party cautiously attributes the saying to Anon. Blake, R. N. W., *The Conservative Party from Peel to Churchill* (London, 1970), p. 272.
[2] Taylor, A. J. P., 'The Thing', *The Twentieth Century*, Oct., 1957, p. 295.
[3] Bealey and Pelling, *Labour and Politics, 1900–1906*, pp. 3–4.

1850s	1890s
Leicester	
Lincoln	
Monmouth	Monmouth
Northumberland	
	Nottingham
Stafford	Stafford
	Warwick
Yorkshire	Yorkshire (N & W ridings only)

Except for the 'Cromwellian' counties of Eastern England, these represent the country's principal mining and industrial areas. In political representation they were overwhelmingly Liberal. The outstanding change between the middle and the end of the century took place in Lancashire, where there was not only a successful Anglican counter-reformation but a marked swing to the Conservatives: between 1865 and 1906 the Liberals only once gained a majority of seats there.

These facts do not, by themselves, answer the question whether the left-wing affiliation of Nonconformists simply reflects their social composition, or whether there is an additional, independent denominational factor at work. For the nineteenth century the evidence is suggestive, but incomplete. Almost all Dissenters active in politics were Liberals or Radicals and many of the leaders of Radicalism – John Bright, Joseph Chamberlain, Lloyd George – were Dissenters. Nonconformist ministers were overwhelmingly Liberal,[1] and on those occasions where Church–State relations dominated political debate, as over school control in the elections of 1874 and 1906, the rank-and-file Dissenting vote could no doubt be mobilized. There were some areas – Lancashire in particular – where we can trace a correlation between denomination and party, transcending class.[2] But it is worth remembering that even at the height of the Victorian religious revival the urban masses remained largely untouched by religious observance, let alone sectarian disputes.[3] At the present day there is nothing to suggest that Labour, nationally, benefits from any residual dissenting radicalism (which has in any case declined in this century), but the Liberals continue to enjoy disproportionately high support from, at any rate the older, middle-class Nonconformists.[4] National aggregates can, of course, hide local variations.

[1] Vincent, op. cit., pp. 67–9.

[2] Pelling, op. cit., xxiii-v; Kinnear, M., The British Voter. An Atlas and Survey since 1885 (London, 1968), pp. 82–5, 125–9.

[3] Inglis, K. S., Churches and the Working Classes in Victorian England (London, 1963), pp. 11–16, 329–30.

[4] Gallup Political Index B. 9. (March, 1966); Alford, op. cit., pp. 154–5; Butler and Stokes, op. cit., pp. 124–34.

In the old-established cotton town of Glossop, with its traditional community ties, working-class members of the various churches voted as follows in 1951:[1]

	% Con.	% Lib.	% Lab.	% did not vote
Active Anglicans	55	5	29	12
Inactive Anglicans	43	5	36	15
Nonconformist	25	16	44	15
Roman Catholic	20	4	54	21
No religion	20	–	40	40

thus illustrating popular, and largely out-of-date stereotypes.

One of the reasons for the swing to Church and Toryism in Lancashire was the influx of Irish immigration. Catholicism has coloured voting behaviour much more clearly than any other religious factor. From the beginning of the nineteenth century onwards most Catholics in Britain were either Irish labourers or their descendants. The Tories were the party of the Protestant ascendancy in Ireland, the Liberals the party of the Home Rule. As a consequence in the areas of heaviest Irish settlement, round Liverpool and Glasgow, sectarian feeling has tended to dominate politics and not only politics, as any spectator at a Celtic-Rangers match may observe. And of Liverpool one American observer has remarked that it is the only English city he visited in which 'religious imprecations' outnumbered the wall-slogans of CND and Fascists combined.[2] In these areas the Conservatives have emerged as the 'Orange' party, supported by Protestants of all classes. Here, and to a lesser extent throughout the country, working- and middle-class Catholics are more strongly pro-Labour than working- and middle-class Protestants.[3] The exceptionally heavy swing to Labour on Clydeside and Merseyside over the last fifteen years suggests that Protestant sectarianism is a

[1] Birch, A. H., *Small-Town Politics* (Oxford, 1959), p. 112.

[2] Thayer, G., *The British Political Fringe. A Profile* (London, 1965), p. 236.

[3] Budge, I. S. and Urwin, D. S., *Scottish Political Behaviour. A Case Study in British Homogeneity* (London, 1966), pp. 63, 69–70; Bochel, J. M. and Denver, D. J., 'Religion and Voting: a Critical Review and a New Analysis', *Political Studies* XVIII (June, 1970), pp. 206, 211, 214; Berry, D., 'Party Membership and Social Participation', *Political Studies* XVII (June, 1969), pp. 201–2; Butler and Stokes, *op. cit.*, p. 127. Professor Alford's discussion of the possible influence on Catholic voters of the Church's conservatism seems hardly relevant to Britain (*Party and Society*, pp. 139–41). The Church's connection with monarchical absolutism disappeared too long ago, and its link with the aristocracy is too tenuous, for this to count for very much. The same applies to the 'anti-Socialist political tendencies of the Church' (*ibid.*, p. 140). These are rooted in the experience of continental Europe, and arise out of the anti-clerical, rationalist and revolutionary character of the Liberal and Marxist movements. When a Catholic hierarchy was re-established in England after a lapse of 400 years, its first major intervention in social policy was in favour of the dock strikers in 1889.

declining force, but the revival of Ulster troubles has served to keep the Catholic population faithful to Labour. In Scotland Catholics appear to have withstood even the blandishments of the Scottish National Party.[1]

It would probably be more helpful to classify Catholic electors, given their overwhelmingly Irish origins, as an ethnic rather than a religious minority. Politically they are a low-status immigrant group with a historic grievance against the Conservative Party. For long they were the only such group in Britain but they have recently been joined by coloured immigrants from the New Commonwealth (mainly the Caribbean, India and Pakistan), now numbering one and a quarter million. The coloured immigrants' first political impact, like that of the Irish, was to produce a nativist back-lash, most noticeable in 1964.[2] By 1970 immigration seems to have declined as an issue affecting the white electorate, while it has succeeded in politicizing the immigrants. All the (limited) evidence shows that in 1970 immigrants turned out to vote in unprecedented numbers and voted preponderantly for Labour, irrespective of the local Conservative candidate's stand on race relations. In several constituencies only their intervention can explain exceptionally small drops in the turn-out and exceptionally small swings to the Conservatives.[3]

Though religion and race may counteract class as a voting determinant, it is more difficult to conclude that region does so. Scotland and Wales, East Anglia and Durham certainly have their distinctive voting characteristics. But is it really possible to distinguish the politics of coal, agriculture or shipbuilding from the party preferences of Durham, Norfolk and Clydeside? The first comprehensive analysis of regional voting habits, based on a sample of 120,000 over three years (1963–6) showed what seemed to be quite substantial variations over and above those that class would account for. The proportion of skilled manual workers (C2) supporting the Conservatives ranged from 42·5 per cent in South-Central England to 15·2 per cent in Wales; the proportion of white-collar employees supporting Labour ranged from 21·6 per cent in the South-West to 46·0 per cent in Wales.[4]

Yet we must look for other causes than provincial predilections to account for these fluctuations. We know, for instance, that the type of neighbourhood people live in influences their political outlook. In a heavily industrialized area the proportion of both manual and nonmanual workers who vote Labour is greater than in rural or suburban

[1] McLean, I. S., *op. cit.*, p. 367.
[2] See below, p. 126.
[3] *Nuffield 1970*, pp. 406–7. Deakin, N. and Bourne, J., 'Powell, The Minorities and the 1970 Election', *Political Quarterly* LXI (October, 1970), pp. 402–4, 407–9.
[4] Butler and Stokes, *op. cit.*, pp. 140–1.

areas.[1] We know that workers in some types of community show much greater solidarity than those in others. Butler and Stokes found that in mining towns Labour got 91 per cent of working-class support and 36 per cent of middle-class support; in seaside resorts 48 per cent of working-class support and 7 per cent of middle-class support.[2] We know from relating the 1966 census data to the 1970 voting figures that in certain types of constituency Labour polled 'above average' for class composition, e.g. in seats where heavy industry or council housing predominate, and that in others the Conservatives poll 'above average', e.g. agricultural constituencies. These variables go a long way towards cancelling out regional accident though they do not do so entirely: mining seats in Durham and Northumberland support Labour more heavily than those in Derbyshire and Nottinghamshire. Agricultural seats in the North and South-West support the Conservatives more heavily than those in East Anglia.[3] Regional variations, therefore, suggest less that region plays an important, independent role in forming political opinion than that we should beware of an over-simplified, dichotomous view of the class structure. The type of industry in which one is employed, the type of community in which one lives is as important an occupational criterion as the distinction between 'manual' and 'non-manual' jobs, in determining the individual's consciousness. Because industries and residential patterns vary from one part of the country to another, manual and non-manual workers support the parties in different proportions from region to region. But the patterns *within* each industry and *within* each community type vary much less from one part of the country to another.

Any statement about the nation-wide homogeneity of social characteristics applies to England only. Wales and Scotland, with their separate cultural identities and, in part, separate institutions, cannot be classified as mere regions. The most striking contrast with England lies in the long-term weakness of the Conservative Party. Its Anglican and monarchist connections have made the Tory Party predominantly English. It has failed to gain a majority of English seats in only four of the twenty-two elections since 1885: in 1906, 1929, 1945 and 1966, the years of its worst defeats. In Scotland, on the other hand, it has gained a majority of seats only five times, in 1900 (the first time ever), 1924, 1931, 1935 and 1955. In Wales the Tories have been in a minority since 1857; since 1885 they have only four times exceeded a quarter of the seats (1895, 1924, 1931, 1935); once, in 1906, they held none at all.

---

[1] Bealey, Blondel and MacCann, *op. cit.*, pp. 182–3; Berelson, B. R., Lazarsfeld, P. F., McPhee, W. N., *Voting. A Study of Opinion Formation in a Presidential Campaign* (Chicago, 1954) – hereafter cited as *Voting* – pp. 98–101.
[2] Butler and Stokes, *op. cit.*, p. 145.
[3] *Nuffield 1970*, pp. 427–30.

Wales, therefore, represents the clearest example of political localism in Britain. Its nationalism is radical and based on the chapel. Until 1918 this radicalism was expressed through the Liberal Party and found its greatest expression in David Lloyd George. The major constitutional grievance of Welsh Dissent was removed with the disestablishment of the Church in 1920. But the populist radicalism survived unweakened; Labour inherited its legacy not merely in the industrial South, where its natural social base was reinforced by the Depression, but in the rural areas also. Since the war the Liberals have lost five of their six remaining rural seats, all to the benefit of Labour. Only in Wales does Labour consistently hold such non-industrial constituencies as Anglesey, Merioneth or Carmarthen; only in Wales do the Conservatives frequently come bottom, even losing their deposits, in such seats. Outside the coastal resorts and the border counties Conservatism is still regarded, as it was sixty years ago, as foreign, even hostile to the interests of Wales.

Popular radicalism was a much less important ingredient of Scottish Liberalism than of Welsh. Until well into the nineteenth century its leaders and parliamentary representatives were overwhelmingly aristocratic; their social outlook was correspondingly more conservative. The hegemony of Scottish Liberalism came to an end in 1885 under the dual impact of the Third Reform Act (which emancipated the crofters) and the Irish Home Rule controversy. Significantly, the Conservatives in Scotland were until 1965 officially known as Unionists (i.e. favouring union with Ireland). But separatist feeling has kept Scottish Conservatism weak. Most of Labour's strength is derived from the industrial belt of Central Scotland, but of the remaining nineteen Border or Highland constituencies outside this belt the Conservatives held only eleven in 1966; five went to Liberals, three to Labour. As in Wales, the Liberal Party is associated with aspirations to self-government and is to that extent a rival to the self-confessedly nationalist parties. The association is, however, of long standing: it dates from the beginnings of the Church disestablishment controversies in the mid-nineteenth century and Liberal espousal of Irish Home Rule.

Political separatism in Scotland and Wales is dominated by national sentiment. This, as well as the long-term aversion to voting Conservative, helps to explain why it was Nationalist parties rather than – as in England – the Conservatives, that benefited from the Labour government's unpopularity in by-elections and local elections between 1966 and 1970. The special role of the Liberal Party in expressing this Celtic discontent has meant that in rural Scotland and Wales there is three-party rather than two-party competition; the rise of the Nationalist parties has even led to quadripartite competition. The only area of England in which the Liberals compete on tolerably equal terms is the

South-West, in particular the counties of Cornwall, Devon, Dorset and Hereford. It shares, with Scotland and Wales, remoteness from London and, outside the towns, the survival of a nineteenth-century social structure and of Nonconformity.

The class basis of politics explains one of the minor curiosities of the British electoral system, namely a flaw in the 'cube law'. The cube law states that if the parties' votes are in the proportions of A:B, their seats in parliament will be in the proportions of $A^3:B^3$. Put differently, it means that a swing of 1 per cent will cause between fifteen and twenty seats to change hands. Post-war elections have borne out the general validity of this law.

Swing and Seat changes, 1945–66

	Swing	Net gain in seats	Seats per 1% swing
1945–50	2·9	81	28★
1950–51	1·1	23	21
1951–55	1·8	24	13★
1955–59	1·1	21	19
1959–64	3·1	59	19
1964–66	2·7	46	17
1966–70	4·8	75	16

★Indicates that there was a redistribution of seats.

However, on four occasions since the war (1950, 1951, 1955, 1959) there appeared a bias in the system in favour of the Conservatives of about 1½ per cent – that is, to secure the same number of seats as the Conservatives, Labour would need about 1½ per cent (or 500,000 votes) more than the Conservatives. There are two reasons for this. One is the uneven distribution of Labour support: Labour voters are mainly industrial workers and industry, especially heavy industry, tends to be concentrated in compact areas. Labour therefore 'wastes' more votes than the Conservatives. In 1951, when Labour won more votes, but fewer seats, than the Conservatives, thirty-seven out of forty-eight majorities over 20,000 were in Labour seats. The other is the influence of community on voting behaviour. The pressure of environment can influence not only party allegiance but its intensity. For instance, in 1950, when class feeling ran more highly than it does today, the group of seats with the highest median turn-out were the forty-eight in which Labour had majorities of 40 per cent or over.[1] Since 1964 this bias has disappeared. It might be tempting to attribute this to migration. The average electorate of Labour-held seats in 1970 was several thousands smaller than in Conservative-held seats. There is, however, no convincing evidence that

[1] *Nuffield 1950*, p. 318.

Labour gained more seats *through migration alone* (i.e. through New Town or council estate development) than it lost (i.e. through middle-class commuter development). The main reason appears to be an above-average drop in the turn-out in safe Labour seats.[1] All that has happened is that Labour is under-polling about 1-1½ per cent of its potential support.

PARTY CHOICE

If it is true that social characteristics determine most people's party allegiance, what has happened to the concept of an election as choice? No two elections produce identical results. *Some* choice, therefore, does take place. Sociology in the main explains the reasons for long-term loyalty; psychology is more useful in explaining why some people change. Both emphasize the non-rational elements involved in political choice. A pioneer in this field was Graham Wallas, who in 1908 launched the much-abused term 'political image':

'The origin of a political party may be due to a deliberate intellectual process. It may be formed, as Burke said, by "a body of men united for promoting by their joint endeavours the national interest upon some particular principle in which they are all agreed". But when a party has once come into existence its fortunes depend upon facts of human nature of which deliberate thought is only one. It is primarily a name, which, like other names, calls up when it is heard or seen an "image" that shades imperceptibly into the voluntary realization of its meaning. As in other cases, emotional reactions can be set up by the name and its automatic mental associations. It is the business of the party managers to secure that these automatic associations shall be as clear as possible, shall be shared by as large a number as possible, and shall call up as many and as strong emotions as possible.'[2]

One important variable is missing from this catalogue, however. The association needs not to be not only clear, widespread and strong, it must also be favourable. This is the most difficult one to guarantee, for the same image may stand the party in good stead one year and harm it in another. This applies, in particular, to a party's class image. The most important difference between Labour and Conservative supporters in their 'images' of the parties is that Labour people tend to see parties in terms of class interest or general aims ('for the working class', 'for the rich', 'for the man in the street'), while Conservatives do so in terms of issues or competence ('against nationalization', 'for individual freedom',

---

[1] See above, p. 93.
[2] Wallas, G., *Human Nature in Politics* (London, 1908), pp. 83–4.

'having a clear policy').[1] This leaves wide open the question of how potent this image is under differing circumstances. The 'cloth-cap' image may well have helped Labour in 1945 or 1950; it was probably a liability by 1959, when memories of unemployment had faded and consumer affluence had eroded proletarian solidarity. The 'grouse-moor' image may well have helped the Conservatives in tapping the reserves of deference for most of this century; but in 1964 or 1966, when administrative failure and the leadership squabble had tarnished it, it became, temporarily at any rate, a vote-loser.

'Image' is also used, rather confusingly, to describe transient aspects of parties and political leaders which influence the mood of the moment. We may read that one man's 'television image' is unfavourable, perhaps because he has not mastered the techniques of the medium; or that a party's 'image' is one of disunity or lack of policies. Such factors change from one year to the next. They may well help to explain why people change their opinions, but they are not what Graham Wallas had in mind. His 'images' consisted of long-term attributes; their purpose is to establish a permanent brand-loyalty 'in the dim and shadowy region of emotional association'.[2] Image, as conceived by Wallas, is therefore more useful in explaining political loyalty than political change. There is, indeed, a good deal of evidence, both from this country and the United States, that many habitual supporters are either ignorant of their parties' programmes or in substantial disagreement with them. In one Bristol survey Conservative, Liberal and Labour voters scored respectively 60, 58 and 53 per cent in attributing policy statements to the main parties: even completely random answers would have scored 50 per cent.[3] Perception of issues is one matter, slavish adhesion to the party line is another. Party preference tends, after all, to be a relative rather than an absolute matter. It is sufficient to agree with a majority of the party's stands on major issues, especially since some policy statements are themselves the outcome of bitter controversy within the party – one thinks of nationalization or defence in the Labour Party, decolonization or crime and punishment among Conservatives. Moreover, issues are not of equal importance. One person may be more concerned with the abolition of health service prescription charges, another with Rhodesia. Even so, the degree to which party policy is accepted is remarkably low and it tends to be lower among Labour than Conserva-

[1] Bealey, Blondel and MacCann, op. cit., pp. 206–13; Milne and Mackenzie, op. cit., pp. 131–40; Butler and Stokes, op. cit., pp. 80–95; McKenzie and Silver, op. cit., pp. 107–13; See also, Dahrendorf, R., Class and Class Conflict in Industrial Society (2nd edn, Stanford, 1959), p. 284.
[2] Wallas, op. cit., p. 86.
[3] Milne and Mackenzie, op. cit., p. 121. cf. Voting, p. 230; Trenaman and McQuail, op. cit., pp. 166, 215; McKenzie and Silver, op. cit., pp. 114–20.

tive supporters. In Greenwich, for instance, the largest group of supporters within each party agreed with only 40–60 per cent of official policies; 7 per cent of Conservatives and 21 per cent of Labour supporters were actually more in agreement with their opponents than with their own party.[1] Similarly, the assessment of party leaders is not necessarily translated into electoral preference. In 1966, 55 per cent thought that Mr Wilson would make the better Prime Minister and 30 per cent that Mr Heath would.[2] But this 25 per cent lead became a lead of only 6 per cent in votes cast. The contrast was even more striking in 1970, when Mr Heath trailed Mr Wilson by 24 per cent even in the polls most favourable to the Conservatives and yet went on to victory:

	Labour lead	Prefer as Prime Minister	
		Wilson	Heath
Harris Poll (*Daily Express*, 17 June)	2%	56%	32%
Gallup (*Daily Telegraph*, 15 June)	2·5%	54%	29%

All in all, the permanent image seems to be a more potent factor than changing issues or successive party leaders. It may even be more potent than rationally considered self-interest. After all, it by no means follows that the same party is at every election the best for the working (or middle) class, as most electors seem to think. There is a lot to be said for Professor Alford's view that it is 'class-based traditionalism', not ruthlessly evaluated economic interest, that is the chief motivator.[3]

Who, then, *does* change his mind? Is there such a creature as the 'floating voter'? It would probably be better if the term had never been invented. In the first place it must be remembered that the electorate itself is constantly changing. Every year approximately 600,000 adults die and 750,000 adolescents come of age. This alone could gradually affect the political balance in the country. But the word also suggests that the electorate can be conveniently divided into two categories, on the one hand the faithful supporter of the big battalions, on the other, earnest individuals seeking after truth. All survey evidence suggests the contrary: that there is a relatively small core of 'thick-and-thin men', shading off, through weak and conditional party-support into neutrality

[1] Mark, Benney and Pear, *op. cit.*, pp. 145–6. cf. Milne and Mackenzie, *op. cit.*, pp. 117–20; Birch, *op. cit.*, pp. 82–5; Donnison, D. and Plowman, D. E. G., 'The Functions of Local Labour Parties: Experiments in Research Methods', *Political Studies* II (Feb., 1954), pp. 162–4; Fienburgh, W. and others, 'Put Party Policy on the Agenda', *Fabian Journal* 6 (Feb., 1952), pp. 29–31; *Voting*, pp. 223–7.
[2] *The Sunday Telegraph*, 27 March 1966.
[3] Alford, *op. cit.*, p. 110, n. 13.

(or apathy). One survey, taken less than a fortnight before the 1966 General Election, illustrates this:[1]

How strongly would you say you support the Conservative/Labour/Liberal Party?

Very strongly	38%
Quite strongly	36%
Not very strongly	20%
Not at all strongly	6%

How much do you personally care which party wins the General Election?

Very much	40%
Quite a lot	32%
Not very much	22%
Not at all	3%

These figures are very similar to those recently found in other countries:

Intensity of Party Identification in USA, Norway, and W. Germany (in per cent)[2]

	USA 1956	Norway 1957	W. Germany 1961
Strong identifiers	36	25	25
Weak identifiers	37	34	46
Independents (identification rejected)	23	25	5
Unpolitical (question not understood)	4	9	19
Not ascertained	—	7	5
	100	100	100

In fact, we can identify no fewer than four types of non-constant electors:

1. those whose involvement with the party of their choice is low and who therefore hesitate between voting and abstention;

[1] *Daily Mail*, 24 March 1966.

[2] American-Norwegian comparison: Campbell, A. and Valen, H., 'Party Identification in Norway and the United States', *Public Opinion Quarterly* XXV (Winter, 1961), p. 510; reprinted in Campbell, A. and others, *Elections and the Political Order* (New York, 1966), p. 251. American-German comparison: Zölnhofer, W. in Scheuch and Wildenmann, *op. cit.*, p. 113.

2. those who experiment with alternative allegiances but generally return to the party of their first choice at election time;
3. those who support a minor party but may be deprived of a candidate of their highest preference;
4. those who experience a genuine conversion and transfer their allegiance.

These four types between them amount to a substantial minority among the electorate; and the total is certainly greater the number who 'float' in any one election. The contrast between the violent fluctuations of opinion polls and the relatively small swing at general elections illustrate how much more numerous the potential waverers are than the actual changers. Constituency surveys agree that anything up to a quarter of electors have not firmly made up their minds at the beginning of an election campaign.[1] Of course, the 'swing' figure is misleadingly small. A 'net swing' of 5 per cent from Conservative to Labour conceals reverse changes from Labour to Conservatives, changes to and from both parties involving the Liberals, as well as changes from abstention to voting and vice versa. Even so, the fact that most waverers in the end revert to their former loyalties[2] is significant, and confirms the existence of a gap between waverers and actual changers.

Those who decide late and hesitatingly how they should vote could be, and in traditional liberal mythology are, the independent-minded, rational élite. Modern evidence, however, points predominantly in the opposite direction. In both Britain and America it has emerged that 'waverers' are on average less well informed on current affairs, less exposed to the political items in the newspapers or on radio or TV, less likely to read election literature or attend meetings, less likely to discuss politics with friends or members of their family.[3] The pressures on them to participate in politics are either weaker than for most other people, or they are contradictory. Electors subject to 'cross-pressures', e.g. whose family votes differently from most of their friends or who are uncertain of their social status, have particular difficulty in making up their minds. The statistical evidence can deal in averages only. There certainly are electors who live up to the liberal idea of the rational, disinterested citizen.[4] But they are in a minority.

[1] Milne and Mackenzie, op. cit., pp. 36–8; Campbell, Donnison and Potter, 'Voting Behaviour in Droylesden', p. 61; Mark, Benney and Pear, op. cit., p. 175.
[2] Milne and Mackenzie, op. cit., pp. 41–2.
[3] Milne and Mackenzie, op. cit., pp. 85, 103–4, 123, 154. Mark, Benney and Pear, op. cit., pp. 176–8; Voting, pp. 306–13; Lazarsfeld, P. F., Berelson, D. and Gaudet, H., The People's Choice. How the Voter Makes up his Mind in a Presidential Campaign (2nd edn, New York, 1948) – hereafter cited as The People's Choice – p. 69.
[4] See above, p. 85.

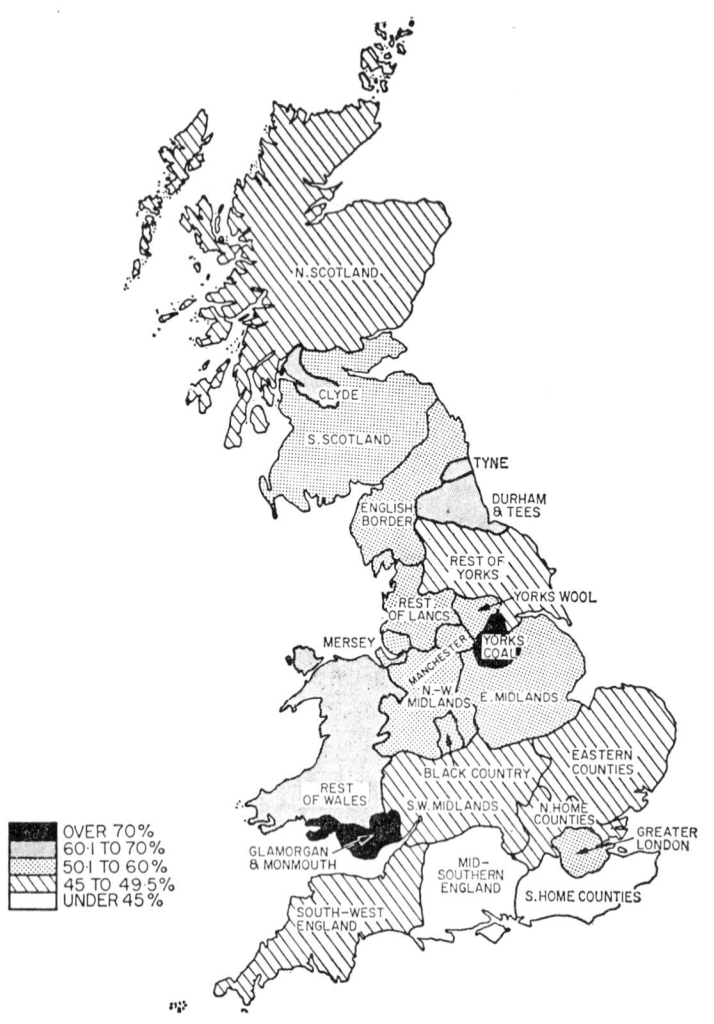

FIGURE IV. 8: Labour Party's share of major Party vote, 1966, by regions (as defined by *The Economist*).

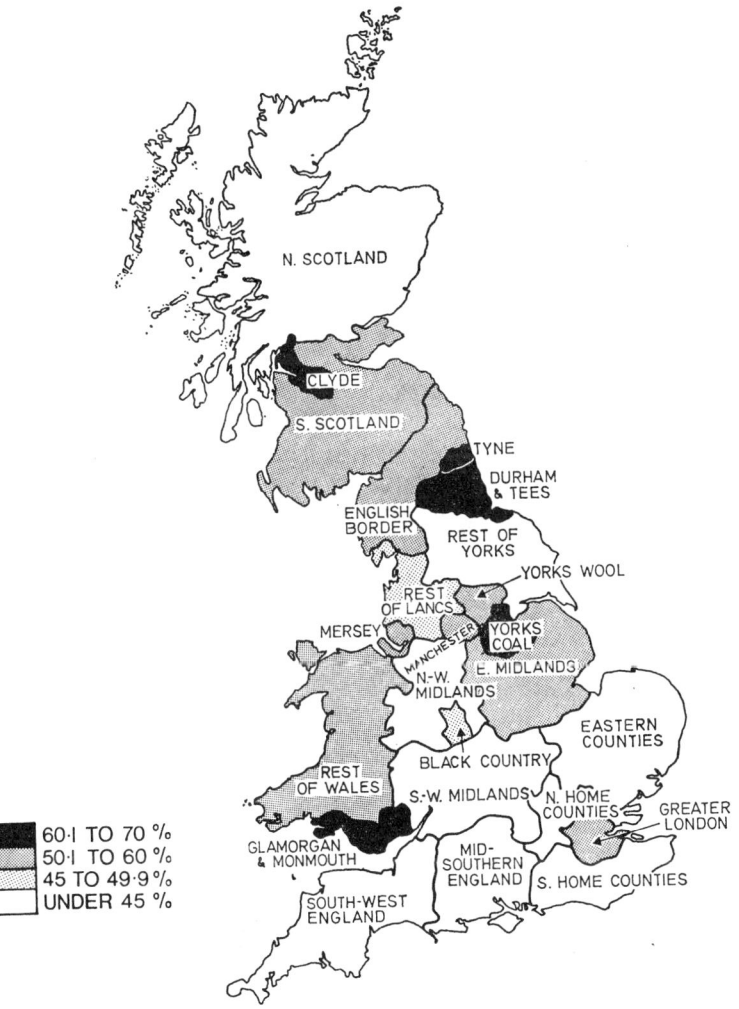

FIGURE IV. 9: Labour Party's share of major Party vote, 1970, by regions
(as defined by *The Economist*).

FIGURE IV. 10: Change in Labour Party's share of major Party vote, 1945–66, by regions (as defined by *The Economist*).

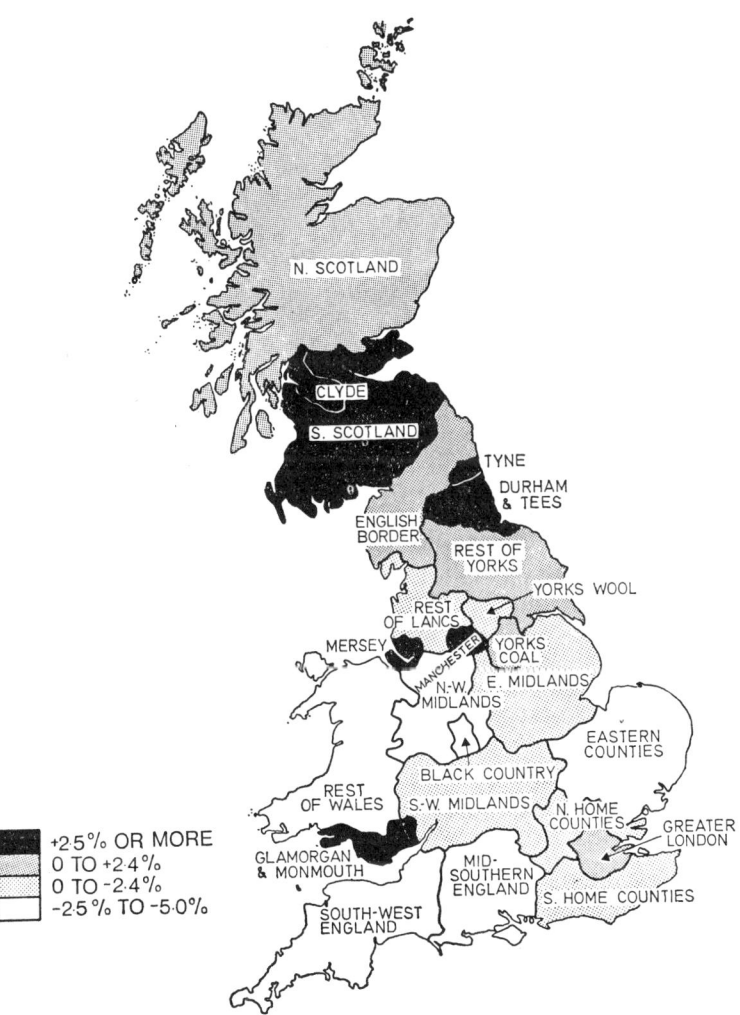

FIGURE IV. 11: Change in Labour Party's share of major Party vote 1955–70, by regions (as defined by *The Economist*).

I

LOCAL ISSUES, PERSONALITIES AND BAND-WAGONS

So far it has been assumed that all political choice in Britain is between parties. The stability of party loyalties and the uniformity of the swing show that this is indeed so. But local issues do arise and there are frequent attempts to exploit them. It is remarkable how seldom this works. Economic grievances are an obvious example of a potential local issue. In 1959 parts of Lancashire and of Scotland swung to Labour against the national trend, presumably because of the depressed state of the cotton industry and shipbuilding, perhaps also because of a general feeling that these areas were not sharing in the growing affluence of the country. Conversely in 1964 the swing to Labour in the West Midlands was below average, presumably because the prosperity of that region gave less reason for discontent with the Conservative Party. Regional deviations of this kind can be explained in terms of spontaneous reaction by voters. Little or no persuasion is needed by candidates or party leaders to bring them about. Moreover, the state of the economy looms so large in most people's thinking about politics that it can hardly be isolated as a separate issue.

Education and immigration are more promising as genuine local issues. In 1964 there was a below-average swing to Labour in the Bristol area and this was attributed to local opposition to the Labour council's comprehensive scheme; at any rate, Conservative candidates emphasized their sympathy with the opponents. Immigration was a more obvious, though by no means uniform, cause of deviant results in 1964. Swings to the Right in Smethwick, Southall and Eton and Slough were obviously connected with resentment at coloured immigration, but other constituencies with equally heavy influxes (e.g. Brixton, Bradford E.) seemed less worried.[1] Anti-immigrant Independents in three constituencies secured between $7\frac{1}{2}$ and 10 per cent, much the same as Sir Oswald Mosley had gained in 1959 in N. Kensington on a similar platform; in subsequent elections they have polled rather less. But the role of the candidate is not the only factor. Mr Griffiths, who gained Smethwick from Labour, emphasized the issue; Sir Anthony Meyer, who gained Eton and Slough, admittedly on a much lower swing, did not. Local issues, it is evident, can influence individual results, but their impact is limited.

The marginality of a seat, too, may affect voting behaviour. Between 1955 and 1966 it helped both to raise turn-out and to depress support for Liberal candidates, though there was no such correlation between 1966 and 1970. But turn-out did increase, contrary to the national trend,

[1] Deakin, N. (ed.), *Colour and the British Electorate, 1964* (London, 1965), Chapters 2 and 7.

where there had been dramatic by-election upsets.[1] Relatively poor Liberal performance in marginal seats is important for any discussion of the function of parties in the British system, and the possible effects of electoral reform. We might expect the 'wasted vote' argument to weigh least in a marginal constituency, for two reasons. Marginal seats have, by definition, a more balanced social composition than safe ones (which are heavily middle-class or heavily working-class), and the Liberal Party has the most evenly spread social following (see Figure IV.7). Moreover a marginal seat offers the best opportunity for victory on a minority vote. Where the parties are evenly balanced a mere 35 per cent may suffice to win a three-cornered fight. In fact, Liberals do exceptionally badly in marginal seats; we have already observed that the greatest Liberal successes have been in seats where the minority major party has no hope of success.[2] In Britain political success depends on the ability to form a strong government, and the elector in a marginal constituency is well placed to bestow or deny such success.

One further conclusion follows, namely that Liberal intervention has less effect on the outcome of a general election than is sometimes thought. Comparison between different types of contests enables us to calculate how Liberals would vote if they had no candidate of their own.[3]

1. In no election did the Liberals take more than 60 per cent of their vote from one of the major parties.

2. Liberal voters are representative of the national trend. When the country is swinging Right their votes are, in the majority, potentially Conservative (1950, 1951, 1955, less so in 1959); when the country is swinging Left, their votes are, in the majority, potentially Labour (1945, 1964, uncertain in 1966).

3. In safe seats Liberal votes are drawn heavily from the minority party, in marginal seats, much more evenly from both major parties, though with some regional variations.

Granted this, and the low Liberal vote in marginal seats, Liberals have had an important effect only twice since 1929. Had they contested no marginal seats in 1950, it is probable that the Conservatives would have become the strongest party, but without an absolute majority (instead of a Labour majority of five). Had they contested no marginal seats in 1964, Labour would probably have had a majority of ten, possible sixteen, instead of four. In 1970 it is probable that Liberal intervention had no net effect.[4]

If local issues count for little, what about the personality of the

---

[1] *Nuffield 1966*, p. 285; *Nuffield 1970*, pp. 409–10.
[2] See above, pp. 59–60.
[3] Berrington, 'The General Election of 1964', pp. 40–8.
[4] *Nuffield 1964*, pp. 349–50; *Nuffield 1970*, pp. 411–12.

candidate? The *obiter dictum* of an anonymous election agent that 'no candidate is worth 500 votes'[1] has become part of British election mythology. Even if it were true it would not reduce the candidate to insignificance. In 1964 twenty-five seats were won by majorities of less than 500. Few personal characteristics of the candidate have any measurable impact on electors. Women fare no worse than men. Jews and Roman Catholics – with very few exceptions – fare no worse than Protestants. There is, however, no doubt that coloured candidates, who have become accepted at the municipal level, are vote-losers in parliamentary elections. Dr David Pitt in Clapham suffered a swing of 10·2 per cent, almost twice as great as any other anti-Labour swing in Inner London. Three Indian candidates who stood as Liberals also did badly. Ideological deviation, or emphasis on specific policies on, say, entry into the Common Market, or law and order, have little effect. Voters vote for the ticket, not for the man or his ideas. There is also strong evidence that at least two types of candidates do have a personal effect. The first consists of minor-party challengers. There is little doubt that most of the Liberals, members of other small parties and Independents who have succeeded in entering parliament since the war have done so, in part at least, on the strength of their personalities. The same applies to exceptionally good performances, especially at by-elections, which fell short of victory. Candidates of major parties can achieve less in this respect. All they can do is to build up a personal following on the basis of conscientious constituency service. This unquestionably does pay off, though there are pitfalls in calculating its exact extent. Different swings in seats defended by incumbents and newcomers could be due to regional bias or constituency-type bias (an excess of surburban over rural seats in the sample). Even taking this into account, it is evident that 'familiar' MPs may at the height of their popularity be worth an extra swing of $1\frac{1}{2}$ to $3\frac{1}{2}$ per cent to their party. This is an average: the exceptionally popular MP will be worth even more than that. There are two caveats, however. Very long-serving MPs may outstay their welcome and begin losing votes for their party. If, however, the MP concerned, like a wise prima donna, retires at the right moment, some of his increment stays with the party: his successor will suffer some loss of support, but not as much as a strict party average would indicate.[2]

The occasionally different behaviour of electors in marginal and safe seats, both in their decision whether to vote at all, and in the support they give to minor parties, is evidence of increasing sophistication – a growing tendency to join in the social scientists' game of standing back and watching individuals react to one another. There has, for instance,

[1] *Nuffield 1955*, p. 3.
[2] Williams, P. M., 'Two Notes on the British Electoral System', *Parliamentary Affairs* XX (Winter, 1966–7), pp. 24–30; *Nuffield 1970*, p. 404.

been much greater interest in opinion polls in the last three elections, and not only because more organizations were making predictions. All social science depends on the assumption that it is possible to make valid generalizations about human behaviour. All sampling techniques depend on the assumption that if a carefully chosen small percentage of individuals are studied, valid conclusions can be drawn about the whole of society. Opinion polls, and the publicity that surrounds them at election time, are subject to two criticisms. The first is that they are unreliable. This charge may be justly levelled at the majority of inexperienced organizations which dabble in this difficult exercise. Of the fifty-four individual constituency surveys conducted during the 1966 election eight had an error of more than 10 per cent in their prediction of the final majority.[1] Even the major polling businesses have their ups and downs. Since their notorious forecast of President Truman's defeat in 1948 they have been improving their technique and performance. Both Gallup and Harris got to within 1 per cent of the result in the Nixon-Humphrey election of 1968.[2] In Britain the polls' record was good in 1964 and 1966 and distinctly patchy in 1970. The organizations that fared best were those with the keenest noses for last-minute switches by the electorate, though even they under-estimated the extent of the Conservative recovery.

Accuracy of eve of poll forecasts
1966[3]

	Actual result (GB only) %	NOP %	Gallup Quota %	Research Services %
Labour	48·7	50·6	49·5	49·7
Conservative	41·4	41·6	41·5	41·6
Liberal	8·6	7·4	8	7·4
Labour Lead	7·3	9·0	8·0	8·1
Error		1·7	0·7	0·8

[1] *The Sunday Times*, 3 April 1966.
[2] White, *op. cit.*, p. 382.
[3] NOP: *Daily Mail*, 31 March 1966; Research Services: *The Observer*, 27 March 1966; Gallup: *The Daily Telegraph Gallup Analysis of the Election '66* (London, 1966), p. 140. The quota method requires the interviewer to collect interviews from persons he selects, provided their numbers are typical of the nation as a whole in age, sex and occupation. The random method requires him to interview respondents whose names have been randomly selected from the electoral register, leaving him no discretion. The eve-of-poll Gallup forecast, as published in *The Daily Telegraph* (31 March 1966) was a combination of the quota survey and a less accurate random survey, giving a Labour lead of 11 per cent – error: 3·7 per cent.

1970[1]

	Actual result (GB only) %	Gallup %	NOP %	Harris %	ORC %
Conservative	46·2	42	44	46	46·5
Labour	43·8	49	48·1	48	45·5
Liberal	7·6	7·5	6·4	5	6·5
Labour Lead	−2·4	7	4·1	2	−1
Error		9·4	6·5	4·4	1·4

That most British polls tripped on the obstacle that felled their American colleagues in 1948 – the assumption that the final lap in the campaign would not affect the outcome – is now beyond doubt.[2] Complacent technique, not the idea of the sample survey, stands condemned.

A second criticism of polls is that their publication influences the outcome. People like to be on the winning side; the polls oblige by showing them which way the band-wagon is rolling. The experience of 1970 has probably killed the band-wagon myth, though 1970 was by no means the first election in which the outcome for the 'favourite' party was less good than the forecast. Foregone conclusions, or apparently foregone conclusions, may rob a contest of the excitement. Consistent prophecies of defeat have a depressing effect on the losing side. They – or, as in 1970, unexpected losers – find in polls a convenient scapegoat.[3] Perhaps 1970 will give birth to an anti-band-wagon myth. But to ban the publication of opinion polls – as has been suggested – would be a quite unjustified act of paternalism and would diminish even further the elector's right of free access to information.

Polls and sampling techniques are among the methods which have enabled us to know much more than even a generation ago how people vote, what conditions their allegiances, why they change their minds. There remains one further, vital, question: how relevant is the whole electoral process to government of a modern industrial state?

[1] Gallup: *Daily Telegraph*, 18 June 1970; NOP: *Daily Mail*, 18 June 1970; Harris: *Daily Express*, 18 June 1970; ORC: *Evening Standard*, 18 June 1970.

[2] The most detailed discussion of the limitations of polling is by Richard Rose, *The Polls and the 1970 Election*. University of Strathclyde Occasional Papers No. 7 (Glasgow, 1971).

[3] After the election 51 per cent of Labour voters thought the polls had harmed Labour; virtually no one thought they had harmed the Conservatives. *Evening Standard*, 13 July 1970.

V

The Relevance
of Elections

THE more we examine the electoral process at work under modern conditions, the more strongly we become aware of two main doubts about it. The first concerns its *efficacy*, the second its *relevance*.

IGNORANCE, IRRATIONALITY AND APATHY

Since elections are a device for expressing choice, we must assume that the participants are capable of making meaningful decisions. Before they can do this, they must have access to the necessary information, they must be willing to absorb it, they must be able to draw conclusions about it. On these counts, all the evidence so far discovered is discouraging. Few people are sufficiently interested in politics to follow or discuss current affairs regularly. Fewer still are accurately informed, or rethink their position in the light of this information from one election to the next. Those who do change their minds, and therefore decide alternations of power are, if anything, even less involved and worse informed than the regular 'ballot-fodder' of the main parties.

At first sight, this would seem to dispose of one of the classical arguments for universal suffrage, namely that most adults are the best judge of their own interests, and to lend weight to the emphasis of Graham Wallas and others on the irrational elements in political allegiance. To these objections, several answers may be given. In the first place, the argument from enlightened self-interest is not the only valid defence of universal suffrage. There is the argument of individual entitlement. No doubt the philosophical basis of the classical doctrine of natural rights, as it flourished in the seventeenth and eighteenth century, has taken some hard knocks; but perhaps the onus of proof is not on those who wish to include individuals within 'the pale of the constitution', but on those who wish to exclude them from it. It is by no means certain that the better-off or the better-educated are more rational and more disinterested in their political behaviour than those who left school at fifteen and earn their living by shovelling sand.

We should also be chary of jumping to conclusions about irrationality in electoral choice. To some extent it is a question of the standards we impose. The rational man, according to one authority,

'is open to new information, no matter whether it comforts or pains him. This means that he must actively seek information which is pertinent to the issues of the day, and it means that must not seek only that which is compatible with his own prejudices. [He] attempts to formulate an opinion on the basis of the best information available, selecting primarily on the basis of reliability and relevance.'[1]

Few of us would clear that hurdle without difficulty. What about the remainder? No doubt our values and attributes, of which political loyalties are a part, are often formed in early childhood by family or school environment. No doubt it is irrational to vote for a candidate because he is handsome or has kissed babies, or to support a party which promises to solve all problems by exterminating the Jews. But is it irrational to vote Labour out of class loyalties, or to vote as one's parish priest advises, if one considers him a well-qualified judge? As means to the desired end these are certainly rational. As for the ends themselves – a government favouring the workers, or a state based on Christian principles – our voters probably adhere to them for emotional and environmental, rather than coolly elaborated reasons. But it is dangerous to dismiss the values of others as unreasonable.

Above all it is a mistake to press the analogy between economic and political choice, as many of the classical Liberals were apt to do. The political market-place is different from the economic market-place. To buy one house rather than another, to prefer a refrigerator to a washing-machine, to invest in equities rather than gilt-edged are all individual and specific choices which require a fairly high degree of rationality. Failure to choose rationally results in measurable disadvantages. Prime Ministers, however, are not like houses and political parties are not like washing-machines. Our electoral choices are not specific, they are general. We choose between groups of politicians, some of whom have been familiar figures for years, perhaps decades. Or we choose between two party leaders on the basis of our broad impression of them. Unless we regard one issue or one sectional interest as overwhelmingly important, it is not much good tooth-combing the manifestoes. No doubt most politicians sincerely believe what they promise in the heat of a campaign. But we elect our rulers for five years at a time. Who knows what the balance of payments will be three years from now? Or what Central Africa may bring? Events which are difficult to foresee and impossible

[1] Lane, R. E. and Sears, D. O., *Public Opinion* (Englewood Cliffs, N. J., 1964), p. 73.

to control may make nonsense of the carefully laid schemes of the parties' pamphleteers. Detailed knowledge of policy statements, correct perception of party attitudes, clear understanding of individual speeches are no doubt admirable; but are they really necessary before an intelligent vote can be cast?

Just as the content and significance of voter ignorance and voter irrationality are often exaggerated, so are the content and significance of voter apathy. Meetings are poorly attended; canvassers and pollsters get luke-warm receptions; turn-out, especially in safe seats and at municipal elections, is often low and has been tending to get lower. What does this reveal about the health of British politics? In the first place it is easy to forget that most people are not very good at expressing themselves. Eager pollsters and fastidious analysts often mistake inarticulateness for ignorance or irrationality. Moreover, observers lump too many different states of mind together under the heading of 'apathy'. Strictly speaking, it should denote indifference. An apathetic person does not care, for reasons of ignorance, disillusionment or cynicism, who governs or by what policies. He has either deliberately opted out of involvement in public affairs in order to pursue some private objective, or considers it quite beyond his capacity to influence 'them' in any way. He is a-political. Apparently apathetic behaviour can, however, have a quite different explanation: it may reflect widespread acceptance of the way in which disputes are resolved. It may, therefore, be a symptom not of alienation or despair, but of homogeneity. If the political structure is in no immediate danger of being overthrown, if the general principles on which the political system is based are not in serious dispute, if the distribution of power between the major groups in society is unlikely to change rapidly or violently, if, therefore, political dispute is limited to ways and means of improving the existing structure – and this seems a fair description of the situation in most advanced, industrial nations – then there is not really very much to get excited about. Political controversy becomes limited, pragmatic and intermittent, rather than fundamental, ideological and endemic. The surface of political life is unruffled, hence the illusion of apathy.

High electoral participation, massive attendance at meetings, enthusiastic processions and heated discussions may, on the other hand, indicate fever, not robust good health. Between 1928 and 1932 participation in German parliamentary elections rose from 75 per cent to 83 per cent, while the Nazi party's share of the vote rose from $2\frac{1}{2}$ per cent to 37 per cent. Increased turn-out did not reflect greater civic consciousness, but panic. It represented the mobilization of the normally a-political (in the sense defined above) in the service of an exceptionally irrational and hysterical political appeal. In countries with stable parliamentary systems above-average turn-out may indeed be a response to a crucial contest, e.g. in a marginal seat, but it can also indicate closely knit inward-looking community ties, e.g. in coal-mining constituencies in Britain[1] or strongly Catholic villages on the continent of Europe. It then becomes an index of the internal homogeneity of a sub-group, not of that sub-group's integration into the national community.

The sudden mobilization of the a-political will almost certainly result in a violent upset of the normal balance of political forces, since the apathetic are, by definition, least strongly attached to traditionally established groups. But these are not the only conditions under which transient political formations may rise and fall in response to the circumstances of the moment. It was argued above that the prospect of violent or rapid change in the relative strengths of major groupings was important in determining the intensity of political strife. Indeed, it is probably the most important single factor, for general acceptance of the system, and consensus about political methods, must rest on the common assumption that cataclysmic changes are neither imminent nor desirable. Stability of this kind, however, is itself a consequence of political habits as well as their cause; it depends on how widespread and how strong is the electorate's sense of party identification. Where it is weak, as, for instance, in France,[2] party strengths, even for the short term, are much less predictable than in systems where strong party identification is widespread.

The stability of political loyalties, which is so marked in Britain, is therefore a source of strength to the British system of government. This might be dismissed as a platitude, but it is also a paradox. Party loyalty is, after all, rooted to some extent in obstinacy. It rests on a reluctance to accept novel arguments or inconvenient facts, on a predilection for fitting thoughts into prearranged categories or stereotypes, on a temptation to judge arguments according to the source from which they emanate, on a readiness to rationalize or ignore inconsistencies. None of these characteristics contributes to rational thought as we have defined it. Yet at the same time stability of institutions discourages the search for oversimplified and extreme solutions, and the appeal to fears and prejudices in the mind of the voter. It is in seasons of chaos that the prophets of unreason flourish. If the twentieth century has taught us nothing else, it is that. The solution to the paradox lies in the intensity of party identification. Without strong – and therefore partly irrational – party loyalties, the system lacks foundations. But an organized interest can contribute to stability only if it recognizes the legitimacy of rival

---

[1] See above, p. 120.

[2] Converse, P. E. and Dupeux, G., 'Politicisation of the Electorate in France and the United States', *Public Opinion Quarterly* XXVI (Spring, 1962), p. 9. Reprinted in Campbell et al., *Elections and the Political Order* (New York, 1966), p. 277.

interests and their right to share in government. Party loyalty which is totally intransigent and self-sufficient leads to a civil-war situation and the break-down of the system.

If British experience is at all significant, then lack of information, poor perception of issues, and allegiances which have at best a partially rational basis are not fatal to the workings of a representative system. The implications of this are raised in the pioneering American study of electoral behaviour, *Voting*:

'If the democratic system depended solely on the qualifications of the individual voter, then it seems remarkable that democracies have survived through the centuries . . .

'Individual voters today seem unable to satisfy the requirements for a democratic system outlined by political theorists. But the system of democracy does meet certain requirements for a going political organization. The individual members may not meet all the standards, but the whole nevertheless survives and grows. This suggests that where classic theory is defective is in its concentration on the individual citizen.'[1]

A theory fitting the known contemporary facts would therefore place less emphasis on institutions or individual psychology, and more on the political culture of a society. To help in balancing conflict against stability a distribution of labour, between the enthusiasts and the passively committed, may be useful. Common sense and inherited habits can operate as substitutes for individual rationality, since political choice is, at best, crudely defined and broadly delineated. Conclusions such as these have their pitfalls. In the first place they are tentative: what exactly is the cut-off point at which enthusiasm undermines political equilibrium? and, at the other end of the scale, the point at which 'apathy' begins to deprive the system of essential support? More importantly, are they intended to be descriptive, or normative? Are we merely to deduce that this is how parliamentary democracy works out in practice in complex, stable societies? Or are we to deduce that this is what, under modern conditions, democracy *ought* to consist of?

If the latter, then there has been a fundamental shift of emphasis. Classical democratic theory concentrated on the individual not only on the grounds of his rights and his intellectual capacity, but on the grounds that democracy was good for him. Democracy meant participation. It was a way of life that meant self-fulfilment and an enhancement of the personality. We therefore test the soundness of a decision by the degree of public participation involved in reaching it. The modern variant of the theory, however, looks on democracy as largely instrumental: 'a

[1] *Voting*, pp. 311, 313.

method', as Schumpeter puts it, 'a certain type of institutional arrange-ment for arriving at political . . . decisions'.[1] It is a way of producing good government rather than good human beings. Schumpeter's is the most ambitious, and one of the most influential, of modern attempts to integrate theoretically the democratic precepts and élitist practices of twentieth-century parliamentary government.[2] We shall encounter its premises again in looking at the problems of the mandate and of the content of electoral choice.

MAJORITIES AND MANDATES

During the eighteenth and nineteenth centuries many Conservatives and Liberals opposed the indiscriminate extension of the suffrage because they feared that the majority of electors were not fitted, intellectually or morally, for the exercise of this right; and that if they were allowed to exercise it without restraint the result would be an end to individual liberty and the rights of property.

'In a democracy [wrote James Madison] where a multitude of persons exercise in person the legislative functions, and are continually exposed, by their incapacity for regular deliberation and concerted measures, to the ambitious intrigues of their executive magistrates, tyranny may well be apprehended, on some favourable emergency, to start up in that quarter.'[3]

His contemporary, Thomas Jefferson, warned:

'It will be no alleviation, that these powers will be exercised by a plural-ity of hands, and not by a single one. One hundred and seventy-three despots would surely be as oppressive as one . . . As little will it avail us that they are chosen by ourselves. An *elective despotism* was not the government we fought for.'[4]

John Stuart Mill, eighty years later, inveighed against 'a government of privilege, in favour of the numerical majority, who alone possess prac-tically any voice in the State'.[5]

[1] Schumpeter, J. A., *Capitalism, Socialism and Democracy* (4th edn, London, 1954), p. 242.
[2] It has, accordingly, evoked critiques to counter the rather pessimistic esti-mate of human behaviour on which it is based, e.g. Bachrach, P., *The Theory of Democratic Élitism: A Critique* (Boston–Toronto, 1967); Pateman, C., *Partici-pation and Democratic Theory* (Cambridge, 1970); Duncan, G. and Lukes, S., 'The New Democracy', *Political Studies* XI (June, 1963), p. 177. For an excellent discussion of the controversy, see Parry, G., *Political Élites* (London, 1969).
[3] *The Federalist* No. 48, p. 309.
[4] Quoted in *The Federalist* No. 48, p. 311.
[5] Mill, J. S., *Representative Government*, pp. 256–7.

Modern research into electoral behaviour has tended to support the pessimists' premises more strongly than their conclusion. We have seen that the political climate of a society can counter-balance the short-comings of institutions or individual voters. But it can do so on one condition: the political system will remain stable only if the main contending forces within it are unable to deal each other knock-out blows, and if the main contestants are confident that this is so. Mill foresaw a different contingency:

'In all countries there is a majority of poor, a minority who, in contradistinction, may be called rich. Between these classes, on many quest-ions, there is complete opposite of apparent interest . . . Is there not a considerable danger lest [the majority] should throw upon the larger incomes, an unfair share, or even the whole, of the burden of taxation; and having done so, add to the amount without scruple, expending the proceeds in modes supposed to conduce to the profit and advantage of the labouring class?'[1]

An ultra-Conservative might be tempted to argue that surtax and the welfare state have borne out Mill's darkest fears; but it can hardly be seriously maintained that all states with universal suffrage have been governed consistently and exclusively for the benefit of wage-earners and 'the poor'. Society is more complex than Mill (or Marx) imagined, and the evolution of industry has made it more, not less, complex. Political loyalties have other sources beside self-interest, correctly or incorrectly perceived. Both sides in the classical debate about Radicalism and Democracy arrived at the wrong answer, because both asked the same, wrong question. Neither the sovereignty of the people, nor the tyranny of the majority, as conceived of a hundred or a hundred and fifty years ago, has come to pass, for if we examine 'the people' and 'the majority' under a microscope we discover that they disintegrate into their component parts.

Concepts like 'the will of the people', and 'majority rule' make political sense only on the assumption that the people or the majority can, through elections, translate their interests into public policy. If they cannot, then the hopes of Tom Paine or J. A. Roebuck will be disappointed, and the fears of James Madison and John Stuart Mill be proved groundless. We therefore have to ask: how effective are elections as determinants of policy? The evidence presented in Chapter IV points against their effectiveness. Most electors, it emerged, vote in accordance with habit rather than the immediate issues at stake (though the one does not, of course, exclude the other); not many electors have clear knowledge of the issues stressed by the candidates; fewer still can identify the

[1] *ibid.*, p. 250.

parties' stands correctly; a significant number wittingly or unwittingly vote contrary to their policy preferences.

No election in Britain is ever fought on a single, overwhelmingly important issue. No party and no major-party candidate ever campaigns on one issue only. The reasons for this are threefold. A British election centres principally on the capacity of the parties to provide effective government over a broad range of topics. Secondly, each of the major parties is trying to appeal to a majority of the electorate, including some who have in the past voted, or might vote, for the other party. It is hardly likely that the same coherent, ideologically consistent, policy statement will appeal with equal strength to all potential supporters. Teachers may want to compare the parties' educational policies, retired people their pensions policies, house-buyers their mortgage policies. But not all teachers, retired persons or house-buyers will give their own sectional considerations priority – anyway a person may be both a teacher and a house-buyer – and they will certainly not all interpret the programmes offered them in the same way. Thirdly, the parties themselves, especially in a two-party system, are coalitions of disparate interests. These interests accept each others' claims in order to be able to press their own, and to secure a share in the benefits that a parliamentary majority can bestow. There is no logical connecting link between the Labour Party's support for the nationalization of steel, the enfranchisement of leaseholds and state aid to Church schools. Each majority that emerges from an election, therefore, turns out not to be a coherent expression of the people's voice, but a successful coalition of groups with differing priorities. This is what Professor Dahl has named 'minorities rule'.

'In no large nation-state [he continues] can elections tell us much about the preferences of majorities and minorities, beyond the bare fact that among those who went to the polls a majority . . . or minority indicated their first choices for some particular candidate or group of candidates. What the first choices of this electoral majority are, beyond that for the particular candidates, it is almost impossible to say with much confidence . . .

'If the majority rarely rules on matters of specific policy, nevertheless the specific policies selected by a process of 'minorities rule' probably lie most of the time within the bounds of consensus set by the important values of the politically active members of the society.'[1]

This hypothesis, while denying that parliamentary elections are a satisfactory way of determining specific questions of policy, leaves open the wider question of whether most voters are swayed by specific policy

[1] Dahl, *A Preface to Democratic Theory*, pp. 128, 129–30, 132.

issues at all.[1] Even this is, however, doubtful. Single issues are more likely to predominate in local than in national elections. An interesting test case of this was the election for governor of Wisconsin, USA, in 1962 which was fought on the issue of a sales tax (supported by the Republican candidate) *versus* higher income tax (supported by the Democrat) and narrowly won by the Democrat. Of voters interviewed, only a quarter claimed that they made their choice primarily on the tax issue. Of these a majority voted for the victorious Democrat; those who switched to him from their normal allegiance were more numerous than normal Democrats who switched to his opponent. Here, it might appear, is an undoubted mandate for higher income taxes. But is this really justified? Against those who voted Democratic solely because of the tax issue must be put the much larger number who voted for the Democrat, simply because he was the Democrat. Indeed, those who voted for him *although they preferred the sales tax* considerably outnumbered the pro-income tax switchers.[2]

If modern representative democracy has any theoretical foundation at all, then it is in the proposition that the wish of the numerical majority should prevail. The majority of Wisconsin voters preferred the Democratic candidate and he was duly elected. But those who preferred him primarily for tax reasons amounted to only 28 per cent of his own supporters and 14 per cent of the total voters. This episode from the Mid-West is of relevance to a question often raised in British constitutional discussion: Does victory in a general election bestow a mandate on those who win it?

The idea of using general elections as plebiscites, or 'appeals to the people' is an old one; certainly the dissolution of 1784 was an attempt to gain a majority for Pitt, whom George III had just appointed Prime Minister. But any time before 1832 such an appeal was less to 'the people' than, as Creevey noted, to the Treasury,[3] and never more so than in the (successful) appeal of 1784.[4] The election of 1831 was fought for or against parliamentary reform, and the overwhelming Whig victory ensured that reform would pass. But it is only since the reform of 1832 that there has been any traceable relationship between the state of public opinion and the composition of the House of Commons; and only since then, therefore, that the theory of the mandate has been at all plausible. Other elections since 1832 have been fought, at any rate in the

---

[1] At one point Dahl implies that they are (*op. cit.*, p. 128).

[2] Epstein, L. D., 'Electoral Decision and Policy Mandate: An Empirical Example', *Public Opinion Quarterly* XXVIII (winter, 1964), p. 569. cf. Milne and Mackenzie, *Straight Fight*, p. 139.

[3] Quoted by Jennings, *Party Politics*, Vol. I, p. xiii.

[4] Laprade, W. T., 'Public Opinion and the General Election of 1784', *English Historical Review* XXXI (April, 1916), pp. 224–37. George, Mrs E., 'Fox's Martyrs. The General Election of 1784', *Transactions of the Royal Historical Society*, 4th Series, XXI (1939), pp. 133–68.

eyes of the contestants, on specific issues: that of 1886 on Irish Home Rule, that of 1906 on free trade, those of 1910 on the powers of the House of Lords. There is no doubt that had these elections resulted differently this would have affected the policies to be pursued: the parties which won and those which lost had both declared in advance what they would do if elected. What we do not know is how many voters were swayed by the dominant issue.

That, however, is the least of the difficulties which such a theory of the mandate raises. We need also to ask: does the mandate extend equally to all items of a party's programme? The Labour Party is committed to steel nationalization and has twice, in 1948 and 1965, attempted to carry this policy into effect. It can no doubt claim that anyone who voted Labour knew – or could easily have found out – that steel nationalization would be a natural consequence of a Labour victory. But it cannot be demonstrated whether Labour voters supported this policy explicitly or merely by implication.

The doctrine of the mandate is clearly more attractive to Radicals and Socialists, who believe that parliament exists to carry out the instructions of the electors, than to Liberals or Conservatives, who lay greater emphasis on the independent judgment of Parliament. The Radical view, however, raises a second difficulty: if a government is under an obligation to carry out its mandate, is it also entitled to exceed it? A great many of the most important decisions by British governments have been introduced without prior leave by the electorate. This is true of the repeal of the Corn Laws in 1846, of Gladstone's first Irish Home Rule Bill in 1886, of the Liberal government's social legislation between 1906 and 1910, of the National Government's introduction of a tariff in 1932, of Mr Macmillan's decision to apply for British membership of the Common Market in 1961. It is on occasions such as these that the doctrine of the mandate becomes attractive to conservatives, for it can then be argued that innovations should await the approval of the electorate. This was the argument used by the Marquess of Salisbury in opposing the abolition of the death penalty, which the Commons had voted to do, in 1956:

'This question of capital punishment has quite definitely not been put before the electorate at the last or, so far as I know, any other General Election. I know, of course, that there are, on occasions, questions, it may be great questions, which blow up suddenly between elections, and on which the electorate cannot, in the nature of things, be consulted . . .

'But this question of the abolition of the death penalty is no sudden issue, utterly unforeseen, which could not possibly have been raised at the General Election . . . I had the curiosity to inquire what mention of capital punishment there had been in the Election addresses of those

Members in all parties who have supported this Bill in the House of Commons. What did I find? Not a single one had ever mentioned the subject in his Election address . . .

'It seems to me quite impossible for Parliament in this country to pay lip-service to democracy in theory and not to accept its implications in practice. To say that we trust the people when the people happen to agree with us, and to fail to trust the people in practice, when the people happen to take a rather different view – that way, to my mind, lies the destruction of free democracy.'[1]

Lord Salisbury is entitled to blame abolitionist MPs for their lack of candour on a topic which they judged to be a vote-loser; but he gets no nearer than any other advocate of the mandate theory to explaining how the electorate's views on this topic could be singled out from their views on any other in the course of a General Election. Nor does an episode from the 1966 election get us much further. An independent candidate who favoured the retention of hanging stood against Mr Sydney Silverman, the Labour promoter of the abolitionist bill. He got 13·7 per cent of the vote, which appeared to be drawn almost equally from Mr Silverman and his Conservative opponent. This demonstrated that 13·7 per cent of the voters in that constituency (Nelson and Colne) felt sufficiently strongly on the issue to desert their normal allegiance. We do not know for certain how they would have voted in the absence of an Independent; nor do we know the views on hanging of the 83·6 per cent who voted Labour or Conservative, or of the 49·3 per cent who voted for the country's chief abolitionist legislator. Similarly, Lord Salisbury's thesis sheds no light on the third major difficulty: how far a government may take policy initiatives on topics which, though of great national importance do not arise overnight. An outstanding example is the dispute over rearmament in the 1930s. Against Stanley Baldwin's defence that the government had had no mandate for such a step, Churchill insisted that 'the responsibility of ministers for the public safety is absolute and requires no mandate'.[2] Events justified him. In April, 1939, Baldwin's successor, Neville Chamberlain, announced peace-time conscription, without a mandate.

THE VOTER'S CHOICE

The emphasis on the individual voter's inadequacy for his responsibilities is one frequently-voiced criticism of the electoral process. But the voter, too, has his complaints, as he perceives how little influence he

[1] Quoted by Nicolson, *People and Parliament*, pp. 97–8.
[2] 12 November 1935. *H. C. Deb.*, *5th series*, Vol. 317, 1105, quoted by Mowat, C. L., *Britain Between the Wars, 1918–1940* (London, 1955), p. 556.

has on the way he is governed. This is not merely an argument about the mandate theory, about whether or not the system allows the voter to answer specific questions. The complaint goes deeper than this: that the questions which voters are asked are not necessarily the ones they wish to answer. They choose between two or three candidates in the constituency, but have little influence in their nomination. They choose between Mr Heath and Mr Wilson, or between Mr Macmillan and Mr Gaitskell, but they were never asked whether they wanted any of these men to be the chief aspirants to the Premiership. On some issues the parties have opposed views; on others not. Both major parties are committed (for instance) to the Atlantic alliance, to compulsory education, to the basic principles of the welfare state, to the maintenance of full employment. The voter who wants a neutralist or pro-Soviet foreign policy, voluntary education or two million unemployed has little chance of casting an effective vote if he wants his views represented.

These are severe limitations on the individual's political power. In part, they illustrate a problem common to all advanced, industrial nations, Eastern or Western. The gap between those who take the decisions and those who have to carry them out is becoming wider everywhere, partly because of the growing centralization of power, whether political or economic, but also because of the increasing reliance on 'technocrats' who command skills which the ordinary man does not understand. The distance between the citizen – however generously the constitution may define his rights – and the real sources of power appears to be getting greater and greater all the time. More and more power seems to be concentrated into the hands of the manager, the planner, the party boss, the trade union leader. But there is a peculiarly British dimension to this international problem. British democracy is highly élitist, more so than that of many other states with parliamentary systems. Britain has never known the referendum, the popular initiative, the nominating convention, the primary or the write-in vote, and the prospects of any of these devices being introduced here seem remote. Not merely the British social structure but the whole evolution of our representative institutions explain why there are so few checks on the behaviour of elected legislators. What has happened is that Parliament, feudal and patrician in origin, has adapted itself to the widening of civil liberties and the extension of the right to vote. Certainly, most of the decisive changes happened under the impulse of popular radicalism. But none has been achieved by revolution, and in the absence of a British revolutionary tradition the slogans and symbols of popular sovereignty, so important in America or France, carry little weight.

Joseph Schumpeter's thesis that democratic elections amount to no more than competition between élites is therefore particularly applicable to Britain:

'In political life there is always some competition, though perhaps only a potential one, for the allegiance of the people. To simplify matters we have restricted the kind of competition for leadership which is to define democracy, to free competition for a free vote. The justification for this is that democracy seems to imply a recognized method by which to conduct the competitive struggle . . .

'Between [the] ideal case which does not exist, and the cases in which all competition with the established leader is prevented by force, there is a continuous range of variation within which the democratic method of government shades off into the autocratic by imperceptible steps . . .'[1]

Arguing that the true function of the electorate's vote is the acceptance of leadership, he concludes, 'The principle of democracy then merely means that the reins of government should be handed to those who command more support than to any of the competing individuals or teams.'[2] This is a substantial modification of Aristotle's definition: we no longer have 'the sovereignty of the majority', but the consent of the majority. Free elections in Britain mean free choice between policies and leaders, but little freedom in establishing the terms of the choice.

Various ways have been proposed of reducing the present distance between ruler and ruled. The contemporary protest movements – CND in Britain, or civil rights in America – have their roots in the belief that existing parliamentary institutions are useless for bringing about major policy changes. In this they merely take at their word the defenders of parliamentarism, who point out that parliamentarism can function only if there is agreement on essentials. Regional devolution, workers' control in industry, community projects, 'participatory democracy' have been urged on normative grounds: that without them life is insufficiently democratic; and on pragmatic: that the present system leads to bad, ill-informed decisions, e.g. in town planning. But are these remedies intended to replace or to supplement elected, central parliaments? If the first, they look suspiciously like pre-industrial utopias, nostalgic for simple, self-sufficient communities. The technical arguments against them are formidable, and are acknowledged by the more realistic critics of 'democratic élitist' orthodoxy, like Peter Bachrach. 'The theorist', he argues, 'must fully recognize the élite-mass nature of modern industrial society and implications of this fact for democratic theory'.[3] 'The main thrust of the élitist argument is incontestable . . . participation in key political decisions on the national level must remain extremely limited.'[4] Referenda, community projects, joint consultation committees or

---

[1] Schumpeter, J. A., *op. cit.,* p. 271.
[2] *ibid.,* p. 273.
[3] Bachrach, *op. cit.,* pp. 6–7.
[4] *ibid.,* p. 95.

student power may be desirable on grounds of democratic ethic; they may even contribute to better 'outputs' by government and other authorities, though the argument for the second does not necessarily rest on the argument for the first. One thing they cannot do: co-ordinate policies over several fields, or determine priorities. That must be done centrally, and if public feeling is to be transmitted to the centre in a parliamentary régime it must be through nationally organized bodies willing to execute as well as advocate – in other words, political parties. What direct action bodies, and pressure groups, can do is to make both the executive and the elected representatives more sensitive; to engage in 'political back-seat driving'.[1]

There is an argument of principle behind the prescription of a division of labour between voters and politicians: 'They must understand that, once they have elected an individual, political action is his business, and not theirs.'[2] But there is also a pragmatic defence: most people do not want to be bothered with participation. Most people are not, by nature, political animals. They see democratic elections as a control, as a last-ditch defence against misgovernment, not as an invitation to a continuous town-meeting. Such propositions are difficult to prove or refute; but the present condition of British parties, and the present state of the electorate's confidence in them, are not so wonderful that we can accept without question the pragmatic argument for the *de facto* élitism of British electoral politics.

Since 1950 the turn-out at elections has dropped from 84 per cent to 72 per cent. In the centres of large cities the turn-out has dropped even more sharply. In the sixty-two inner London seats the average poll in 1970 was 58·4 per cent; the decline has been twice the national average over the last decade. In nine London seats the poll was under 50 per cent, and polls under 60 per cent were by no means unusual in other city-centre seats.[3] As I have argued above, one must beware of equating high polls with democratic zeal. The 92·1 per cent poll in Fermanagh and South Tyrone does not, by itself, demonstrate exceptional devotion to parliamentary government in that constituency. But neither does the 44·9 per cent poll in Stepney. Turnout stayed high, or even rose, where there were three- or four-cornered contests; there was a direct correlation between the level of minor-party support and the turn-out.[4] In other words there is now – in contrast with the 1950s – a sector of the electorate that will stay at home when faced with a choice between the two main parties alone.

[1] The phrase is Schumpeter's (*op. cit.*, p. 295) who, on Burkean grounds, disapproves of it.

[2] Schumpeter, *loc. cit.*

[3] Three each in Liverpool, Manchester and Glasgow, two in Birmingham, one each in Leeds and Sheffield.

[4] *Nuffield 1970*, p. 388.

There are other symptoms of declining interest in working through the main parties. Membership of both is down by nearly 50 per cent compared with the early 1950s – in the Conservative Party from 2¼ million to under 1½ million; in the Labour Party from a nominal one million individual members, to a nominal 680,000 and an estimated effective 350,000.[1] Party youth organizations show an even more drastic decline. The Young Conservatives have gone down from a peak of over 150,000 at the end of the 1940s and 80,000 a decade later to not more than 50,000, despite a major membership drive. The young Socialists, always beset with greater doctrinal and organizational disputes, have under 10,000 members, low even by the modest figures of a decade earlier.[2]

It may be argued that such trends are not by themselves a sign of diminishing political vitality; that the mass-mobilization political party dates from an earlier phase of constitutional development and has become redundant in an age of highly-developed communications media and ritualized negotiation among the major producer groups. If we agree, however, that parties retain their importance as aggregators of sectional interest, and codifiers of political choice, their atrophy must cause concern. In one party at least, the Labour Party, the atrophy was well advanced by 1970. Not only was membership unprecedently low, constituency activity was in many cases at a virtual stand-still.[3] In 1969 136 local parties failed to send a delegate to the annual conference, in 1970 172 – mostly because they were behindhand with their subscriptions.[4] No doubt there were particular, short-term reasons for this demoralization and a period in Opposition may remedy some of the damage caused by disillusionment with the Wilson government. But the situation in both parties in 1970 was also the culmination of a long-term trend not so easily reversed.

Party organization remains important for two reasons: both the selection of leaders and the drawing-up of policy continue to depend on it. Both processes illustrate the strength of élitist traditions. The methods by which policy is formulated have always been more controversial in the Labour Party than among Conservatives and Liberals, for reasons

[1] *ibid.*, pp. 265, 279. Labour Party membership figures exclude 'affiliated' members, who belong automatically by virtue of belonging to an affiliated trade union. Official returns of individual membership are based on figures supplied by constituency parties. But since CLPs cannot register with the central organization for fewer than 1,000 members, the official statistics have always over-estimated the real level of membership.

[2] *Nuffield 1970*, p. 287. For a general survey of the situation in the early 1960s, see Abrams, P. and Little, A., 'The Young Activist in British Politics', *British Journal of Sociology* XV (June, 1965).

[3] See Dean, M., 'Is the Labour Party Dying?' *The Guardian*, 18–21 January, 1971; Hindess, B., *The Decline of Working-Class Politics* (London, 1971).

[4] *The Observer*, 3 January 1971.

which have already been discussed.[1] Writing in 1937, shortly after he had become Leader of the Labour Party, Attlee defined the role of the party's annual conference as 'a parliament of the movement':

'In contradistinction to Conservative conferences which simply pass resolutions that may or may not be acted upon, the Labour Party Conference lays down the policy of the Party, and issues instructions which must be carried out by the Executive, the affiliated organizations, and its representatives in Parliament and on local authorities.'[2]

This is not quite how Attlee managed the Labour Government of 1945–51, of which he was Prime Minister; 'You can't', he recalled afterwards, 'have a non-parliamentary body arranging things, saying "You must do this. You mustn't do the other"'.[3] Nor was it an accurate description of the situation in 1937, for the Labour Party had already then been in office twice, and the conflict between a government's responsibility to Parliament or the party outside was not a new one. The way in which Ramsay MacDonald had formed and conducted the first Labour Government in 1924 showed that the Labour Party was as fully part of the established parliamentary system as the Conservative and Liberal Parties, and subsequent attempts to reassert the sovereignty of conference failed. 'I am not going to have ropes around my neck for other people to pull when they like,' MacDonald announced.[4] Indeed the Parliamentary Labour Party has tried, almost from its beginnings in 1906, to emancipate itself from (in Keir Hardie's words) 'definite instructions to introduce this and that'.[5]

It is sometimes argued that the power of the Labour Party Conference varies according to whether the party is in opposition or power. According to this view it is legitimate for the conference to lay down future policy commitments, as it did in 1945, when it itemized the industries to be nationalized, against the wishes of the National Executive Committee; it is not legitimate to dictate policy to H.M. Ministers. This is an unreal distinction. What is the use of recommending policies, if you cannot control those in whose hands lies the decision whether to carry them out when they are in power?

The question of who controls whom in the Labour Party has been debated many times, and it was probably decided conclusively in 1960–1 in the course of the debate on nuclear weapons. In 1960, at Scarborough, the conference reversed official party policy and backed unilateral

[1] See above, pp. 64–5.
[2] Attlee, C. R., *The Labour Party in Perspective* (London, 1937), p. 93.
[3] Williams, F., *A Prime Minister Remembers. The War and Post-War Memoirs of the Rt. Hon. Earl Attlee* (London, 1961), p. 91.
[4] McKenzie, *op. cit.*, p. 428, n. 1.
[5] *ibid.*, pp. 393, 627.

nuclear disarmament, while the majority of Labour MPs did not. Hugh Gaitskell, in his speech at that conference, asked delegates how they envisaged the situation of MPs who disagreed with the conference decision on so fundamental a matter.

'What do you expect of them? You know how they voted in June – overwhelmingly for the policy statement . . . So what do you expect them to do? Change their minds overnight? To go back on the pledges they gave to the people who elected them from their constituencies? And supposing they did do that? Supposing all of us, like well-behaved sheep, were to follow the policies of unilateralism and neutralism, what kind of impression would that make upon the British people?'[1]

It was not merely a scholastic interpretation of the Labour Party's constitution that was involved here; the basic question was one which lies at the centre of all representative systems – is the elected legislator a delegate, and, if so, whose? Since, in the following year at Blackpool, the Conference reversed its 1960 decision and fell into line with official policy, the outcome of this particular dispute was a clear victory for the parliamentary party and Mr Gaitskell. Though the party conference of 1970 celebrated the return to Opposition by reaffirming the primacy of conference decisions over elected governments, the heart has gone out of this particular fight.

In the Liberal and Conservative parties the rights of conference delegates have provoked less controversy. Ever since the newly-formed extra-parliamentary bodies overplayed their hands in the 1880s and 1890s, the parliamentary leadership has been firmly in charge, irrespective of whether it was in power or in opposition. There have, of course, been critical debates at Conservative conferences: that of 1903 on tariff reform, that of 1921 on the Treaty with the Irish Free State, that of 1934 on Baldwin's India policy, and that of 1962 on the Common Market. In 1934 the official policy survived by only 543 votes to 520;[2] but as a rule the challenge to the platform is feeble – so feeble that the chairman of the 1962 conference could commit the Freudian slip of announcing, 'We will take the [hostile] amendment first, and after that has been beaten we will vote on the main question'.[3] When in 1969 there was a demand for a ballot on the question of law-and-order the conference chairman did not know the procedure for complying with so unusual a request.

The *de facto* primacy of the parliamentary leaders over the party conferences has its limits. True, the rank-and-file cannot *instruct* the

[1] Quoted *ibid.*, pp. 615–6.
[2] *ibid.*, p. 204.
[3] Quoted by Berkeley, H., 'Political Party Conferences', *The Listener*, 22 September 1966, p. 411.

leaders, especially when these are also government ministers. But it is not true (as Michels claims it is) 'that the history of parliamentary parties consists of a succession of rejected congress decisions'.[1] Party leaders cannot afford to be frequently disavowed by their own followers, and the appearance of disunity is always bad for the party's public image. For this reason the rebels in the Labour Party during the 1950s saw with some satisfaction that official policy was often trimmed to anticipate their objections. And if the 1961 Labour conference had reaffirmed the 1960 decision in favour of unilateralism it would have been politically, even if not constitutionally, necessary for Mr Gaitskell to resign the leadership – something which he had himself privately acknowledged.[2]

While the internal politics of the Labour Party centre on policy disputes, in the Conservative Party the manner of choosing the leader has been the main source of conflict. Just as Labour has in these matters inherited the radical-democratic tradition, and turns instinctively to election as the normal method, so the Conservatives have acted, as far as they could, in accordance with the hierarchic principle. The mystical qualities with which the leadership is thereby endowed emerge in the famous declaration by Capt. Pretyman, MP, in 1923: 'Great leaders of parties are not elected, they are evolved . . . The leader is there, and we all know it when he is there'[3] This was not a democratic method and it was not meant to be, and for this reason was criticized not only by anti-Conservatives but by reformers within the party. It could not survive the leadership crisis of 1963, when Sir Alec Douglas-Home was chosen to succeed Mr Macmillan, and when, although justice may have been done, it was not seen to have been done. As a result the leader of the Conservative Party, like the leaders of the Labour and Liberal parties, is now elected by his party's members in the House of Commons, Mr Heath succeeded Sir Alec Douglas-Home in this way in 1965.

Who makes policy and who chooses the leader are important questions in determining the degree of intra-party democracy. But whatever the answer the ordinary voter may remain dissatisfied. Whether the leader of the Conservative Party is to be nominated by what Mr Macleod christened 'the magic circle'[4] or by a few hundred MPs is a debate within the élite about the extent of the élite. So is the debate whether party policy should be drawn up with or without the aid of party militants. All that can be said is that the more extensive the élite, the more

[1] Michels, R., *Zur Soziologie des Parteiwesens in der modernen Demokratie* (2nd edn, reprinted Stuttgart, 1957), pp. 138–9.
[2] Jenkins, R. in Rodgers, W. T. (ed.), *Hugh Gaitskell, 1906–1963*, p. 129.
[3] McKenzie, *op. cit.*, p. 34.
[4] Macleod, I. N., 'The Tory Leadership', *The Spectator*, 17 January 1964, p. 66.

sensitive it becomes to indirect pressures from outsiders. Back-bench MPs can be lobbied in a way that Chief Whips cannot; conference delegates are, for the rest of the year, friends and neighbours in a way that Cabinet Ministers (or shadow ministers) are not. It may not be just, but it is surely unavoidable, that those citizens who are politically active have more influence than those who are not; public opinion, after all, consists of 'those opinions held by private persons which governments find it prudent to heed'.[1]

THE RELEVANCE OF ELECTORAL CHOICE

The contemporary British voter who asks himself what say he has in his country's affairs must be assailed with one further doubt. He may agree that he has little chance as an individual of influencing election manifestoes or the choice of leaders; but what of the parliament and the cabinet which emerge from the election? How many of the really important policy decisions do they make? How many of the effective choices are theirs? Who runs Britain? And is it in the first place the elected parliamentarians who do so?

Marxists have always had a ready-made answer to these questions. Real power lies in the hands of those who own the means of production. When their interests are at stake they are always in a position to exert pressure – on MPs, ministers, civil servants or mass media – to ensure a decision in their favour. Electoral competition is therefore a façade, parliamentary debate a farce. It would be difficult to maintain, in the face of the evidence, that all parliamentary politics in the past hundred years has been merely a capitalist racket. But even if this were agreed, it would not answer the further question, namely, where and by whom are the crucial decisions made?

In the course of this century the concept of the self-regulating market in matters of wages and prices has been left further and further behind. Wage negotiations now take place on an industry-wide basis, between representative organizations which enjoy official standing and may be subject to some public scrutiny. In many professions, the standard of qualifications and of conduct is determined by private, monopolistic bodies – the Inns of Court, for instance, or the British Medical Association. Professor Gunnar Myrdal's verdict on these developments is typical of many:

'If it sometimes looks as if the state had left it to the powerful organizations themselves to fight it out and come to an agreement . . . this is only so because it is felt that the balance of strength between the buyers and

[1] Key, V. O. jr., *Public Opinion and American Democracy* (New York, 1961), p. 14.

the sellers in the market has been established by state intervention. These organizations then actually function as organs for public policy . . .

'Many of the most important decisions, then, are taken outside parliament, and put into effect by other organs than those of the state administration.'[1]

A ten per cent wage increase in the engineering industry, or a railway strike, may have more impact on the country's affairs than the whole of one year's legislation. Even when the state is involved with the private partners, its role may be only passive and subordinate. Although manufacturing industries or agriculture may depend on the state for protective tariffs, fixed prices and subsidies they can, if they are sufficiently well organized, often dictate their own terms.

Because there is a general tendency for producer groups – whether of goods or of professional services – to organize in defence of their interests, and because modern governments increasingly depend on such groups for information or expert advice, the biggest lobbies have come to assume important representative functions. Professor Beer is convinced that

'producer groups have a power to affect policy-making that is quite separate from their position in the system of parliamentary representation and party government . . .

'The source of the power is not the fact that the group or its members has a role – for instance, as voters or contributors to party funds – in the system of parliamentary representation, but derives from the group's performance of a productive function.'[2]

In the nineteen-fifties this could lead to a sort of corporative stagnation, where progress was possible 'with near unanimity, or not at all'.[3] Despite the two-party system, therefore, which is supposed to lead to strong governmental leadership, Britain seemed to be immobilized by a multi-party coalition of economic interests, operating by the side of, and through, the state machine. If the economic power of the producer groups were such that they could permanently impose their wishes on both parliament and the civil service, then the voter would certainly be entitled to wonder what his contribution was worth. But if Beer is right, and the groups' power drives precisely from their integration into the modern 'mixed', 'managed' or 'planned' economy, there is no inherent reason why the state should continue in this passive role.

[1] Myrdal, G., *Beyond the Welfare State* (London, 1960), p. 33.
[2] Beer, *op. cit.*, p. 30.
[3] Beer, S. H., 'Pressure Groups and Parties in Britain', *American Political Science Review* L (March, 1956), pl 16.

In the early sixties both parties tried to break out of the corporatist impasse by giving the state a more positive role in its relations with the interest groups. The National Economic Development Council (NEDC or Neddy), set up in 1962, and the Prices and Incomes Board (PIB) of 1965 were designed as steps towards indicative planning as opposed to merely holding the ring. The Labour government declared its intention of maintaining a watching brief on wages, prices and incomes, quite apart from such temporary and panic-inspired expedients as the wages freeze. The then Chancellor of the Exchequer, Mr L. J. Callaghan, declared at the Labour Party Conference of 1966:

'Any group of people who are arguing about their incomes, whether it is workers about their wages or landlords about their rents, must accept and recognize that the bargaining strengths of the two parties is not the only factor that can be allowed to decide these issues in future.

'From the moment the Order in Council [implementing Part IV of the Prices and Incomes Act] is made, the public is in these negotiations as a third party, as an interested party, and . . . when the powers become extinct next August the public interest will remain in the arguments about the level and distribution of income.'[1]

Such a policy, if successfully pursued, would have restored to the politician a degree of initiative that would have greatly enhanced the salience of elections in the individual's political options. The greater the power of the organized group vis-à vis the state, the more the individual must look towards these groups as his most effective representatives. The greater the power of the state vis-à-vis the organized groups, the more the voter comes into his own. When Professor Beer, in the first edition of Modern British Politics, dismissed these new efforts by government as a further 'agency of functional representation',[2] it seemed plausible to accuse him of looking at the 1960s through the spectacles of the 1950s.[3] Now that the 1960s are over, it looks as though the same spectacles will serve both decades: government did not emerge victoriously from the battle and did not achieve the objects it set itself.[4]

Elections were thus restored as the most important direct means of achieving political goals, expectations, or experience, of the parties'

[1] Report of the 65th Annual conference of the Labour Party, Brighton 1966, p. 213.
[2] Beer, Modern British Politics, p. 390.
[3] In the first edition of this book, p. 143.
[4] Beer expands the argument in the second edition of Modern British Politics, esp. pp. 410–11. For the best account of the Government's strategy and the reasons for its defeat, see Jenkins, P., The Battle of Downing Street (London, 1970).

attitudes to different groups would become an important factor in electoral choice. Will a particular minister be tough with the trade unions, lenient with the farmers, conciliatory towards the doctors, unbending towards shipbuilding or the aircraft industry? Such issues can become electorally relevant. They are, no doubt, far removed from the legislative function of parliament, as traditionally conceived; but if, by procedural reforms and an extension of the committee system, Members of Parliament are to share increasingly in the making of national policy, this could transfer even more power to those who are, in the last resort, answerable to the electors and amenable to public complaints.

HOW REPRESENTATIVE? HOW DEMOCRATIC?

Was Rousseau right after all? Are the British people free only once every five years? There have, no doubt, been times when the actions of the government, and of parliament, have gone clearly against the wishes of the public; or when the public have had only inadequate or misleading information on which to judge these actions; or when well-organized minorities have been able to nobble the agencies of the state at the expense of the interests of the majority. But exactly how great is the distance between the individual citizen and the well-springs of power? Exactly how difficult is it for the majority to express and impose their wishes?

In any system of elective representation the rights of the individual voter are of necessity exercised indirectly, not merely because most political communities are too large for the primitive forms of direct self-government, but because the skills and techniques of modern administration need fairly specialized divisions of labour. In addition there are in Britain special local factors which emphasize the strength of the delegate's power. These are

1. *The strong element of élitism in political leadership*, discussed in Chapter III. The prominent members of both major parties are recruited from roughly the same strata and the same is increasingly true of the back-benchers. Leadership within the parties is highly centralized and backed by exceptionally strong discipline. Most of the senior civil servants, many of the top men in industry and finance and the professions share the background and the values of the political leaders; they communicate through a handful of quality media – The Times, The Economist, the BBC – which, at the higher reaches are also staffed by men largely like themselves. This does not mean that they are necessarily out of touch with the opinions of ordinary people: it does mean that they are a socially and intellectually unrepresentatative, and relatively homogeneous, group. The similarity of background is largely provided by the

equally élitist British educational system; in so far as this system is changing it could well lead to a fragmentation of the political élite, but it will clearly be some time before such a development can have a noticeable impact.

2. *The tradition of parliamentary independence,* discussed in Chapter I. Though this has its origins in the parliamentary struggle with the Crown and dates from the pre-reform era, the notion that Parliament is a public forum, but nobody's servant, has survived virtually intact, largely thanks to the gradualness with which the franchise has been democratized. The mystique and ceremony of Parliament help to keep it at one remove from mundane affairs.

3. *The collective character of political representation.* Once this was the direct representation of economic interests or family connections. For the past century the channelling of interest and opinion into workable units has been undertaken by party, so that today the conduct of elections and the working of parliament would be unthinkable without the party struggle.

It is in this inter-party competition that the voter can effectively intervene. A party enters an election in order to win a parliamentary majority; it wants a parliamentary majority in order to govern the country. There is only one, overriding issue in every British general election: the rival parties' fitness to govern. This is recognized by constitutional practice. Until 1868 it was customary for governments to resign only if defeated in a division in the House of Commons. In 1868 Disraeli set the precedent of resigning immediately it was obvious that he had lost the election. Because the choice is essentially between two parties, many of the objections to the electoral method – the irrationality of the voters, the difficulty of disentangling policy issues, the doubts surrounding the mandate theory – miss the point. General elections are useful for broad, not specific, decisions.

Two consequences flow from this. The first is that the personal qualities of the rival politicians, particularly the leaders of the two main parties, intrude very heavily into the campaigning. The second is that the party which is in power, and is therefore daily seen to be governing, has an advantage over the challenger. For the party in power, the art of political management consists of identifying itself, as far as possible, with a supra-partisan national interest. This is often referred to as 'consensus politics', though it is rarely clear whether this is to mean national agreement on specific topics or on ultimate aims (or both). To some extent this consensus, however defined, can be created or influenced by the government, in its choice of problems to tackle, and the way in which it decides to approach them. The party in power generally has the propaganda initiative, and it must try to use its leader's non-political position as head of the national administration to its full advantage. President Johnson exemplified the art of consensus-management when he told the citizens of Providence, Rhode Island, during the 1964 election campaign, 'We're in favour of a lot of things, and we're against mighty few'[1]. In Britain, analysis of the candidates' election addresses testifies to the special vote-getting power of the party leader when he is also Prime Minister. In 1964 41 per cent of Conservative candidates mentioned Sir Alec Douglas-Home, while in 1966 only 19 per cent mentioned Mr Heath; on the other hand the percentage of Labour candidates mentioning Mr Wilson rose from eight in 1964 to forty-seven in 1966.[2] Ironically, in 1970, Conservative candidates mentioned Mr Wilson (36 per cent) more often than Mr Heath (20 per cent), and more often than Labour candidates (21 per cent).[3]

If it is the personality of the incumbent Prime Minister, and the administrative record of the outgoing government, that are really at stake in an election, then the parties start rather unevenly in the race. The plebiscite is not so much between equally poised rivals, as between rewarding or punishing the party in power. The onus of proving that he can govern better is laid on the challenger, and this is, in the nature of things, a difficult proposition to prove. Hence a government, however dim its record, can reckon on staying in power as long as its opponents do not inspire confidence; and to spend a lengthy period in opposition can in itself be a disadvantage, since it brings with it lack of administrative experience.

For Rousseau's objection to be valid, it would have to be shown that even if the voter can intervene effectively at election time, he cannot intervene effectively at any other time. But this, as should have emerged by now, is an untenable distinction. It is absurd to say to people: you may elect your leaders at intervals of five years, but you may not control, or are incapable of controlling, their actions during the intervals. For in that case the elections either do not impress the elected with a sense of public responsibility, which makes them pointless, or they do, in which case the public is involved at other times than the quinquennial consultations. In other words: *either* the British people are, in Rousseau's sense, 'free' even when elections are not taking place, *or* they are not free at all.

It is as a device for controlling political leaders that elections fulfil their most important function; it is by their effectiveness in doing so that their utility in British politics must in the last resort by judged. If they are effective, then the whole political culture is thereby transformed.

[1] White, T. H., *The Making of the President 1964* (London, 1965), p. 347.
[2] *Nuffield 1966*, p. 103.
[3] *Nuffield 1970*, p. 442.

Power, as a result, comes to be regarded as a trust, not as a right, and the politician's tenure of office as probationary, not permanent. The party struggle becomes a non-violent way of resolving a type of conflict which exists in all except the most primitive societies – the rivalry between different interests for state power. Elections become a non-violent way of solving a difficulty common to all political systems – how to organize the succession from one group of men holding authority to another. For this reason any electoral choice is better than none, even if the policy differences between the parties are trivial or their attitudes on major issues overlap. It is still worth while to be able to choose between contestants of whom one is younger, or abler, or more honest than the other; indeed, it may be very important to be able to do so.

It has been argued earlier in this chapter that a political culture favourable to peaceful alternations of power is necessary before such a system can reliably function. It is equally true that the experience of reliable functioning reinforces public faith in the habits of tolerance and compromise. Political institutions and political manners are inseparable from each other as contributors to the characters of a régime. If this is true, we shall have to revise some of our earlier tentative conclusions. If elections are an effective control on political leaders, and are widely believed to be effective, then the voter does have an indirect influence on the content of the choice that he is given. Any party, whether in power or in opposition, which knows that it has to face an election within a given term of years, must take some trouble to draw up policies that look like being successful; and it will get rid of its leaders, often very ruthlessly, if their public rating sinks too far, as happened with Sir Alec Douglas-Home in the summer of 1965.

'No man could act with effect' thought Burke, 'who did not act in concert.'[1] All political choice, to be effective, has to be limited. In Britain it is limited to two major parties, highly disciplined, with loyal mass followings. At the same time the 'daily plebiscite' of public relations, policy statements and parliamentary debate keep the activities of the political élite in the public eye. The purpose of this activity is to urge the public to accept one of two rival leaderships; but the activity is necessary only because the final verdict is in the hands of the individual citizen. There can be no government by consent without the ritual of voting; and the right to vote periodically opens up countless indirect methods of expressing wishes and grievances at other times.

[1] Burke, E., 'Thoughts on the Cause of the Present Discontents', *Works*, Vol. II, p. 81.

The following editions of standard classical texts have been used:

ARISTOTLE, *Politics,* translated with notes by Ernest Barker, Oxford University Press, 1948.

BAGEHOT, W., *The English Constitution,* introduction by R. H. S. Crossman, M.P., The Fontana Library, Collins, London, 1962.

BURKE, E., *Works,* The World's Classics, 6 vols, Oxford University Press, 1906–7.

HAMILTON, A., JAY, J., and MADISON, J., *The Federalist Papers,* Introduction by Clinton Rossiter, Mentor: New American Library, New York, 1961.

MICHELS, R., *Political Parties,* introduction by Seymour Martin Lipset, The Free Press, Glencoe, 1962.

MILL, J. S., *Utilitarianism, Liberty and Representative Government,* Everyman Library, J. M. Dent, London, 1910.

ROUSSEAU, J-J., *Social Contract,* The World's Classics 511, Oxford University Press, 1947.

The following works are recommended for further reading. The titles of frequently cited periodicals have been abbreviated, viz.,

APSR	– *American Political Science Review*
BJS	– *British Journal of Sociology*
EHR	– *English Historical Review*
PQ	– *Political Quarterly*
PS	– *Political Studies*

BACKGROUND READING
Constitutional

BIRCH, A. H., *The British System of Government,* 2nd edn, London, 1969.

BLONDEL, J. F., *Voters, Parties and Leaders: The Social Fabric of British Politics,* London, 1963.

KING, A. S. (ed.), *British Politics: People, Parties and Parliament,* New York, 1966.

MACKINTOSH, J. P., *The Government and Politics of Britain,* London, 1970.

ROSE, R., *Politics in England,* London, 1965.

ROSE, R. (ed.), *Studies in British Politics: A Reader in Political Sociology,* 2nd edn, London, 1969.

SMELLIE, K. B., *A Hundred Years of English Government,* 2nd edn, London, 1950.

Social and Cultural

CARR-SAUNDERS, A. M., CARADOG-JONES, D. and MOSER, C., *Social Conditions in England and Wales,* Oxford, 1958.

GLASS, D. V. (ed.), *Social Mobility in Britain*, London, 1954.

HARRISON, J. F. S., *Society and Politics in England, 1780–1960*, New York, 1966.

HOGGART, R., *The Uses of Literacy*, London, 1957.

INGLIS, K. S., *Churches and the Working Classes in Victorian England*, London, 1963.

JACKSON, B. and MARSDEN, D., *Education and the Working Class*, London, 1962.

MARWICK, A., *Britain in the Century of Total War: War, Peace and Social Change, 1900–1967*, London, 1968.

RUNCIMAN, W. G., *Relative Deprivation and Social Justice: A Study of Attitudes to Social Inequality in Twentieth-Century England*, London, 1966.

THE BRITISH REPRESENTATIONAL SYSTEM

History

BLEWETT, N., 'The Franchise in the United Kingdom, 1855–1939', *Past and Present* 32 (Dec., 1965).

BUTLER, D. E., 'The Redistribution of Seats', *Public Administration*, XXXIII (summer, 1955).

BUTLER, D. E., *The Electoral System in Britain since 1918*, 2nd edn, Oxford, 1963.

BUTLER, J. R. M., *The Passing of the Great Reform Bill*, London, 1914.

DUNBABIN, J. P. D., 'Parliamentary Elections in Great Britain, 1858–1900: a Psephological Note', *EHR* LXXXI (Jan. 1966).

FOORD, A. S., *His Majesty's Opposition, 1714–1830*, Oxford, 1964.

GASH, N., *Politics in the Age of Peel: A Study in the Technique of Parliamentary Representation, 1830–50*, London, 1953.

HANHAM, H. J., *Elections and Party Management: Politics in the Time of Disraeli and Gladstone*, London, 1959.

JENNINGS, SIR IVOR, *Party Politics, I: Appeal to the People*, Cambridge, 1960.

LEONARD, R. L., *Elections in Britain*, Princeton-London, 1968.

LOWELL, A. L., *The Government of England*, 2nd edn, New York, 1926.

MORRIS, H. L., *Parliamentary Franchise Reform in England from 1885 to 1918*, New York, 1921.

NAMIER, SIR L. B., *England in the Age of the American Revolution*, 2nd edn, London, 1961.

NAMIER, SIR L. B., *The Structure of Politics at the Accession of George III*, 2nd edn, London, 1957.

NEALE, SIR J. E., *The Elizabethan House of Commons*, London, 1949.

PORRITT, E. and A. G., *The Unreformed House of Commons: Parliamentary Representation Before 1832*, Cambridge, 1903.

ROKKAN, S. and MEYRIAT, J. (eds.), *International Guide to Election Statistics*, Vol. I, The Hague, 1969.

SEYMOUR, C. S., *Electoral Reform in England and Wales*, New Haven, 1915.

SMITH, F. B., *The Making of the Second Reform Bill*, Cambridge, 1966.

WILLIAMS, P. M., 'The Politics of Redistribution' *PQ* XXXIX (July, 1968).

WILLIAMS, P. M., 'Two Notes on the British Electoral System', *Parliamentary Affairs* XX (winter, 1966–7).

Election Results

BUTLER, D. E. and FREEMAN, J., *British Political Facts, 1900–1968*, London, 1969,

CRAIG, F. W. S. (ed.), *British Parliamentary Election Results, 1918–1949*, Glasgow, 1969.

CRAIG, F. W. S. (ed.), *British Parliamentary Election Results, 1950–1970*, Chichester, 1971.

MITCHELL, B. R. and BOEHM, K., *British Parliamentary Election Results, 1950–1964*, Cambridge, 1966.

Political Companion (quarterly) (ed. F. W. S. Craig: Political Reference Publications).

Times, The [of London], *Guide to the House of Commons*, London, 1918, 1929, 1931, 1935, 1945, 1950, 1951, 1955, 1959, 1964, 1966, 1970.

THEORIES OF REPRESENTATION

AMERY, L. S., *Thoughts on the Constitution*, Oxford, 1947.

BACHRACH, P., *The Theory of Democratic Élitism: A Critique*, Boston-Toronto, 1967.

BEER, S. H., *Modern British Politics*, 2nd edn, London, 1969 [U.S.: *British Politics in the Collectivist Age*, New York, 1969].

BENEWICK, R. J., BIRCH, A. H., BLUMLER, J. G. and EWBANK, A., 'The Floating Voter and the Liberal View of Representation', *PS* XVII (June, 1969).

BIRCH, A. H., *Representative and Responsible Government: An Essay on the British Constitution*, London, 1964.

BRYCE, VISCOUNT, *Modern Democracies*, New York, 1924.

CHRISTOPH, J. B., 'Consensus and Cleavage in British Political Ideology', *APSR* LIX (Sept., 1965).

DAHL, R. A., *A Preface to Democratic Theory*, Chicago, 1956.

DUNCAN, G. and LUKES, S., 'The New Democracy', *PS* XI (June, 1963).

EPSTEIN, L. D., 'Electoral Decision and Policy Mandate: An Empirical Example', *Public Opinion Quarterly* XXVIII (winter 1964.)

GIBBONS, P. A., *Ideas of Political Representation in Parliament, 1651–1832*, Oxford, 1914.

LOWI, T., 'The Public Philosophy: Interest-Group Liberalism', *APSR* LXI (March, 1967).

MAY, J. D., 'Democracy, Organization, Michels', *ASPR* LIX (June, 1965).

MILNOR, A. J., *Elections and Political Stability*, Boston, 1969.

MYRDAL, G., *Beyond the Welfare State*, London, 1960.

PITKIN, H. F., *The Concept of Representation*, Berkeley-Los Angeles, 1967.

PLAMENATZ, J. and SARTORI, G., 'Electoral Studies and Democratic Theory', *PS* VI (Feb., 1958).

RUNCIMAN, W. G., *Social Science and Political Theory*, Cambridge, 1963.

SCHATTSCHNEIDER, E. E., *Party Government*, New York, 1942.

SCHUMPETER. J. A., *Capitalism, Socialism and Democracy*. 4th edn, London, 1954.

ELECTION SURVEYS

British

BUTLER, D. E., *The British General Election of 1951*, London, 1952.

BUTLER, D. E., *The British General Election of 1955*, London, 1955.

BUTLER, D. E. and ROSE, R., *The British General Election of 1959*, London, 1960.

BUTLER, D. E. and KING, A. S., *The British General Election of 1964*, London, 1965.

BUTLER, D. E. and KING, A. S., *The British General Election of 1966*, London, 1966.
BUTLER, D. E. and PINTŌ-DUSCHINSKY, M., *The British General Election of 1970*, London, 1971.
BERRINGTON, H. B., 'The General Election of 1964', *Journal of the Royal Statistical Society* Series A, CXXVIII (1965).
BERRINGTON, H. B., 'The 1966 Election; An Analysis of the Results', *Swinton Journal* XII (autumn, 1966).
CRICK, B., 'Some Reflections on the Late Election', *Public Law*, (spring, 1966).
HANSON, A. H. and WRIGHT, E., 'The Election in Retrospect: The Future of the Labour Party; The Future of the Conservative Party', *PQ* XLI (Oct., 1970).
KENDALL, M. G. and STUART, A., 'The Law of Cubic Proportion in Election Results', *BJS* I (Sept., 1950).
MCCALLUM, R. B. and READMAN, A., *The British General Election of 1945*, Oxford, 1947.
NICHOLAS, H. G., *The British General Election of 1950*, London, 1951.
RASMUSSEN, J. S., 'The Disutility of the Swing Concept in British Psephology', *Parliamentary Affairs* XVIII (autumn, 1965).
SHARPE, L. J. (ed.), *Voting in Cities: The 1964 Borough Elections*, London, 1967.

Comparative

CHAPMAN, R. M., JACKSON, W. K. and MITCHELL, A. V., *New Zealand Politics in Action: The 1960 General Election*, Oxford, 1962.
GOGUEL, F. and others, *Le Référendum d'Octobre et les Elections Législatives de Novembre 1962* [Cahier de la Fondation Nationale des Sciences Politiques, 142] Paris, 1965.
KITZINGER, U. W., *German Electoral Politics. A Study of the 1957 Campaign*, Oxford, 1960.
RAWSON, D. W., *Australia Votes*, Melbourne, 1961.
WHITE, T. H., *The Making of the President, 1960*, London, 1961.
WHITE, T. H., *The Making of the President, 1968*, London, 1969.

ELECTORAL SYSTEMS

CAMPBELL, P. W., *French Electoral Systems and Elections since 1789*, 2nd edn, London, 1965.
DUVERGER, M. (ed.), *L'Influence des Systèmes électoraux sur la Vie politique*, Paris, 1950.
HERMENS, F. A., *Democracy or Anarchy? A Study of Proportional Representation*, Notre Dame, 1941.
HOGAN, J., *Election and Representation*, Cork, 1945.
LAKEMAN, E., *How Democracies Vote: A Study of Majority and Proportional Electoral Systems*, London, 1970.
RAE, J. D., *The Political Consequences of Electoral Laws*, New Haven, 1967.
ROSS, J. F. S., *Elections and Electors: Studies in Democratic Representation*, London, 1955.
STEED, M., 'Alternative Vote and Speaker's Conference', *New Outlook* 49 (Nov.–Dec., 1965).

POLITICAL PARTIES

British: Major Parties

ATTLEE, C. R., *The Labour Party in Perspective*, London, 1937.
BEALEY, F. and PELLING, H., *Labour and Politics, 1900–1906 : A History of the Labour Representation Committee*, London, 1958.
BEATTIE, A., *English Party Politics*, 2 vols, London, 1970.
BLAKE, R. N. W., *The Conservative Party from Peel to Churchill*, London, 1970.
BURNS, J. M., 'The Parliamentary Labour Party in Great Britain', *APSR* XLIV (Sept., 1950).
COOKE, G. W., *The History of Party : From the Rise of the Whig and Tory Factions in the Reign of Charles II to the Passing of the Reform Bill*, London, 1836–7.
HARRISON, M., *Trade Unions and the Labour Party since 1945*, London, 1960.
HOFFMAN, J. D., *The Conservative Party in Opposition, 1945–51*, London, 1965.
JENNINGS, SIR IVOR, *Party Politics, II : The Growth of Parties*, Cambridge, 1961.
LIPSON, L., 'The Two-Party System in British Politics', *APSR* XLVII (June, 1953).
MACLEOD, I. N., 'The Tory Leadership', *The Spectator* (London), 17 January, 1964.
MILIBAND, R., *Parliamentary Socialism : A Study of the Politics of Labour*, 2nd edn, London, 1971.
MCKENZIE, R. T., *British Political Parties*, 2nd edn, London, 1963.
PELLING, H., *The Origins of the Labour Party, 1880–1900*, 2nd edn, Oxford, 1965.
RASMUSSEN, J. S., *The Liberal Party : A Study of Retrenchment and Revival*, London, 1965.
ROSE, R., 'Parties, Factions, and Tendencies in Britain', *PS* XII (Feb., 1964).
ROSE, S., MCKENZIE, R. T. and MILIBAND, R., 'Policy-Making in Opposition; Party Democracy and Parliamentary Government', *PS* IV–V (June, 1956; June, 1957; June, 1958).
TREVELYAN, G. M., *The Two-Party System in English Political History*, Romanes Lecture, Oxford, 1926.
VINCENT, J. R., *The Formation of the Liberal Party, 1857–1868*, London, 1966.

British: Minor Parties, Regionalism

BUDGE, I. S. and URWIN, D. W., *Scottish Political Behaviour : A Case Study in British Homogeneity*, London, 1966.
CORNFORD, J. P. and BRAND, J. A., 'Scottish Voting Behaviour' ed. J. N. Wolfe, *Government and Nationalism in Scotland*, Edinburgh, 1969.
CROSS, C., *The Fascists in Britain*, London, 1961.
DOWSE, R. E., *Left in the Centre : The Independent Labour Party, 1893–1940*, London, 1966.
MCLEAN, I., 'The Rise and Fall of the Scottish National Party', *PS* XVIII (Sept., 1970).
MORGAN, K. O., *Wales in British Politics, 1868–192?*, Cardiff, 1963.
de PAOR, L., *Divided Ulster*, London, 1970.
PELLING, H., *The British Communist Party : A Historical Profile*, London, 1958.
THAYER, G., *The British Political Fringe : A Profile*, London, 1965.

Comparative

DAHL, R. A. (ed.), *Political Oppositions in Western Democracies*, New Haven and London, 1966.
DUVERGER, M., *Political Parties*, London, 1954.
ELDERSVELD, S. J., *Political Parties: A Behavioural Analysis*, Chicago, 1964.
EPSTEIN, L. D., 'British Mass Parties in Comparison with American Parties', *Political Science Quarterly* LXXI (March, 1956).
EPSTEIN, L. D., *Political Parties in Western Democracies*, New York, 1967.
KEY, V. O. jr., *Politics, Parties and Pressure Groups*, 5th edn, New York, 1964.
LA PALOMBARA, J. and WEINER, M., *Political Parties and Political Development*, Princeton, 1966.
LEISERSON, A., *Parties and Politics: An Institutional and Behavioural Approach*, New York, 1958.
LOWELL, A. L., *Governments and Parties in Continental Europe*, Boston–New York, 1896.
NEUMANN, S. (ed.), *Modern Political Parties*, Chicago, 1956.
OSTROGORSKI, M., *Democracy and the Organization of Political Parties*, London, 1902.
P.E.P., *European Political Parties* (ed. S. Henig and J. Pinder), London, 1969.

POLITICAL RECRUITMENT

BUCK, P. W., *Amateurs and Professionals in British Politics 1918–59*, Chicago, 1963.
CRITCHLEY, J. and MAGEE, B., 'Candidates: How They Pick Them', *New Statesman*, 5 February 1965.
GUTTSMAN, W. L., *The British Political Élite*, London, 1963.
MCKITTERICK, T. E. M., REES-MOGG, W. and SKELSEY, P., 'Selection of Parliamentary Candidates', *PQ* XXX (July, 1959).
MEYNAUD, J. et al., 'The Parliamentary Profession', *International Social Science Journal* XIII/4 (1961).
PATERSON, P., *The Selectorate: The Case for Primary Elections in Britain*, London, 1967.
RANNEY, A., *Pathways to Parliament: Candidate Selection in Britain*, London, 1965.
ROTH, A., *The Business Background of M.P.s*, 5th edn, London, 1965.
RUSH, M., *The Selection of Parliamentary Candidates*, London, 1969.
WATT, D., 'Picking and Choosing', *The Spectator*, 1 May 1964.

PARTY COHESION

British

BERKELEY, H., 'Party Political Conferences', *The Listener*, 22 September, 1966.
BERRINGTON, H. B., 'Partisanship and Dissidence in the Nineteenth-Century House of Commons', *Parliamentary Affairs* XXI (autumn, 1968).
DONNISON, D. and PLOWMAN, D. E. G., 'The Functions of Local Labour Parties: Experiments in Research Methods', *PS* II (June, 1954).
DOWSE, R. E. and SMITH, T., 'Party Discipline in the House of Commons', *Parliamentary Affairs* XVI (spring, 1963).
EPSTEIN. L. D., 'British M.P.s and their Local Parties: the Suez Cases', *APSR* LIV (June, 1960).
EPSTEIN, L. D., 'New M.P.s and the Politics of the PLP', *PS* X (1962).

FINER, S. E., BERRINGTON, H. B. and BARTHOLOMEW, D. J., *Backbench Opinion in the House of Commons, 1955–1959*, Pergamon Press, 1961.
HINDELL, K. and WILLIAMS, P., 'Scarborough and Blackpool: An Analysis of Some Votes at the Labour Party Conferences of 1960 and 1961', *PQ* XXXIII (July, 1962).
HOUGHTON, D., 'Trade Union M.P.s and the British House of Commons', *The Parliamentarian*, IL/4. (Oct., 1968.)
JACKSON, R. J., *Rebels and Whips*, London, 1968.
JANOSIK, E. G., *Constituency Labour Parties in Britain*, London, 1968.
MARTIN, L. W., 'The Bournemouth Affair: Britain's First Primary Election', *Journal of Politics* XXII (Nov., 1960).
NICOLSON, N., *People and Parliament*, London, 1958.
POTTER, A. M., 'The English Conservative Constituency Associations', *Western Political Quarterly* XI (June, 1956).
RASMUSSEN, J. S., *The Relations of the Profumo Rebels with their Local Parties*, Tucson, Arizona, 1966.
RICHARDS, P. G., *Honourable Members*, London, 1959.
RICHARDS, P. G., *Parliament and Conscience*, London, 1971.
ROSE, R., 'The Policy Ideas of English Party Activists', *APSR* LVI (June, 1962).

Comparative

FROMAN, L. A., *Congressmen and their Constituencies*, Chicago, 1965.
MCCLOSKY, H. *et al.*, 'Issue Conflict and Consensus among Party Leaders and Followers', *APSR* LIV (June, 1960).

PRESSURE GROUPS

British

ALLEN, V. L., *Trade Unions and the Government*, London, 1960.
BEER, S. H., 'Pressure Groups and Parties in Britain', *APSR* L (March, 1956),
ECKSTEIN, H., *Pressure Group Politics* [The British Medical Association], London, 1960.
FINER, S. E., *Anonymous Empire*, London, 1966.
HOWARTH, R. W., 'The Political Strength of British Agriculture', *Political Studies* XVII, 4 (1969).
MCKENZIE, R. T., 'Parties, Pressure Groups and the British Political Process', *PQ* XXIX (Jan., 1958).
MOODIE, G. C. and STUDDERT-KENNEDY, G., *Public Opinions and Pressure Groups*, London, 1970.
POTTER, A., *Organized Groups in British National Politics*, London, 1961.
SELF, P. and STORING, H., *The State and the Farmer*, London, 1962.
STEWART, J. D., *British Pressure Groups*, Oxford, 1958.
WILSON, H. H., *Pressure Group: The Campaign for Commercial Television*, London, 1961.

Comparative

EHRMANN, H. W. (ed.), *Interest Groups on Four Continents*, Pittsburgh, 1958.
LA PALOMBARA, J., *Interest Groups in Italian Politics*, Princeton, 1964
MEYNAUD, J., *Les Groupes de Pression* [Que Sais-Je? 895], Paris, 1960.
TRUMAN, D. B., *The Governmental Process*, New York, 1951.

SPECIAL ISSUES

BARNETT, M. J., *The Politics of Legislation: The Rent Act of 1957*, London, 1969.
CHRISTOPH, J. B., *Capital Punishment in British Politics*, London, 1962.
DRIVER C., *The Disarmers: A Study in Protest*, London, 1965.
DEAKIN, N. D. (ed.), *Colour and the British Electorate, 1964*, London, 1965.
EPSTEIN, L. D., *British Politics in the Suez Crisis*, London, 1964.
SPIERS, M. and LELOHE, M. J., 'Pakistanis in the Bradford Municipal Election of 1963', *PS* XII (Feb., 1964).

VOTING BEHAVIOUR

British

ABRAMS, M., 'Social Class and British Politics', *Public Opinion Quarterly* XXV (fall, 1961).
ABRAMS, P. and LITTLE, A., 'The Young Activist in British Politics', *BJS* XV (June, 1965).
ALLEN, A. J., *The English Voter*, London, 1964.
BEALEY, F., BLONDEL, J. and MCCANN, W. P., *Constituency Politics: A Study of Newcastle-under-Lyme*. London, 1965.
BENNEY, M., GRAY, A. P. and PEAR, R. H., *How People Vote* [Greenwich], London, 1956.
BERRY, D., 'Party Membership and Social Participation', *PS* XVII (June, 1969).
BIRCH, A. H., *Small-Town Politics* [Glossop], Oxford, 1959.
BIRCH, A. H. and CAMPBELL, P. W., 'Voting Behaviour in a Lancashire Constituency', *BJS* I (Sept., 1950).
BOCHEL, J. M. and DENVER, D. J., 'Religion and Voting: A Critical Review and a New Analysis', *Political Studies* XVIII (1970).
BONHAM, J., *The Middle-Class Vote*, London, 1954.
BUTLER, D. and STOKES, D., *Political Change in Britain: Forces Shaping Electoral Choice*, London, 1969.
GOLDTHORPE, J., LOCKWOOD, D., BECHOVER, F., and PLATT, J., *The Affluent Worker: Political Attitudes and Behaviour*, Cambridge, 1968.
GOODHART, C. A. E. and BHANSALI, R. J., 'Political Economy', *PS* XVIII (March, 1970).
HINDESS, B., *The Decline of Working Class Politics*, London, 1971.
KINNEAR, M., *The British Voter: An Atlas and Survey since 1885*, London, 1968.
MCKENZIE, R. T. and SILVER, A., *Angels in Marble: A Study of Working-Class Conservatism in England and Wales*, London, 1968.
MILNE, R. S. and MACKENZIE, H. C., *Straight Fight* [Bristol, N-E], London, 1954.
MILNE, R. S. and MACKENZIE, H. C., *Marginal Seat* [Bristol, N-E], London, 1958.
NOSSITER, T., 'Voting Behaviour 1832–1872' *PS* XVIII (Sept., 1970).
PELLING, H. *The Social Geography of British Elections, 1885–1910*, London, 1967.
SAMUEL, R., 'The Deference Voter', *New Left Review* No. 1 (Jan.–Feb., 1960).
STACEY, M., *Tradition and Charge: A Study of Banbury*, Oxford, 1960.
VINCENT, J. R., *Pollbooks: How Victorians Voted*, Cambridge, 1967.

Comparative

ALFORD, R. R., *Party and Society: The Anglo-American Democracies*, London, 1964.

ALMOND, G. A. and VERBA, S., *The Civic Culture: Political Attitudes and Democracy in Five Nations*, Abridged edn, Boston–Toronto, 1965.

BERELSON, B. R., LAZARSFELD, P. F. and MCPHEE, W. M., *Voting: A Study of Opinion Formation in a Presidential Campaign*, Chicago, 1954.

CAMPBELL, A., CONVERSE, P. E., MILLER, W. E. and STOKES, D. E., *The American Voter*, New York, 1960.

CAMPBELL, A., CONVERSE, P. E., MILLER, W. E. and STOKES, D. E., *Elections and the Political Order*, New York, 1966.

LANE, R. E., *Political Life: Why and How People Get involved in Politics*, 2nd edn, New York, 1964.

LAZARSFELD, P. F., BERELSON, B. and GAUDET, H., *The People's Choice: How the Voter Makes up his Mind in a Presidential Election*, 2nd edn, New York, 1948.

LIPSET, S. M., *Political Man*, New York, 1960.

LIPSET, S. M. and ROKKAN, S. (eds.), *Party Systems and Voter Alignments*, New York, 1966.

MEYNAUD, J. and LANCELOT, A., *La Participation des Français à la Politique.* [Que Sais-Je? 911], 2nd edn, Paris, 1965.

MILBRATH, L. W., *Political Participation*, Chicago, 1965.

RAE, D. W. and TAYLOR, M. J., *The Analysis of Political Cleavages*, New Haven, 1970.

ROKKAN, S. (ed.), *Approaches to the Study of Political Participation*, Bergen, 1962.

ROKKAN, S. *et al.*, 'Citizen Participation in Political Life', *International Social Science Journal* XII/I (1960).

TINGSTEN, H., *Political Behaviour*, Stockholm, 1937.

SCHEUCH, E. K. and WILDENMANN, R. (eds.), 'Zur Soziologie der Wahl', *Kölner Zeitschrift für Soziologie und Sozialpsychologie*, Sonderheft 9, Cologne, 1965.

POLITICAL COMMUNICATION AND CAMPAIGN MANAGEMENT

British

ABRAMS, M., 'The Opinion Polls and the British Election of 1970', *Public Opinion Quarterly* XXXIV (fall, 1970).

ABRAMS, M., 'Opinion Polls and Party Propaganda', *Public Opinion Quarterly* XXVIII (spring, 1964).

ABRAMS, M., 'Why the Parties Advertise', *New Society*, 6 June, 1963.

ABRAMS, M., ROSE, R. and HINDEN, R., *Must Labour Lose?*, London, 1960.

BLUMLER, J. G. and MCQUAIL, D., *Television in Politics: Its Uses and Infleunce*, London, 1968.

CRAIG, F. W. S. (ed.), *British General Election Manifestoes, 1918–1966: Conservative, Labour, Liberal*, Chichester, 1970.

HARRISON, M., 'Political Finance in Britain', *Journal of Politics* XXV (1963).

KAVANAGH, D. A., *Constituency Electioneering in Britain*, London, 1970.

ROSE, R., *Influencing Voters: A Study of Campaign Rationality*, London, 1967.

ROSE, R., 'Money and Election Law', *PS* IX (Feb., 1961).

ROSE, R., *The Polls and the 1970 Election,* University of Strathclyde Survey Research Centre, Occasional Paper No. 7, Glasgow, 1970.

SEYMOUR-URE, C., *The Press, Politics and the Public,* London, 1968.

TRENAMAN, J. and MCQUAIL, D., *Television and the Political Image* [two Leeds constituencies], London, 1961.

TUNSTALL, J., *The Westminster Lobby Correspondents: A Sociological Study of National Political Journalism,* London, 1970.

WINDLESHAM, LORD, *Communication and Political Power,* London, 1966.

Comparative

HEIDENHEIMER, A. J. (ed.), *Comparative Political Finance,* Lexington, Mass., 1970.

KELLEY, S., *Professional Public Relations and Political Power,* Baltimore, 1956.

KELLEY, S., *Political Campaigning: Problems in Creating an Informed Electorate,* Washington, D.C., 1960.

KEY, V. O., *Public Opinion and American Democracy,* New York, 1961.

LANE, R. E. and SEARS, D. O., *Public Opinion,* Englewood Cliffs, N.J., 1964.

NEWMAN, F. C., 'Money and Election Law in Britain – Guide for America', *Western Political Quarterly* X (Sept., 1957).

WALLAS, G., *Human Nature in Politics.,* London, 1908.